KT-569-728

# Children's Human Rights

## Progress and Challenges for Children Worldwide

Edited by
Mark Ensalaco and Linda C. Majka

ROWMAN & LITTLEFIELD PUBLISHERS, INC.
*Lanham • Boulder • New York • Toronto • Oxford*

323.352
ENS

DEPT. COPY

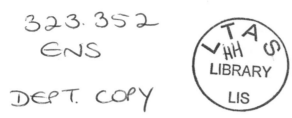

LTAS
HH
LIBRARY
LIS

2699437

ROWMAN & LITTLEFIELD PUBLISHERS, INC.

Published in the United States of America
by Rowman & Littlefield Publishers, Inc.
A wholly owned subsidary of The Rowman & Littlefield Publishing Group, Inc.
4501 Forbes Boulevard, Suite 200, Lanham, Maryland 20706
www.rowmanlittlefield.com

P.O. Box 317, Oxford OX2 9RU, UK

Copyright © 2005 by Rowman & Littlefield Publishers, Inc.


*All rights reserved.* No part of this publication may be reproduced, stored
in a retrieval system, or transmitted in any form or by any means, electronic,
mechanical, photocopying, recording, or otherwise, without the prior permission
of the publisher.

British Library Cataloguing in Publication Information Available

**Library of Congress Cataloging-in-Publication Data**

Children's human rights : progress and challenges for children worldwide / edited by
  Mark Ensalaco and Linda C. Majka.
    p. cm.
  Includes bibliographical references and index.
  ISBN 0-7425-2987-8 (cloth : alk. paper) — ISBN 0-7425-2988-6 (pbk. : alk. paper)
  1. Children's rights. I. Ensalaco, Mark. II. Majka, Linda C.
HQ789.C454 2005
323.3'52—dc22

                                                        2004029609

Printed in the United States of America

∞™ The paper used in this publication meets the minimum requirements of American
National Standard for Information Sciences—Permanence of Paper for Printed Library
Materials, ANSI/NISO Z39.48-1992.

# Children's Human Rights

T.A.S.C. LIBRARY LEEDS

269943 7

# Contents

Acknowledgments vii

Introduction: A Human Rights Approach to the Needs of Children 1
 *Linda C. Majka and Mark Ensalaco*

## PART I: CHILDREN'S RIGHTS IN INTERNATIONAL LAW 7

**1** The Right of the Child to Development 9
 *Mark Ensalaco*

**2** Transforming Visions into Reality: The Convention on the
 Rights of the Child 31
 *Jill Marie Gerschutz and Margaret P. Karns*

**3** Strengthening the Framework for Enforcing Children's Rights:
 An Integrated Approach 53
 *Ursula Kilkelly*

## PART II: CHILDREN IN A DANGEROUS WORLD 81

**4** The Problem of Sexual Trafficking in Postcommunist Europe 85
 *Jaro Bilocerkowycz*

**5** Three Prints in the Dirt: Child Soldiers and Human Rights 111
 *Mary B. Geske with Mark Ensalaco*

**6** Children's Rights and the Tenuousness of Local Coalitions:
 A Case Study in Nicaragua 127
 *Richard Maclure and Melvin Sotelo*

**7** Protecting Children on the Margins:
Social Justice and Community Building 149
*Laura M. Leming, FMI, and Bro. Raymond L. Fitz, SM*

**PART III: CHILDREN'S RIGHTS IN THE UNITED STATES** **169**

**8** Child Farm Workers in United States Agriculture 173
*Linda C. Majka and Theo J. Majka*

**9** Human Rights and Juvenile Justice in the United States 197
*Rosemary C. Sarri and Jeffrey J. Shook*

**10** The Challenges of Human Rights Education and the
Impact on Children's Rights 229
*Joyce Apsel*

Conclusion: Some Progress, Many Challenges 247
*Mark Ensalaco and Linda C. Majka*

Index 261

About the Contributors 275

# Acknowledgments

The authors wish to thank the Sesquicentennial Committee of the University of Dayton for financial support and clerical assistance to bring together an interdisciplinary group of scholars to begin our dialogue through an international symposium on the UN Convention on the Rights of the Child, which was held at the University of Dayton on March 2–3, 2001. We also wish to thank Paula Braley for secretarial support through all stages of this project. The encouragement of our editor Jennifer Knerr at Rowman & Littlefield was critical in the evolution of this volume. We are grateful to our partners Maria Messer and Theo Majka for their advice and assistance. This book is dedicated to our fellow contributor Dr. Mary Geske, whose untimely death in 2001 prevented her from seeing the publication of the volume her scholarship helped to realize.

# Introduction: A Human Rights Approach to the Needs of Children

## Linda C. Majka and Mark Ensalaco

> Each day, countless children around the world are exposed to dangers that hamper their growth and development. They suffer immensely as casualties of war. . . . Each day, millions of children suffer from the scourges of poverty and economic crisis—from hunger and homelessness, from epidemics and illiteracy, from the degradation of the environment. . . . Each day 40,000 die from malnutrition and disease, including immunodeficiency syndrome (AIDS), from lack of clean water and inadequate sanitation.
>
> —World Declaration on the Survival, Protection, and Development of Children and Plan of Action for Implementing the World Declaration (adopted by the World Summit for Children in New York, 30 September 1990)

Children are the future. Investing in children's education, health, and well-being and protecting them from harm and exploitation strengthens local communities and contributes to sustainable national development. Nothing could be simpler. But the reality for children in much of the world is stark, and powerlessness obscures their condition. In 1990 world leaders taking part in the World Summit for Children noted that "each day, countless children around the world are exposed to dangers that hamper their growth and development." Twelve years later, when the UN General Assembly met in a special session to renew the appeal to the international community to give every child a better future, the condition of many of the world's children had not appreciably changed.

Appearing fifteen years after the United Nations World Summit for Children in 1990 and three years after the UN General Assembly special session on children in 2002, this book is an edited collection of ten chapters of original interdisciplinary research conducted by scholars from the social sciences, law, education, and public administration. The book takes as its frame of reference the Convention on the Rights of the Child, the two optional protocols to the CRC, other treaties and resolutions, and the declarations and plans of action of the 1990 World Summit and the 2002 UN General Assembly special session on children (found in *A World Fit for Children*). Using different methodologies and theoretical frameworks, the researchers examine the global challenges to the well-being of children, as well as the public policies, community initiatives, and advocacy strategies that best protect children and promote their development.

The chapters in the book reflect different disciplinary, theoretical, and methodological perspectives but share two core assumptions. First, it is critically important to take a human rights approach to the problems confronting children. This premise defines the normative dimension of the research presented here. A human rights approach to the problems confronting children rejects the presumption that children are entitled to only those rights that governments grant them, that the dominant culture will tolerate, or that the market will bear. States have the individual obligation to implement all the provisions of the Convention on the Rights of the Child through effective national action, and the international community has the collective obligation to honor all the resolutions adopted at the 1990 World Summit on Children and the 2002 special session of the UN General Assembly through effective international cooperation.

The human rights approach transforms the cost-benefit analysis that too often dominates public policy debates about children. While it is critically important to implement cost-effective programs to promote the education, health, and nutrition of children and to protect them from harm and exploitation, cost cannot be the overriding criterion in the public policy debates about investments in children. For states, fulfilling their obligations under the CRC means redefining budgetary priorities—for example, by redirecting military expenditures to education, health care, nutrition, and other social programs. For the world's wealthiest states, honoring the commitments of the World Summit and UN General Assembly special session means allocating more development assistance for poor countries and taking other measures to ensure that globalization ameliorates rather than exacerbates the problems affecting children.

Ultimately, the survival, protection, and development of children depend on poverty reduction and the narrowing of the social and economic inequalities that adversely affect children around the world. Poverty and inequality hamper the development of children everywhere and force them into situations that expose them to harm and exploitation. The reality described in this volume is that poverty and inequality harm children in rich states as well as poor ones. A human rights approach to the problems affecting children reaffirms the principle of the indivisibility of human rights: it is impossible to give a better life to all children without promoting their economic, social, and cultural rights, as well as protecting their civil and political rights.

Second, interdisciplinary research is indispensable for policymaking and human rights advocacy. This premise defines the empirical dimension of the chapters in this book. Empirical research into the condition of the world's children is critical to situate both policy analysis and human rights analysis in the real-life circumstances of children, to document the many systemic injustices that harm children and hamper their development, and to give specificity and force to abstract human rights principles and norms. Interdisciplinary research is necessary to reveal the gulf between human rights theory and the reality in which children live. Moreover, interdisciplinary research can evaluate the human rights impact of public policies, as well as the effectiveness of human rights advocacy strategies and community-based initiatives intended to promote the well-being of children. These research streams are complementary because human rights advocacy is primarily oriented toward altering or improving public policy. A core assumption of this book, in other words, is that knowledge is a prerequisite of the effective action that the international community must take to complete the unfinished agenda of the 1990 World Summit for Children.

Part I, Children's Rights in International Law, examines the evolution of international norms relating to children and the critical role of nongovernmental organizations in drafting the Convention on the Rights of the Child (CRC) and litigating on behalf of children in the European and American courts for human rights using the CRC as the interpretive guide. As noted in chapter 1, the drafting and near-universal ratification of the CRC represent real progress. (To date, only Somalia and the United States have not ratified the convention.) It had taken the international community more than sixty years, since the League of Nations adopted the first Declaration on the Rights of the Child in 1924, to establish children's rights in international law. Similarly, the ability of nongovernmental organizations to push for the conclusion of two optional protocols to the CRC on, one, the sale of children, child prostitution, and child pornography; and, two, the involvement of children in armed conflict strengthens the normative framework for children's rights and therefore represents real progress. Moreover, human rights NGOs have succeeded in incorporating references to children in the declarations and plans of action of six world conferences since the adoption of the CRC. As a result of all these efforts, the best interests of children are now squarely on the international agenda. Finally, in this regard, the willingness of the European and American courts of human rights to use the CRC in making its rulings on a range of issues indicates that the convention is beginning to acquire the force of law in practice as well as theory. However, global implementation of the CRC and achievement of the goals of the 1990 World Summit for Children and the 2002 UN General Assembly special session will ultimately require that the rights of children be integrated into national and international strategies of economic development.

Part II, Children in a Dangerous World, examines two grave challenges to the survival, protection, and development of children—the trafficking of children for sexual exploitation and the use of child soldiers—as well as efforts of nongovernmental and civic organizations to improve the well-being of children in three specific settings. Chapters 4 and 5 document the physical and psychological harm to children resulting from the economic dislocation that makes children vulnerable to traffickers and the ethnic conflicts that expose children to the scourge of modern war. These chapters reveal the huge gap between the norms codified in the CRC; the optional protocols on the sale of children, child prostitution, and child pornography and the involvement of children in armed conflict; and the reality in which thousands of children live and die. Chapters 6 and 7 examine the efforts of nongovernmental and civic organizations to confront dangers to children at the local level in Nicaragua, Mexico, and the United States. These chapters highlight the need for civil society to take action to implement the CRC and to protect and promote the well-being of children. Ultimately, they speak to the need to build communities around the principles of social justice and human rights. The challenges are immense. Nongovernmental organizations are forced to take action where local and national governments have neglected their obligations to children and to struggle against the tide of globalization. The authors consider an array of strategic choices and forms of engagement in a realistic assessment of the opportunities and challenges of promoting compliance with the CRC. The ability of human rights NGOs to develop innovative advocacy strategies and community-based initiatives is going to be critical to the achievement of the goals of the UN General Assembly special session on children.

Part III, "Children's Rights in the United States," examines two practices that harm the life chances of children in the United States—the exploitation of children in migrant farm labor and the disturbing trends in the administration of juvenile justice—as well as efforts to promote human rights education in American schools. The refusal of the United States to ratify the Convention on the Rights of the Child does not mean that human rights and children's rights advocates cannot make normative judgments about the failures of the world's wealthiest advanced democracy to protect children. To the contrary, the United States' moral obligation to children, if not its treaty obligation, is sharpened by its insistence on criticizing the human rights records of other states. The research presented in chapters 8 and 9 reveals failure to meet those obligations. The unacceptably high levels of risk and harm to minor teen and child farm workers violate the norms established in the CRC, as well the International Labour Organization's Convention 182 on the worst forms of child labor. The widespread practice of processing juveniles as adults, sentencing them to lengthy prison terms, incarcerating them with adults, and sentencing minors to life without parole violate the CRC's provisions relating to juvenile justice as well as provisions of the Covenant on Civil and Political Rights. Chapter 10 discusses the challenges of human rights education in the world's most advanced democracy. Two facts stand out about education in America. The U.S. education system is marked by vast disparities of funding and quality of education, a fact with obvious human rights implications. At the same time, human rights education has yet to be meaningfully incorporated into the K-12 curriculum in the United States, perhaps because of the unsettling issues related to the United States' refusal to ratify all the major human rights treaties or to implement fully the treaty commitments the United States has assumed.

Global implementation of the provisions of the Convention on the Rights of the Child is the measure of the international community's professed commitment to making a world fit for children. Implementation is the central concern of this book, as the chapters look backward and forward. We look backward to assess the progress made in the decade between the adoption of the CRC and the World Summit for Children and the subsequent UN General Assembly special session on children. We look forward to 2015, when the international community will again report on the progress made—and identify the obstacles that obstruct more speedy achievement. At this midway point, educators, advocates, and policymakers need to understand the importance of taking a human rights approach to the problems affecting the well-being of children.

*Part I*

# CHILDREN'S RIGHTS IN INTERNATIONAL LAW

In 1989 the international community adopted the Convention on the Rights of the Child as the common standard of achievement of children's human rights—to paraphrase the Universal Declaration of Human Rights. The three chapters in part I cover the central aspects of the human rights movement's continuing struggle to persuade states—and, increasingly, corporations and other transnational actors—to address children's needs: standard setting, monitoring of implementation, judicial enforcement, and advocacy.

Chapter 1, "The Right of the Child to Development," traces the efforts to set the standards defining the state's obligations to children, from the first declaration of the rights of the child in 1924 to the adoption of the Convention on the Rights of the Child in 1989. The chapter emphasizes state obligations to undertake all necessary measures to realize the economic, social, and cultural rights of children as well as their civil and political rights. The transformation of the declaratory language of two declarations of the rights of the child—one adopted by the League of Nations, the other by the United Nations—into the legal language of a multilateral treaty represents important progress. The chapter then summarizes the goals of the 1990 World Summit for Children and the 2002 United Nations General Assembly special session. These, too, represent actionable standards of achievement. But, as the chapter argues, realization of many of the goals articulated in 1990 and 2002 requires accelerated international cooperation to promote the sustainable human development of the world's poorest states, an undertaking that is consistent with the nearly forgotten Declaration on the Right to Development.

Chapter 2, "Transforming Visions into Reality: The Convention on the Rights of the Child," analyzes the critical role that nongovernmental organizations (NGOs) have played, working closely with multilateral institutions, to transform the dream of children's human rights into a reality. NGOs performed a critical role in setting the common standard of achievement for children's human rights, first by guiding the drafting and adoption of the CRC and then by guiding the drafting and adoption of the two optional protocols—one on the involvement of children in armed conflict and the other on the sale of children, child prostitution, and child pornography. Chapter 2 also discusses the critical role NGOs continue to perform in monitoring compliance with the CRC in collaboration with the Committee on the Rights of the Child, the convention's treaty body, and UNICEF. As important, this chapter discusses how NGOs have forced the best interests of the child onto the agendas of the world conferences that followed the World Summit for Children.

Chapter 3, "Strengthening the Framework for Enforcing Children's Rights: An Integrated Approach," examines the incremental progress that human rights and children's rights advocates have made to enforce the norms of the CRC through litigation before the European and American courts for human rights. The CRC has no enforcement mechanisms (a weakness it shares with the other major human rights treaties); it requires that states submit only periodic reviews of the progress they have made toward the full implementation of the convention. Therefore, as the chapter argues, litigation in domestic courts as well as regional human rights courts represents an important advocacy strategy. The success of human rights and children's rights advocates in convincing the European and Inter-American courts of human rights to accept the CRC as an authoritative interpretive guide is therefore a significant development because such an achievement promises to set legal precedents.

The adoption of the CRC and the two additional protocols, the expression of children's interests in the declarations of world conferences, the beginning of jurisprudence based on the CRC—all these represent meaningful progress for a human rights movement that has struggled for the better part of the twentieth century to codify societal obligations to children in international law. Although significant, the progress also has to be measured against the wide array of formidable challenges confronting children around the world in developed and developing nations. A selection of those challenges are analyzed in parts II and III.

*Chapter One*

# The Right of the
# Child to Development

## Mark Ensalaco

The measure of a state's respect for a treaty is the implementation of its treaty obligations. International legal scholars have a Latin term for this common sense idea: *pacta sunt servanda*—treaties are to be observed. As a legal doctrine, it holds that "treaties are binding upon the parties to it and must be performed by them in good faith."[1] The proposition that states have special obligations toward children that supersede the responsibilities of society in general is hardly controversial. Children are the most vulnerable members of any society and are therefore "entitled to special care and assistance."[2] The Convention on the Rights of the Child (CRC) demands good faith from the states. But because of the nature of state obligations under the CRC and the enormity of the challenges with respect to the survival, protection, and development of children, the good faith of the poorest states is practically meaningless without the commitment of substantial resources by the wealthiest. For this reason, the CRC recognizes the "importance of international cooperation for improving the living conditions of children in every country, in particular in developing countries." Unfortunately, in the decade following the adoption of the CRC, the commitment of resources has been influenced by political and geopolitical exigencies. Predictably, the consequences of this reality for children have been tragic.

This chapter provides an overview of the major documents related to the rights of the child. The first section briefly summarizes the evolution of norms related to the rights of the child and identifies the material and spiritual development of the child as the moral foundation of those rights. The second section examines state obligations under the CRC and emphasizes the importance of international development assistance for the progressive realization of the rights of the child. The third section reviews the global implementation of goals of the World Summit for Children, the secretary-general's decade-end review of the World Summit's plan of action, and the declaration and plan of action of the UN General Assembly's Special Session on Children, and it calls attention to disturbing trends in international development assistance. The fourth section argues that taking the rights of the child seriously requires serious reconsideration of the nearly forgotten right to development, which seeks to establish a duty to provide international cooperation.

## THE EVOLUTION OF CHILDREN'S RIGHTS NORMS

### The Geneva Declaration of the Rights of the Child, 1924

The first attempt to frame the norms later codified in the CRC preceded the Second World War and the founding of the United Nations. In 1924 the League of Nations adopted the Declaration of the Rights of the Child, drafted in Geneva in 1923 by Eglantyne Jebb, founder of Save the Children. The declaration contained a mere five paragraphs, but it covered a full array of concerns, including food, health care, delinquency, shelter, emergency relief, work, exploitation, and the "child's service to mankind." Noteworthy here is the explicit connection between children's needs in these areas and the development of the child. Paragraph 1 of the Geneva declaration framed the issue: "The child must be given *the means requisite for normal material and spiritual development*" (italics added).[3] Future declarations of the rights of the child would connect the realization of those rights to the full development of the child in much the same way that the Universal Declaration of Human Rights and other human rights treaties connect human rights and fundamental freedoms to the inherent dignity of all human beings.[4]

Tragically, the decades that followed the League of Nations' Declaration of the Rights of the Child saw the rise of fascism, the extinction of the League of Nations, and the outbreak of world war with catastrophic consequences for children. In the aftermath of the Second World War, the international community would strive to place the protection of human rights on par with the maintenance of peace and security. The survival, protection, and development of children would be an integral part of that effort.

### The UN Declaration on the Rights of the Child, 1959

The United Nations was established in 1945 and immediately took steps to protect children. At the end of 1946 the United Nations created the United Nations International Children's Emergency Fund; in 1953 it was renamed

UNICEF and made a permanent part of the UN system.[5] The creation of a specialized agency for the protection, development, and well-being of children was in recognition of the fact that the dangers facing children did not end with the war. There was still the need to articulate the special entitlements of children and families.

The Universal Declaration of Human Rights (UDHR) of December 1948, the first major statement of human rights in the postwar era, contained only brief references to the family and children that reflected the principles articulated by the League of Nations in Geneva and were later codified in the CRC. Article 16.3 recognized that "the family is the natural and fundamental group unit of society and is entitled to protection by the society and the State." Article 25, which recognizes an individual's and a family's rights to health and well-being, is explicit about mother and child: "Motherhood and childhood are entitled to special care and assistance." The UDHR was intended only as a general manifesto requiring elaboration in the form of a treaty that would set down legally binding obligations for states, so it is perhaps not surprising that the UDHR did not elaborate on the rights of the child.[6] Thus the special needs of the child demanded independent articulation.

In 1959, more than a decade after the unanimous adoption of the UDHR, the United Nations General Assembly adopted its own Declaration of the Rights of the Child in recognition that "mankind owes to the child the best that it can give."[7] The 1959 UN declaration cites the 1924 declaration in its preamble, and the correspondence between the two documents is obvious, beginning with the fundamental concern for the material and spiritual development of the child; there is only one area of concern in the 1924 declaration—delinquency—that is not addressed in the 1959 UN declaration.[8] However, normative standards related to the child had evolved in the thirty-five years since the League of Nations adopted the 1924 declaration. The evolution of standards is most noticeable with respect to education and work.

The 1924 declaration does not even explicitly mention education, although paragraph 4, which notes that a child must be put in a position to earn a livelihood, implies that society or the state must provide vocational training. By contrast, the 1959 UN declaration mentions education twice: principle 5 concerns, inter alia, education for the handicapped, and principle 7 calls for free and compulsory primary education and connects education to the promotion of culture, equal opportunity, and the development of abilities, judgment, and moral and social responsibility. The League of Nations adopted the 1924 declaration at a time when the International Labour Organization was just beginning to formulate labor standards that would eventually encompass protections for children. As noted, the 1924 declaration raises the issue of vocational training to put children in a position to earn a livelihood. That same paragraph demands that the child "must be protected against every form of exploitation." The juxtaposition of work and exploitation is not coincidental. By 1959, the international community had made progress in defining standards with respect to the employment of children and had identified other forms of exploitation. Thus, principle 9 of the 1959 declaration demands the child's protection from *all forms* of neglect, cruelty, and exploitation as well as trafficking. That same principle addresses a yet-to-be-defined minimum age for employment and notably calls for the prohibition of "any occupation or employment which would prejudice [the child's] health or education, or interfere with his physical, mental or moral development."[9]

The 1959 declaration also raises issues that were not addressed thirty-five years earlier by the League of Nations, attesting to the evolution of norms and a recognition of emerging dangers. However, there is a fundamental similarity between the 1924 and 1959 declarations: in both, the notion of the child's development figures as the moral foundation for the rights of the child. The first paragraph of the 1924 declaration is most explicit: "The child must be given the means requisite for normal material and spiritual development." Similarly, principle 2 of the 1959 declaration states: "The child shall enjoy special protection, and shall be given opportunities and facilities, by law and by other means, to enable him to develop physically, mentally, morally, spiritually and socially in a healthy and normal manner in conditions of freedom and dignity."

## The Convention on the Rights of the Child, 1989

On 20 November 1989, the General Assembly of the United Nations adopted the CRC. When the treaty was opened for signature on 26 January 1990, sixty-one states signed it without hesitation. By September, forty states had ratified it—twice as many as the requisite twenty for the treaty to enter into force—and the Convention on the Rights of the Child became a binding legal instrument. By 1995 the number of states to ratify or accede to the CRC had risen to 176.[10] By 2002, 192 states had become party to the CRC. This was near-universal ratification: as is so frequently commented, only two states have yet to ratify the CRC, the United States of America and Somalia.

The CRC encompasses a set of autonomy, development, and protection norms that relate to the following: the rights and responsibilities of parents; the best interests of the child; nondiscrimination; the child's right to life, survival, and development; protection from harmful influences, abuse, and exploitation; respect for the views of the child; and the full participation of the child in family, cultural, and social life. It also recognizes a comprehensive

**Table 1.1.   Evolving Standards Related to the Rights of the Child**

| *Geneva Declaration (1923)* | *UN Declaration (1959)* |
|---|---|
| 1. The child must be given the means requisite for normal material and spiritual development. | Physical, mental, moral, spiritual development in freedom and dignity (principle 2). |
| 2. The child that is hungry must be fed, the child that is sick must be helped, the child that is backward must be helped, the delinquent child must be reclaimed, the orphan and the waif must be sheltered and succored. | Adequate nutrition (principle 4). Medical care, prenatal and postnatal care (principle 4). Special treatment, education, and care for physical, mental, social handicaps (principle 5). Social or state assistance to children without a family (principle 6). Adequate housing (principle 4). |
| 3. The child must be the first to receive relief in times of distress. | First to receive protection and relief (principle 8). |
| 4. The child must be put in a position to earn a livelihood and must be protected against every form of exploitation. | Minimum age for employment; no employment prejudicial to physical, mental, or moral development (principle 9). Neglect, cruelty, exploitation, trafficking (principle 9). |
| 5. The child must be brought up in the consciousness that its talents must be devoted to the service of its fellow man. | Understanding, tolerance, friendship among peoples. Service to mankind (principle 10). Nondiscrimination. Protection from practices promoting racial, religious, or other discrimination (principles 1 and 10). Name and nationality (principle 3). Best interest of the child (principles 2 and 7). Rights and responsibilities of parents (principle 6). Play and recreation (principle 7). Education (principle 7). |

list of rights and corresponding state obligations. The Geneva Declaration of the Rights of the Child of 1923 contains only five paragraphs; the UN Declaration on the Rights of the Child of 1959 states a mere ten principles. The CRC, extrapolating from the basic principles enunciated in the earlier declarations, contains forty-one substantive articles covering a range of issue-areas, including those not specifically addressed in the earlier conventions but clearly deducible from their principles.

The CRC's view of the child differs significantly from that of the 1924 Geneva declaration and is only implicit in the 1959 UN declaration. In effect, the CRC considers the child to be the "subject of rights" rather than the "object" of concern for the state or private philanthropy. The CRC portrays the child as the subject of rights who is entitled to special care and safeguards by reason of his or her physical and mental immaturity (paragraphs 4 and 9) but who is also entitled to expect respect for his or her views as well as full participation in family, cultural, and social life in accordance with his or her evolving capacities (article 12). The rights to which a child is entitled are all necessary for his or her survival, protection, and development.

The differences between the 1924 and 1959 declarations and the 1989 CRC aside, each of the documents articulates the belief that the physical, mental, spiritual, moral, and social development of the child is the moral foundation of the rights of the child. The CRC explicitly makes the connection in several contexts: "the child, for the full and harmonious development of his or her personality, should grow up in a family environment, in an atmosphere of happiness, love and understanding" (preamble, paragraph 6); due account should be taken of "the importance of traditions and cultural values of each people for the protection and harmonious development of the child" (preamble, paragraph 12); "states shall ensure to the maximum extent possible the survival and development of the child" (article 6); "states shall use their best efforts to ensure recognition of the principle that both parents have responsibilities for the upbringing and development of the child" (article 18); assistance should be extended to the disabled child to ensure "the child's achieving the fullest possible social integration and individual development, including his or her cultural and spiritual development" (article 23); "states recognize the right of every child to a standard of living adequate for the child's physical, mental, spiritual, moral and social development" (article 27); "states parties recognize the right of the child to be protected from economic exploitation or any work that is likely . . . to be harmful to the child's health or physical, mental, spiritual, moral or social development" (article 32). Given that the child's survival and protection are the sine qua nons of development, it becomes apparent that developing the child's full potentialities is the transcendent objective of the CRC and that development is the moral foundation of the rights recognized in the convention.

## State Obligations under the CRC

State obligations under the CRC are specified in articles 2 through 4.[11] States incur the fundamental obligation to "respect and ensure" the rights set forth in the CRC, "without discrimination of any kind," taking into account "the best interests of the child" and the "rights and duties of his or her parents" or of others who have legal responsibility for the child. States also incur two sets of actionable obligations that parallel the differing obligations under the Covenant on Civil and Political Rights and the Covenant on Economic, Social, and Cultural Rights. First, states are obligated to "undertake all appropriate legislative, administrative and other measures for the implementation of the rights recognized in the present Convention." Second, "with regard to economic, social, and cultural rights," states are obligated "to undertake such measures to the maximum extent of their available resources, *and where needed, within the framework of international cooperation*" (italics added).[12]

These obligations involve the core elements of governance: laws, policies, institutions, staffs, and budgets. States party to the CRC are obligated to enact its provisions into law at the national level and, where required, the state or provincial level. The enactment of legislation that brings national legal codes into conformity with international human rights treaties that are not self-executing can be an arduous process. Unfortunately, states often fail to meet their treaty obligations at this initial stage. But even where legislatures enact laws that respect and protect certain rights, state agencies must craft and implement policies to promote them. Article 3, section 3 of the CRC elaborates on the obligations: "States Parties shall ensure that the institutions, services and facilities responsible for the care or protection of children shall conform with the standards established by competent authorities, particularly in the areas of safety, health, in the number and suitability of their staff, as well as their competent supervision." Institutions, services, staff, competent supervision—each of these demand budgetary allocations, whether the rights in question are civil or political; economic, social, or cultural; "negative" or "positive." Rights demand resources at every level of obligation: the obligations to respect, protect, and promote human rights.[13]

Owing to the scarcity of developing countries' resources, article 4 of the CRC stipulates that states should undertake "such measures to the maximum extent of their available resources" to promote the economic, social, and cultural rights of the child and, "where needed, within the framework of international cooperation." Arguably, the phrase "where needed" applies to virtually the entire developing world. The CRC repeats the call for international cooperation in article 24, which recognizes "the right of the child to the enjoyment of the highest standard of health" and stipulates that "States shall undertake to promote and encourage international cooperation with a view to achieving progressively the full realization of the right" to the attainment of highest attainable standard of health and that "particular account shall be taken of the needs of developing countries." As subsequent documents related to the implementation of the CRC make plain, the appeal to international cooperation is really a call for official development assistance and other transfers of resources from the wealthiest to the neediest states. The fact of the matter is that the neediest states, even where they act in good faith, lack adequate resources to ensure that institutions, services, facilities, and staff are available to children and families. The commitment to undertake measures to the maximum extent of available resources is practically meaningless when the available resources are minimal. Thus, while the CRC places the primary obligation for the progressive realization of children's rights on states themselves, its underlying premise is that the survival, protection, and development of the child are the shared duties of the international community. The CRC, then, is a legal rearticulation of the moral imperative stated in the 1959 Declaration of the Rights of the Child: "mankind owes to the child the best it has to give."

The Committee on the Rights of the Child, the treaty body created to supervise implementation of the CRC, comments on these state obligations in its fifth General Comment in 2003, issued after the secretary-general and the General Assembly had an opportunity to assess the global implementation of the CRC.[14] Fundamentally, the committee emphasizes that "States must see their role as fulfilling clear legal obligations" and that "implementation of the human rights of children must not be seen as a charitable process" (paragraph 11). Consequently, the committee emphasizes the justiciability of the child's rights. Thus, with respect to the CRC's provisions being incorporated into domestic law, the committee observes that "incorporation should mean that the provisions of the Convention can be directly invoked before the courts and applied by national authorities and that it will prevail where there is a conflict with domestic legislation or common practice" (paragraph 20). The committee further emphasizes the justiciability of economic, social, and cultural rights as well as civil and political rights and therefore finds it "essential that domestic law sets out entitlements in sufficient detail to enable remedies for non-compliance to be effective" (paragraphs 25–26). The committee also notes that federal states have the obligation to require state or provincial governments to "legislate within the framework of the Convention," thereby ensuring uniformity across jurisdictions (paragraph 20).

On the critical matter of funding, the committee stresses the importance of "making children visible in budgets." As part of its implementation and reporting requirements, states must "identify the proportion of the national and other budgets devoted to the social sector and within that, to children, both directly and indirectly." The committee goes on to comment on the need to align economic policy to obligations under the convention. "Economic and social planning and decision-making and budgetary decisions" should be "made with the best interests of children as a primary consideration," and children should "be protected from adverse effects of economic policies or financial downturns" (paragraph 51).

With respect to international cooperation, the committee comments on the language contained in the CRC. The committee says that states party to the CRC "take on the obligations not only to implement it within their jurisdiction but to contribute through international cooperation to global implementation" (paragraph 7). This is the strongest indication that the committee views international cooperation as a legally binding obligation, amplifying the committee's comment that "implementation of the human rights of children must not be seen as a charitable process." The committee stresses this point a second time, noting that the implementation of the CRC "is a cooperative exercise for the States of the world." Thus, the committee reworks the original language in article 4 of the CRC: "With regard to economic, social and cultural rights, States Parties shall undertake [all appropriate measures] to the maximum extent of their available resources and, where needed, *within* the framework of *international cooperation*." To emphasize the obligatory nature of article 4, the committee now rephrases the article's language to urge that states "*should form* the framework for *international development assistance*" (paragraphs 60–61; italics added).[15] The implications are obvious: international cooperation means international development assistance, and because a framework of international cooperation is needed almost everywhere to implement the economic, social, and cultural rights of the child, states should undertake to form that framework. The major documents concerning the global implementation of the CRC confirm this nexus between state obligations, international cooperation, international development assistance, and global implementation.

## GLOBAL IMPLEMENTATION OF THE CRC

The drafting of the CRC marked the culmination of eight decades of standard setting with respect to the rights of the child.[16] But it was only the beginning of an exceptional effort to translate concern for the child into measurable actions. After the adoption of the CRC, the UN convened two extraordinary conferences—the World Summit in 1990 and a special session of the General Assembly in 2002—to formulate plans of action to counter the dangers that children confront daily. On both occasions, the international community appealed for political will, the expenditure of resources, and international development assistance.

## Declaration and Plan of Action of the
## World Summit for Children, 1990

In September 1990, only weeks after the CRC entered into force, representatives of 159 nations—71 of them heads of state—assembled in New York City to participate in the World Summit for Children and to issue a declaration and plan of action.[17] Nearly seven decades after the Geneva Declaration of the Rights of the Child, the situation of many of the world's children was deplorable. The declaration begins by noting, "Each day, countless children around the world are exposed to dangers that hamper their growth and development . . . millions of children suffer from the scourges of poverty and economic crisis . . . [and] 40,000 die from malnutrition and disease, including immunodeficiency syndrome (AIDS), from the lack of clean water and inadequate sanitation and from the effects of the drug problem." In view of the seriousness of the condition of children, the 1990 World Summit declaration expresses the participants' determination to "undertake a joint commitment and to make urgent appeal . . . to give every child a better future"[18] and endorses a ten-point program that, beginning with efforts to promote ratification of the CRC, addresses issues of health, nutrition, the status of women, the role of the family, reduction of illiteracy, amelioration of the plight of children in especially difficult circumstances, armed conflict, the environment, and global poverty.

The 1990 World Declaration and Plan of Action set forth twenty-seven specific, measurable, time-bound goals. Achievement would require "political action at the highest level" and, more tangibly, "transfers of appropriate additional resources to developing countries as well as improved terms of trade, further trade liberalization and measures for debt relief."[19] If the challenges were enormous, the UN could note reasons for optimism, including "recent improvements in the international political climate" that might facilitate "international cooperation and solidarity." The CRC was adopted with great optimism and ratified in record time. The end of the Cold War created the hope that meaningful international cooperation in the form of a diversion of resources from weapons to children's welfare was not wildly utopian. Basically, the heads of state present in New York for the World Summit for Children were counting on a peace dividend that never materialized.

The 1990s saw the end of apartheid, the fall of the Iron Curtain, the end of bloody civil conflicts in Central America, and perceptible movement on the Palestinian–Israeli issue—to mention just a few of the positive developments. But the 1990s also saw the eruption of the Gulf War, ethnic cleansing in the former Yugoslavia and in Rwanda, violent civil conflicts in West Africa, and a humanitarian crisis in Somalia. The 1990s also became the "sanctions decade" as the UN Security Council voted to punish a set of states economically. The secretary-general's decade-end review of the progress made toward the goals of the World Summit would reflect these sad realities.

## The Secretary-General's Decade-End Review: *We the Children*

In May 2001, Kofi Annan, the UN secretary-general, submitted a report on the progress achieved in the implementation of the goals proclaimed eleven years earlier at the World Summit for Children. Entitled *We the Children*, the secretary-general's detailed 153-page report is based primarily on national reports, and the secretary-general comments that the very fact that some 130 countries had prepared reports represents an achievement.[20] Yet *We the Children* reflects mixed results: there was "real and significant progress" but also "setbacks, slippage and in some cases, real retrogression, some of it serious enough to threaten earlier gains" (paragraphs 16–17). The optimism of the World Summit for Children—"held at the time of the end of the Cold War and the high hopes for a peaceful world"—was gone. The facts showed that "many of the survival and development goals set by the Summit, especially in the areas of health, nutrition and education, remain unfulfilled" (paragraph 26). The survival, protection, and development of children remained as the results of chronic poverty aggravated by the widening disparities between rich and poor nations.

> At a time of unprecedented global prosperity and in a $30 trillion global economy, half of humanity is desperately impoverished, with 3 billion people subsisting on $2 a day or less. Of these, some 1.2 billion souls live in what the World Bank categorizes as absolute poverty, stripped of all human dignity as they struggle to survive on $1 a day in conditions of almost unimaginable suffering and want. Half of them are children. (paragraph 30)

So, if the goals of the World Summit for Children remain unfulfilled eleven years after world leaders pronounced them, it is "not because they were too ambitious or technically beyond reach" but simply because of "insufficient investment" in children. The appropriate additional resources were not made available. *We the Children* calls attention to the widening gulf between rich and poor nations and laments that "never in the history of development cooperation have we seen overall aid to the world's neediest countries fall to levels as low as they have been in recent years" (paragraph 32).

## The 2002 UN General Assembly Special Session: *A World Fit for Children*

In May 2002, the UN General Assembly met in a special session to consider a draft of yet another declaration and plan of action concerned with the well-being of children. Eleven years had passed since the World Summit for Children, and a year had passed since Kofi Annan's report *We the Children*. The 2002 declaration and plan of action, entitled *A World Fit for Children*, acknowledges "much progress" even while it affirms that "overall gains have fallen short of national obligations and international commitments."[21] The General Assembly meeting in a special session would reaffirm its commitment "to complete the unfinished agenda of the World Summit for Children."

The 2002 declaration sets ten urgent imperatives, and the accompanying plan of action specifies a set of measurable goals to be achieved, in most cases, by 2015. There is notable continuity between the 1990 declaration of the World Summit for Children and the 2002 special session in the areas of health, nutrition, education, poverty, and environment. But there are also obvious differences of emphasis. In 1990, the World Summit gave priority to the universal ratification of the CRC; by 2002, that goal had been achieved but for the failure of the United States and Somalia to ratify the treaty. In 1990 the World Summit deemed it important to explicitly state the principles that the role and status of women should be strengthened and the role of the family promoted; in 2002 the General Assembly's special session addressed the issue of women in the context of supporting goals elaborated in the appendix. In 2002 the General Assembly deemed it important to explicitly reiterate the principles that children should be heeded and their participation ensured. These principles were integral to the CRC, but the World Summit did not restate them.

One danger facing children that warrants attention is HIV/AIDS.[22] The 1990 declaration of the World Summit for Children begins by noting that each day some forty thousand children die from malnutrition and disease. It laments that many childhood diseases are preventable. But the AIDS pandemic represents a challenge of an entirely different order. The number of children who are orphaned or who die as a result of AIDS is staggering, but the declaration notes other dimensions of the AIDS crisis: the drain on public health resources that, in turn, affects the provision of other urgently needed health services, and the social stigmatization associated with the disease.

For present purposes, the most important contrast between the 1990 declaration and plan of action (World Summit) and the 2002 declaration and plan of action (UN special session) concerns each one's tone with respect to the availability of resources. If in 1990 the participants in the World Summit could hope for a peace dividend, in 2002 they were compelled to plead for "renewed political will" and "the mobilization and allocation of additional resources at both the national and international level." At the level of national policy, children's advocates contend that even poor states can make more of their scarce resources available by reallocating resources currently directed, for example, to the military. But as the secretary-general's end-of-decade review makes clear, there are failures at the international level as well. Thus, although "the 1990s was a decade of great promises," it was in reality one of "modest achievements for the world's children" because "the resources promised at the Summit at both the national and international levels have yet to fully materialize" (paragraph 11–12). Later the document expresses appreciation to those developed countries that made good on their pledges to provide official development assistance (ODA) amounting to 0.07 percent of their gross national product, but it implicitly criticizes those whose ODA fell short, while expressing concern about declining trends in ODA (paragraph 52). Moreover, the 2001 declaration calls for the implementation of the enhanced heavily indebted poor countries initiative as outlined in the General Assembly's December 2000 Millennium Declaration and the cancellation of all bilateral official debts of indebted countries, "without delay."

The 2002 declaration could not avoid the question of globalization. The language of the declaration attempts to strike a balance between the advocates and critics. It acknowledges that "globalization and interdependence are opening new opportunities through trade, investment and capital flows, and advances in technology . . . for the growth of the world economy, development and improvement of living standards around the world." However, it calls attention to "exclusion and inequality between and within societies" and warns that "unless the benefits of social and economic development are extended to all countries, a growing number of people in all countries and even entire regions will remain marginalized from the global economy" (paragraph 19). The disturbing trends in ODA and the potentially deleterious effects of globalization affect the rights of the child in two ways: the decline in resource transfers impedes progress in the realization of the goals set during the World Summit for Children and restated during the General Assembly Special Session, and globalization could actually aggravate the already perilous situation of children in many regions of the planet.

Despite, or perhaps because of, these trends, the 1990 and 2002 declarations and plans of action are forward-looking and seek to sustain the political momentum generated in the years since the adoption of the CRC and the World Summit for Children. Whereas the plan of action from the 1990 summit issued an urgent appeal to "make a better life for all children," the 2002 declaration and plan of action emanating from the UN General Assembly special session calls for the creation of "a world fit for children," a world in which

all girls and boys can enjoy childhood—a time of play and learning, in which they are loved, respected, cherished, their rights are promoted and protected, without discrimination of any kind, where their safety and well being are paramount and *where they can develop in health, peace and dignity.* (paragraph 9 [italics added])

For all the time that passed in between, the world called for by the UN General Assembly would provide exactly what the League of Nations called for almost eighty years earlier: a world in which the child is given the "means requisite for normal material and spiritual development."

## THE RIGHTS OF THE CHILD AND THE RIGHT TO DEVELOPMENT

Taking the rights of the child seriously requires serious reconsideration of the right to development as articulated in a now nearly forgotten 1986 United Nations Declaration on the Right to Development.[23] The Declaration on the Right to Development is pertinent for two reasons. First, like the CRC, the Declaration on the Right to Development views human development as the foundation of human rights. Second, it seeks to establish a duty to provide the international assistance that the declaration and plan of action of the 1990 World Summit for Children, *We the Children*, and *A World Fit for Children* deem necessary for the global implementation of the CRC.

The development of the child is the moral foundation of the rights of the child. The language of the 1924 and 1959 declarations and the 1989 CRC make the connection between development and the rights of the child.

* Declaration of the Rights of the Child, 1924: "The child must be given the means requisite for normal material and spiritual development" (paragraph 1).
* Declaration of the Rights of the Child, 1959: "The child . . . shall be given opportunities and facilities, by law and by other means, to enable him to develop physically, mentally, morally, spiritually and socially in a healthy and normal manner in conditions of freedom and dignity" (principle 2).
* Convention on the Rights of the Child, 1989: "States recognize the right of every child to a standard of living adequate for the child's physical, mental, spiritual, moral and social development" (article 27).

This connection between development and the rights of the child is so strong that it is possible to conceive of the rights of the child as the right of the child to development. The CRC recognizes as universal the enjoyment of certain conditions that the specialized sciences have determined as those necessary for child development: an upbringing in a family environment full of happiness, love, and understanding (preamble, paragraph 6); enrichment of traditions and cultural values (preamble, paragraph 12); interaction with both parents (article 18); an adequate standard of living (article 27); protection from exploitation (article 32); and special care for disabled children (article 23).

But child development comprises only the early phases of a continuing process of human development. Indeed, human development should be seen as the moral foundation of human rights in general. John O'Manique frames this argument in a series of seminal articles that advances a defense for the universality of human rights in terms of the propensity of all organisms to develop.[24]

> A right is a claim to something that is needed for the development of an individual human being. Its moral foundation is the virtually universal belief that, since development is good, one ought to develop and have or do what is required to develop. This is the transcendent human articulation of the propensity found in all organisms, to develop.

Fundamentally, this approach to human rights is grounded in the ontology of the human person.[25] This human development approach to human rights holds that every individual has a claim to the economic, social, cultural, civil, and political rights recognized in the Universal Declaration of Human Rights and the major human rights treaties because the enjoyment of those rights is needed for the integral development of the physical, mental, spiritual, moral, and social dimensions of the human person.

This concept of integral human development is also at the core of the 1986 Declaration on the Right to Development, which defines development as "a comprehensive economic, social, cultural and political process, which aims at *the constant improvement of the well-being of the entire population and of all individuals*" (preamble, paragraph 2; italics added). The declaration asserts that the right to development is "an inalienable human right" (article 1); that "the human person is the central subject of development" (article 2, paragraph 1); and that "respect for human rights and fundamental freedoms" is necessary "to ensure the free and *complete fulfillment of the human being*" (article 2, paragraph 2; italics added). The preamble of the declaration specifically refers to the concept of the "integral development of the human being" (preamble, paragraph 5), just then being articulated by the United Nations' specialized agencies. The United Nations Development Programme later defined this concept as *human development* and began preparing human development reports in 1990.

Arjun Sengupta, the UN independent expert on the right to development, has repeatedly stated that "the right to development essentially integrates the human development approach into the human rights–based approach to development."[26] The human development approach goes beyond traditional development theory—which focuses on the maximization of per capita gross national product—by stressing the realization of an individual's freedoms and the enhancement of an individual's capabilities, for which economic growth is necessary but not sufficient.[27] Thus, the human development approach is consistent with the idea framed in the Declaration on the Right to Development that "the human person is the central subject of the development process." The human rights–based approach goes further still by asserting an individual's human rights claims to development of individuals vis-à-vis the state. As Sengupta notes in his very first report, the purpose of "the recognition of the right to development as an inalienable human right is to confer on its implementation a claim on national and international resources and to oblige states and other agencies of society, including individuals, to implement that right."[28]

Indeed, the Declaration on the Right to Development declares that states have "the duty to formulate appropriate national development policies that aim at the constant improvement of the well-being of the entire population and of all individuals" (article 2, paragraph 3), as well as the primary responsibility for the "creation of national and international conditions favourable to the realization of the right to development" (article 3, paragraph 1). It asserts that "sustained action is required to promote the more rapid development of developing countries" and that "as a complement to the efforts of developing countries, effective international cooperation is essential in providing these countries with appropriate means and facilities to foster their comprehensive development" (article 4, paragraph 2).

The CRC and the Declaration on the Right to Development essentially make the same assertions. The CRC recognizes in the preamble "the importance of international cooperation for improving the living conditions of all children" and the "harmonious development of the child" (preamble, paragraphs 12 and 13); the Declaration on the Right to Development is concerned with "the constant improvement of the well-being . . . of all individuals" and "the complete fulfillment of the human being" (preamble, paragraphs 2 and 10). The CRC calls on states to "undertake [all appropriate measures] to the maximum extent of their available resources and, where needed, within the framework of international cooperation" and to "promote and encourage international cooperation with a view to achieving progressively the full realization of the right of the child to the enjoyment of the highest attainable standard of health" (articles 4 and 24); the Declaration on the Right to Development holds that states have the responsibility "for the creation of national and international conditions favourable to the realization of the right to development" and to "cooperate with each other in ensuring developing and eliminating obstacles to development" (article 3).

The critical issue with respect to both the CRC and the Declaration on the Right to Development pertains to the degree of obligation they confer on international cooperation. The obligation established by the CRC in the preamble and in articles 2 and 24 is tenuous; the Declaration on the Right to Development is just that, a nonbinding declaration rather than a convention. The Declaration on the Right to Development has been criticized, precisely because it seeks to lay the foundation for an eventual treaty obligation.[29]

Jack Donnelly, for example, argues against establishing "a right not to be economically underdeveloped, transforming human rights concerns related to development into little more than a device to gain economic concessions on largely spurious grounds."[30] But there is nothing spurious about calls for international cooperation, including the transfer of additional economic resources from the wealthiest states to the poorest, to address the human rights concerns of children related to development. Each of the three major documents on the global implementation of the CRC—the declaration and plan of action of the 1990 World Summit on Children, *We the Children*, and *A World Fit for Children*—makes it absolutely clear that the good-faith efforts of the planet's poorest states are not enough to make the rights of the child a reality. Without the transfer of substantial resources to developing nations—as well as other measures of international cooperation such as improved terms of trade, trade liberalization, and measures for debt relief—poor states acting in good faith and to the maximum of their available resources simply cannot fulfill their obligations under the CRC. The Committee on the Rights of the Child likewise emphasizes this fact in its 2003 General Comment on the implementation of the CRC (General Comment No. 5).

Moreover, it is important to note that the right to development has been reaffirmed on a number of occasions. The 1993 declaration of the World Conference on Human Rights reaffirms that the right to development is "a universal and inalienable right and an integral part of human rights."[31] The 1995 declaration of the World Summit for Social Development proclaims that "our societies must respond more effectively to the *material and spiritual needs* of individuals, their families and the communities in which they live," and it calls for the realization of social and people-centered sustainable development."[32] The 2000 United Nations Millennium Declaration calls attention to the duty of world leaders to making "the right to development a reality for everyone and to freeing the entire human race from want."[33]

The clear implication is that taking the rights of the child seriously demands the reconsideration of an international obligation to cooperate in promoting the child's development.

## CONCLUSION

The Convention on the Rights of the Child represents the culmination of decades of standard setting. The 1924 Declaration on the Rights of the Child declares that "the child must be given the means requisite for normal material and spiritual development." The 1959 Declaration on the Rights of the Child declares that "mankind owes the child the best it has to give." The 1989 Convention on the Rights of the Child recognizes "the importance of international cooperation for improving the living conditions of children in every country, in particular in the developing countries."

The near-universal ratification of the CRC as a legally binding treaty establishes an international commitment of states to take all appropriate measures to promote the survival, protection, and development of the child. The declarations and plans of actions of the 1990 World Summit for Children and the 2002 special session of the General Assembly, as well as the secretary-general's decade-end review of the World Summit, reach the same conclusion: In an increasingly globalized economy marked by growing disparities, the planet's wealthiest states must complement the poorest states' good-faith efforts to realize the rights of the child to the maximum extent of their available resources. The creation of a framework for international cooperation for improving the living conditions of children in all countries is more than sound economics. It is an obligation arising from the near-universal ratification of the Convention on the Rights of the Child. The measure of the international community's commitment to the survival, protection, and development of children is the implementation of its obligations under the convention. *Pacta sunt servanda*— treaties are to be observed, and states must act on them in good faith.

## NOTES

1. The Vienna Convention on the Law of Treaties (1969), article 26.
2. Convention on the Rights of the Child (A/RES/44/25/25, 20 November 1989), preamble, paragraph 3.
3. Declaration of the Rights of the Child (1923), available at www.crin.org.
4. The Universal Declaration of Human Rights connects human rights and dignity in multiple contexts, including the preamble and article 1.
5. General Assembly resolution 57.I of 11 December 1946.
6. The International Covenant on Economic, Social, and Cultural Rights (UN Doc A/6316, 1966) sets forth the norms vis-à-vis the family, mother, and child in article 10, sections 2 and 3. Section 3 obligates states to take "special measures of protection and assistance . . . on behalf of all children and young persons." It goes on to obligate "protections from economic and social exploitation" and calls for legal punishment

for "employment in work harmful to their morals or health or dangerous to life or likely to hamper their normal development." The importance of the phrase "normal development" is elucidated in this chapter.

7. General Assembly resolution 1386.14 of 20 November 1959.

8. The UN addressed the matter of juvenile justice in 1985. The United Nations Standard Minimum Rules for the Administration of Juvenile Justice (Beijing Rules) states, with relevance to the argument developed here, that "juvenile justice shall be conceived as an integral part of the national development process of each country . . . and shall be implemented in the context of the economic, social and cultural conditions prevailing in each Member State" (1.5–1.6).

9. The exploitation of child labor was first addressed in 1930 in the International Labour Organization Forced Labour Convention (no. 29). In 1973 the ILO specifically addressed the minimum age in the Minimum Age Convention (no. 138).

10. Department of Public Information, *The United Nations and Human Rights, 1945–1995* (New York: United Nations), 81.

11. Article 44 also requires states to submit periodic reports to the Committee on the Rights of the Child, established by the CRC. The Committee on the Rights of the Child possesses additional tools to supervise a state's compliance—for example, consultation with UN-specialized agencies, such as UNICEF and the ILO. These are unique among the UN's other treaty-body mechanisms. See Cynthia Price Cohen, Stuart H. Hart, and Susan M. Kosloke, "Monitoring the United Nation's Convention on the Rights of the Child: The Challenge of Information Management," *Human Rights Quarterly* 18 (1996): 445–46.

12. These parallel the differing obligations set forth in article 2 of the Covenant on Civil and Political Rights and in article 2 of the Covenant on Economic, Social, and Cultural Rights. However, the latter covenant also incorporates the concept of progressive realization. This concept is specifically stated in the article 24 of the CRC, in connection with the attainment of the highest attainable standard of health.

13. Ashbjorn Eide, "Realization of Social and Economic Rights and the Minimum Threshold Approach," in *Human Rights in the World Community: Issues and Action*, ed. Richard Pierre Claude and Burns H. Weston (Philadelphia: University of Pennsylvania Press, 1992), 159.

14. Committee on the Rights of the Child, "General Measures of Implementation for the Convention on the Rights of the Child," General Comment No. 5 (2003) (CRC/GC/2003/5). The committee's four previous general comments were "Aims of Education" (General Comment No. 1, 2001), "The Role of Independent National Human Rights Institutions in the Promotion and Protection of the Rights of the Child" (General Comment No. 2, 2002), "HIV/AIDS and the Rights of the Child" (General Comment No. 3, 2003), and "Adolescent Health and Development in the Context of the Convention on the Rights of the Child" (General Comment No. 4, 2003).

15. In its General Comment No. 4, on adolescent health and development, the committee stresses that the promotion of adolescent health "will not be effective without international cooperation" (paragraphs 42 and 43). Committee on the Rights of the Child, "Adolescent Health and Development in the Context of the Convention on the Rights of the Child," General Comment No. 4. (2003) (CRC/GC/2003/4).

16. In May 2002 the UN opened two optional protocols to the CRC for signature: the Optional Protocol to the Convention on the Rights of the Child on the Sale of Children, Child Prostitution, and Child Pornography (A/RES/54/263 of 25 May 2000); and the Optional Protocol to the Convention on the Rights of the Child on the Involvement of Children in Armed Conflict (A/RES/54/263, 25 May 2000). These entered into force in January and February 2002, respectively. Although not directly pertinent to this chapter, they provide the normative bases for later chapters.

17. World Declaration on the Survival, Protection, and Development of Children and Plan of Action for Implementing the World Declaration (adopted by the World Summit for Children in New York, 30 September 1990).

18. World Declaration and Plan of Action, declaration paragraphs 1, 4–6.

19. World Declaration and Plan of Action, paragraphs 18–20.

20. *We the Children: End-Decade Review of the Follow-Up to the World Summit for Children. Report of the Secretary-General* (A/S-27/3, 4 May 2001).

21. *A World Fit for Children: Declaration and Plan of Action of the UN General Assembly Special Session* (A/S-27/19/Rev.1, adopted 10 May 2002), section 1, declaration, paragraph 2.

22. See also Committee on the Rights of the Child, "HIV/AIDS and the Rights of the Child," General Comment No. 3 (CRC/GC/2003/3, 17 March 2003.)

23. Declaration on the Right to Development (adopted by General Assembly resolution 41/128 of 4 December 1986).

24. John O'Manique, "Universal and Inalienable Rights: A Search for Foundations," *Human Rights Quarterly* 12 (1990): 465–85; and O'Manique, "Human Rights and Development," *Human Rights Quarterly* 14 (1992).

25. Similarly, Diarmuid Martin argues that the right to development in this context reflects "the integration of various human rights into one overarching concept, which mirrors the concept of integral human development." See Martin, "Comprehensive Development Strategies and the Right to Development," in *Right to Development: Reflections on the First Four Reports of the Independent Expert on the Right to Development*, ed. Franciscans International (Geneva, Switz.: Franciscans International, 2003), 5.

26. *Fourth Report of the Independent Expert on the Right to Development, Mr. Arjun Sengupta, Submitted in Accordance with Commission Resolution 2001/9* (E/C.4/2002/WG.18.2, 20 December 2001), paragraph 8. Sengupta later elaborates on "the right to human development, defined as a process that expands substantive human freedoms and thereby realizes all human rights." Sengupta, "On the Theory and Practice of Development," *Human Rights Quarterly* 24, no. 4 (November 2002): 851. Similarly, Nobel laureate Amartya Sen defines *development* as freedom, "a process of expanding the real freedoms that people enjoy" (*Development as Freedom* [New York: Anchor Books, 1999], 3).

27. The first report defines *human development* as "a process of widening people's choices and the level of their achieved well being," a process that involves among other things "the formation of human capabilities and the use people make of their acquired capabilities." United Nations Development Programme, *Human Development Report 1990: Concept and Measurement of Human Development* (Oxford: Oxford University Press, 1990), 10.

28. *Study on the Current State of Progress in the Implementation of the Right to Development Submitted by Mr. Arjun K. Sengupta, Independent Expert, Pursuant to Commission Resolution 1998/72 and General Assembly Resolution 53/155* (E/CN.4/WG.18/2, 27 July 1999), paragraph 20.

29. The Declaration on the Right to Development has its origins in the polemics surrounding the call for a New International Economic Order (NIEO), with its demands to "correct inequalities and redress existing injustices . . . to make it possible to eliminate the widening gap between the developed and developing countries." UN Commission on Human Rights, Res. 4 (XXXIII), 1977. General Assembly Declaration and Program of Action on the Establishment of a New International Economic Order RES 3201 (S-VI) 1 May 1974.

30. Jack Donnelly, "The 'Right to Development': How Not to Link Human Rights and Development," in *Human Rights and Development in Africa*, ed. Claude E. Welch and Ronald I. Meltzer (Albany: State University of New York Press, 1984), 267.

31. Vienna Declaration and Programme of Action (adopted at the World Conference on Human Rights, A/CONF.15724, 25 June 1993), paragraphs 8 and 10.

32. Copenhagen Declaration on Social Development and Programme of Action of the World Summit for Social Development (adopted at the fourteenth plenary meeting, on 12 March 1995), resolution 1.

33. United Nations Millennium Declaration (A/RES/55/2, 18 December 2000), paragraphs 2 and 11.

## Chapter Two

# Transforming Visions into Reality: The Convention on the Rights of the Child

## Jill Marie Gerschutz and Margaret P. Karns

In January 1990, the Convention on the Rights of the Child (CRC) was signed by eighty-one heads of state and government at an extraordinary summit meeting in New York. In sum, 197 states had ratified the convention as of early 2004, making it the most widely ratified treaty in history, with only the United States and Somalia having not yet ratified it. The rapid and near-universal endorsement of this human rights instrument, focusing exclusively on children's rights, makes its implementation an interesting case study. Since the convention incorporates a number of positive rights, the question becomes, has there been measurable progress in improving the well-being of children in many parts of the world? Have the egregious problems of child soldiers, child trafficking, and child prostitution received a higher level of attention than they might have otherwise?

The history of international human rights, as Paul Lauren notes, "has always been and always will be a struggle against authority."[1] It is also a struggle of competing concerns. The effort to implement children's rights since the CRC went into effect coincides with the period of greatest human rights activity and of humanitarian disasters associated with post–Cold War conflict and failed states. More than ever, children are both victims and perpetrators of egregious human rights violations. In addition, HIV/AIDS is taking a horrific toll on children and their parents, as well as undermining progress in improving child health. Deepening poverty in Africa, economic crises in Asia, and the uneven effects of globalization have added to the number of children living in poverty and being forced to work. To what extent, we must ask, have the strategies for promoting the rights of the child actually transformed the convention's visions into reality?

This chapter introduces a broad framework for analyzing the implementation of a human rights convention such as the CRC. That framework encompasses not only the legal aspects of implementation, such as ratification and national legislation, but also the efforts of key actors, such as intergovernmental and nongovernmental organizations, to widen the acceptance of particular rights, to fill gaps in the rights protected by a convention, and to secure positive rights (such as improved socioeconomic well-being) for protected groups. Among the key actors in the CRC's implementation are the UN Committee on the Rights of the Child, established under the monitoring provisions of the convention; the United Nations Children's Fund (UNICEF); the UN Special Representative on Children and Armed Conflict; and nongovernmental organizations (NGOs) such as the International Save the Children Alliance and the Defense for Children International, which are part of the NGO Group for the Convention on the Rights of the Child. National governments, the UN Security Council, the World Bank, the World Health Organization (WHO), and the Bill and Melinda Gates Foundation are also among the list of actors.

## A FRAMEWORK FOR ANALYZING IMPLEMENTATION

From a legal standpoint, implementation of an international human rights convention such as the CRC entails getting the largest possible number of states to sign and ratify the convention as a first step. Human rights conventions do not depend on universal acceptance for their effectiveness, but human rights activists certainly aim to achieve universality. Six human rights conventions (torture; racial discrimination; women; children; political and civil rights; and social, economic, and cultural rights) call for the establishment of treaty-monitoring bodies by the UN to review reports of ratifying states on their implementation efforts. Judicial implementation of human rights takes place through adoption of appropriate changes in domestic law and its enforcement.

In general, the global human rights system based in the UN provides only limited means for individuals or groups to submit formal complaints against governments for rights violations or to impose sanctions on states for failure to implement the treaties. The European human rights system has much stronger provisions for complaints and enforcement. The tasks of monitoring governments' compliance, publishing data on violations, lobbying for governmental action, educating people about human rights conventions, and organizing grassroots initiatives fall largely to networks of human rights NGOs, making them key actors in the implementation process.

Since human rights treaties, like treaties in general, may deal with some aspects of an issue but not others, the processes of implementation frequently include efforts to expand the definition of protected rights, first, by increasing awareness and, second, by negotiating supplementary protocols. A common strategy for the former has entailed the use of UN-sponsored global conferences, working groups, and special rapporteurs to promote new norms. For example, the 1979 Convention on the Elimination of Discrimination against Women (CEDAW) did little to address problems of violence against women. In the 1980s and 1990s, women's groups used the world conferences on women and the 1993 Vienna World Conference on Human Rights to dramatize issues of violence against women. In 1994, the UN General Assembly overwhelmingly approved the Declaration on the Elimination of Violence against Women, and UN secretary-general Boutros Boutros-Ghali appointed Radhika Coomaraswamy as the first UN special rapporteur on violence against women. In 1998, the Rome Statute for the International Criminal Court (ICC) defined rape and other gender-based violence as crimes against humanity and war crimes. The Optional Protocol to CEDAW, providing procedures for hearing individual and group complaints of violations, came into effect in 2000 and the Protocol to Prevent, Suppress, and Punish Trafficking in Persons, Especially Women and Children came into force in late 2003.

Implementation of international human rights is thus best conceived as a process not only of giving legal effect to conventions but also of expanding the protected rights through additional legal steps such as optional protocols and through the activities of a special rapporteur, a working group of an intergovernmental organization, or an NGO coalition in order to expand awareness of and promote respect for human rights and to press for action to stop violations. Because human rights are not limited to negative rights, however, implementation also includes efforts to achieve positive rights, such as by improving the economic and social well-being of protected groups such as women and children. In theory, it should be easier to analyze implementation in this context using indicators such as health, literacy, income, and mortality than it is to gauge nondiscrimination or rights protection in broader terms. In practice, however, it is difficult to establish a causal link between changes in socioeconomic indicators and greater respect for human rights resulting from ratification of an international human rights convention.

## DRAFTING THE CONVENTION ON
## THE RIGHTS OF THE CHILD

The UN Commission on Human Rights, an ad hoc group of NGOs, and UNICEF played important roles in the ten-year process of drafting the Convention on the Rights of the Child. NGOs have historically been key actors in efforts to protect children's rights. For example, the world's largest independent movement for children, the International Save the Children Alliance, evolved out of the organization that first developed the concept of children's rights in the 1920s. It is still the leading NGO promoting children's rights and consists of thirty autonomous organizations serving one hundred countries worldwide.[2] NGOs' role in drafting the CRC evolved from a few inexperienced representatives of narrowly focused organizations to a highly respected alliance of some twenty NGOs known as the Ad Hoc NGO Group on the Drafting of the Convention on the Rights of the Child, with Defence for Children International serving as secretariat.[3] As of 2004, the Ad Hoc NGO Group has a membership of over fifty international nongovernmental organizations.[4]

The Ad Hoc NGO Group provided basic draft text for a number of articles, raised support and consciousness for the convention, and effected compromises between states during especially difficult negotiations. Indeed, NGO advocacy and lobbying were described by participants as "both quite unprecedented in degree and particularly useful and constructive."[5] This was the first time NGOs played such a key role in drafting a human rights convention. Among the keys to the NGO group's success were its focus on securing a draft convention, its relatively greater professional expertise in the field of children's rights, its support from UNICEF, and its effective use of lobbying and negotiating skills.[6]

UNICEF was also an important actor, although little has been written about its role in the CRC drafting and negotiation process.[7] Beginning in 1979, the International Year of the Child, UNICEF began publishing annually *The State of the World's Children* reports. These reports have provided a cumulative statistical record of the well-being of the world's children and "compelling arguments in favour of stronger measures [to protect children's rights] than mere 'declaration.'"[8] UNICEF's executive director from 1980 to 1995, James P. Grant, provided strong leadership for the organization and played an instrumental role in bringing the CRC and the World Summit to fruition. World leaders' pledges at the 1990 summit to meet specific numerical goals by the year 2000 became UNICEF's operational focus in the 1990s, and the CRC became, in effect, UNICEF's "unofficial constitution."[9]

The CRC is the first international document with legally binding force to set forth specific rights for children and the methods for their implementation. The document enumerates forty-one civil, political, economic, social, and cultural rights linked to four key principles: the child's right to survival and development; respect for the best interests of the child as a primary consideration; the right of children to express their views freely on all matters affecting them; and the right of all children to enjoy all the rights of the convention without discrimination. The articles not only protect children from discrimination, abuse, neglect, exploitation, abduction, and the death penalty but also guarantee positive rights: the right to a name, nationality, an adequate standard of living, health care, education, and voice—all proportionate to children's maturity levels. The convention aims to abolish the concept that children are possessions of their guardians, recognizing them instead as human beings of equal value.[10] Furthermore, unlike previous children's rights documents, the CRC includes specific measures for implementation of its standards. Given the roles of NGOs and UNICEF in drafting the convention, it is not surprising that they were assigned key roles in implementation. Indeed, the CRC is the only human rights treaty that specifically gives NGOs a role in monitoring its implementation by providing that the treaty-monitoring committee could invite UNICEF and "other competent bodies . . . to provide expert advice . . . in areas falling within the scope of their respective mandates" (article 45a). As one analyst notes, "This provision provides NGOs with a platform in the international arena. From this platform NGOs can contribute to the jurisprudence of the Convention."[11] Among other things, they have used that platform, as we shall see shortly, to address what many children's rights activists consider a key omission from the treaty—namely, protection of children in armed conflict and particularly recruitment of child soldiers under the age of eighteen. The issue became the focus of major efforts to develop additional international norms in the 1990s.

## IMPLEMENTING THE CONVENTION

In analyzing the CRC's implementation process, we will examine the reporting process established by the convention and the key roles of NGOs and UNICEF, including efforts to incorporate references to children's rights into the declarations and programs of action of global conferences in the 1990s as a way of broadening support and action. We will also look at the efforts to expand the CRC's legal scope through two optional protocols and through an International Labour Organization (ILO) core convention, the appointment of a UN special rapporteur and special representative. In addition, we examine some of the programs and activities that have been undertaken to implement the CRC's positive rights provisions by improving children's well-being and developmental opportunities.[12]

## THE CONVENTION-MONITORING AND REPORTING PROCESS

To monitor progress in implementing the CRC, article 44 calls on states to submit periodic reports. Initial reports are due two years after states' ratification, and follow-up reports are due every five years thereafter. To review the reports, the UN General Assembly established the Committee on the Rights of the Child in 1991, a group of eighteen independent experts elected by the assembly.[13] This paralleled the process established for the Covenant on Civil and Political Rights as well as the conventions on the elimination of racial discrimination, torture, and discrimination against women. In addition to reviewing state reports, the committee serves as a forum in which governments, NGOs, and other concerned members of the international community can discuss the CRC's implementation.

State reporting helps to determine the degree of recognition for children's rights among citizens and governments as well as establish priorities for implementation and benchmarks for evaluation. Eight areas linked to articles in part I of the convention must be covered in the initial report, including general measures of implementation; the state's definition of a child; guiding principles for the state; civil rights and freedoms; family environment and alternative care; basic health and welfare; education, leisure, and cultural activities; and special protection measures. In addition, states must explain both the coordination of national law and policy with the CRC and their dissemination strategies.

Representatives from UNICEF, other UN agencies, and NGOs frequently assist states in preparing their CRC reports and by informally reviewing them before the committee receives them. These representatives and the committee itself may put questions to state parties before formal review. Government officials and committee members then meet in a public session, after which the committee forwards its recommendations and concluding observations to the UN Economic and Social Council (ECOSOC).[14]

As of early 2004, 254 reports had been submitted, 27 were due, and 224 were overdue; but the committee itself lags in its report reviews, owing to the extensive time and attention the process requires.[15] For example, in its fall 2000 session, the committee reviewed eight initial reports and two second-round reports. Given the near-universal ratification of the convention, the committee's goal of reviewing reports within a year of receipt is impossible to meet. An added problem is the extensive amount of paper and data that the state reports generate. In short, the scope of the CRC and the reporting requirements pose an enormous information management challenge for the Committee on the Rights of the Child and the UN's Centre for Human Rights, which manages human rights data and is responsible for disseminating them to the largest number of groups—a key to enhancing the monitoring process.

Additionally, the CRC provides for submission of separate reports by non-state actors, which UNICEF and others now routinely do. This has put them in the position of assisting with reports and commenting on them in some cases, thereby creating a potential conflict of interest.[16] In fact, UNICEF has increasingly taken on a de facto monitoring role with respect to the CRC, one that risks politicizing its work and jeopardizing its relationships with host governments whose consent it depends on to carry out its other activities.[17]

Unlike four other human rights treaties, the CRC monitoring and reporting process makes no provision for individuals or groups to submit formal complaints against governments nor for sanctioning governments that fail to make progress toward implementation. Implementation, therefore, depends primarily on individual governments and on pressure from citizens, NGOs, and the international community. In addition to UNICEF's role, children's rights efforts have benefited from NGO proliferation and the globalization of information. Networks established by the largest international NGOs link them to grassroots groups around the world that collect data on children's conditions and the extent to which their rights are respected. The data then form the basis for NGO reports that may influence public opinion or be used as a basis for mobilizing action within countries and transnationally.[18]

Changing domestic law is clearly a key aspect of implementing international human rights treaties, but a systematic examination of efforts in the 197 state parties to the CRC is far beyond the scope of this chapter. As of 2000, fifty states had undertaken legal and constitutional reforms to improve children's rights, and twenty-three others were undergoing legal reviews.[19] Over twenty countries had established independent posts, such as children's ombudsmen or national commissions to serve watchdog roles.[20] Ten (mostly developing) countries had developed children's parliaments.[21] The reality, however, is that governmental implementation of the CRC generally involves lengthy political debates.

## IMPROVING RESPECT FOR CHILDREN'S RIGHTS THROUGH EDUCATION

Education and increased awareness have been the province of a largely NGO-composed coalition, the Children's Rights Information Network (CRIN), established in 1995 with UNICEF sponsorship. Through its website, e-mail lists, and newsletter, CRIN offers a wealth of information to NGOs, UN agencies, and other international organizations, educational institutions, and children's rights experts globally. It focuses on children's rights in general and on more specific concerns such as AIDS and children in armed conflict. Fifty-five percent of CRIN's eleven hundred members come from the South, making it a truly global network.[22] The online accessibility and wealth of information offered by CRIN have greatly aided monitoring and implementation.

In addition, Childwatch International established a network of research institutions.[23] These networks multiply what single NGOs could perform only with significant resources. Furthermore, they reduce redundancy and facilitate transnational conversations between groups to improve existing standards and implementation mechanisms. Some educational tasks are carried out by individual NGOs, such as Defense for Children International, which has taken responsibility for wide distribution of the CRC text and a graphic description of children's basic rights.

Arguably, education is the most effective way to implement the CRC. It is fundamental to the respect of children's rights that they and their guardians understand them. Yet, in most states, the CRC has not become part of school curricula, and Save the Children asserts that the "vision of children's rights is failing to filter down from central to local government," which is often the primary provider of children's services.[24] NGOs continue to pressure national and local governments to raise awareness of the CRC among children and adults. They have also been key actors in the process of incorporating children's rights into the documents produced by various global conferences in the 1990s as a strategy to galvanize action.

## LINKAGES WITH GLOBAL CONFERENCE OUTCOMES

The 1990 World Summit on Children initiated a decade of global conferences and summits focused on the environment, human rights, population, women, social development, human settlements, food, and education. To increase public awareness and promote further implementation, NGOs concerned with children's rights lobbied extensively to include children's rights language into global conference declarations and programs of action. They recognized the opportunity that these global conferences afforded to increase awareness of children's rights among governments and other NGO networks.

Four common themes emerge from an analysis of the children's rights included in six global conference outcomes: discrimination against children, the particular needs of the girl child, child labor, and education (see table 2.1). Additionally, the 1992 UN Conference on the Environment and Development incorporated a child's right to a clean environment, which is not guaranteed by the CRC. The 1993 World Conference on Human Rights stressed a number of positive rights, such as reduced infant and maternal mortality rates, malnutrition, and illiteracy, as well as basic education and safe drinking water. The Beijing Declaration of the 1995 Fourth Conference on Women in Beijing, in a move important for further elaborating children's rights, called for the drafting of an optional protocol on child prostitution and pornography.

The 1995 Copenhagen Summit on Social Development provided impetus for a new convention on child labor. Almost all the conferences stressed education and equal access for girls, but the April 2000 World Forum on Education focused particularly on children often excluded from education, such as girls, working children, children of minorities, and children affected by violence, disabilities, and AIDS, and it reiterated the goal of education for all by 2015.[25]

The inclusion of children's rights in global conference outcomes illustrates the multidimensional nature of efforts to implement the CRC. The proposals for expanding the CRC's scope through optional protocols on child prostitution and pornography and on children in armed conflict and through a convention on child labor were taken up by the UN Commission on Human Rights and the ILO, respectively.

**Table 2.1. Global Conferences and Children's Rights**

*1992 UN Conference on the Environment and Development (Rio de Janeiro)*
- Called for the increased participation of children in caring for the environment
- Recognized the environment and children as important future resources

*1993 World Conference on Human Rights (Vienna)*
- Called for the investigation of children in armed conflict
- "First Call for Children" grants children priority
- Urged removal of reservations to the CRC and universal ratification by 1995

*1994 International Conference on Population and Development (Cairo)*
- "Best interest of the child" should guide decision making
- Called for increased welfare and decreased discrimination of the girl child
- Focused on children's health

*1995 World Summit on Social Development (Copenhagen)*
- Stressed importance of families, noting vulnerability of children
- Called for equal access for the girl child
- Noted the importance of labor rights
- Called for the increased participation of children in education and rights awareness

*1995 World Conference on Women (Beijing)*
- Suggested the drafting of the optional protocol on the sale of children, child prostitution, and child pornography
- Called for the elimination of discrimination, negative cultural attitudes and practices, and economic exploitation against the girl child
- Promoted education, skills, and development training, as well as health and nutrition
- Called for the promotion, protection, and increased awareness of the rights of the girl child

*2000 World Education Forum (Dakar)*
- Agreed to focus on children victims of discrimination: girls, minorities, working, disabled, AIDS, and victims of violence
- Set goal of free education

## EXTENDING THE LEGAL SCOPE OF CHILDREN'S RIGHTS

As with many conventions, the legal scope of the CRC has now been reinforced or complemented by two optional protocols and by an ILO convention, thanks to the efforts of NGOs and UNICEF in pressing for action. In addition, the UN appointed a special rapporteur and a special representative to focus attention on the issues of child prostitution and child soldiers, respectively, and these individuals were important actors in the efforts to strengthen legal norms.

### Child Labor

According to *The State of the World's Children 2000*, 250 million children below age fourteen work; up to 60 million of those are between ages five and eleven and work in hazardous conditions. The ILO estimates that half of them work full-time.[26] Following the CRC's conclusion, the ILO pressed to put child labor at the forefront of the international agenda on children. Eleven surveys conducted by the ILO's International Programme on the Elimination of Child Labour in 1992, plus three international conferences (Amsterdam 1997, Oslo 1998, and Geneva 1999) raised international awareness of the extent of child labor. In addition, aided by UNICEF, the ILO established the Statistical Information and Monitoring Programme on Child Labour to assist governments in tracking child labor trends. This strategy culminated in the unanimous approval of ILO Convention 182, the Convention Concerning the Prohibition and Immediate Action for the Elimination of the Worst Forms of Child Labour, at the June 1999 General Conference session. The convention outlaws the severest forms of child labor (including child soldiering), furthers CRC article 32, and, like the CRC, came into force in record time, with ratifications by 143 states. It also brings to bear ILO mechanisms for monitoring states' compliance with ILO core conventions. In addition, UNICEF has designed its role at the national level to cooperate with governments in monitoring compliance with ILO Convention 182.[27]

### Sale of Children, Child Prostitution, and Child Pornography

Article 35 of the CRC requires "all appropriate national, bilateral and multilateral measures to prevent the abduction of, the sale or traffic in children for any purpose or in any form." The relative brevity and ambiguity of this article suggest the taboos on the subject. Prevention of these abominable forms of child labor requires the cooperation not only of states but also of transnational corporations and criminal groups. "Sex tourism" has become a lucrative business, especially in Southeast Asia and in Latin American countries such as Costa Rica. The program, End Child Prostitution in Asian Tourism, attempts to decrease the demand by improving measures to prosecute sex offenders upon their return home.[28] UNICEF has made public education about child prostitution in Southeast Asia a priority and aids NGO efforts to bring children out of the sex trade.[29]

The UN Commission on Human Rights first appointed the special rapporteur on the sale of children, child prostitution, and child pornography in 1990. It subsequently drafted optional protocol 1, the first international legal document regarding these topics. The protocol was opened for signature at the UN Millennium Assembly in June 2000 after its adoption by the General Assembly on May 25, 2000. As of early 2004, sixty-six states had signed optional protocol 1, and forty-seven had ratified it. The protocol requires that the sale of children, child prostitution, and child pornography be prosecuted as criminal offenses, and it strengthens grounds for jurisdiction and extradition to facilitate prosecution.[30] The Millennium Assembly also approved a second optional protocol, on children and armed conflict. The issue of child soldiers has, in fact, received far more attention.

## Children and Armed Conflict

As noted, the NGO group for the CRC failed to secure provision in the treaty to protect children in armed conflict and, in particular, to ban recruitment of child soldiers under the age of eighteen. Not surprisingly, then, these issues were raised at the first session of the Committee on the Rights of the Child in 1991 and an entire day of meetings was devoted to the subject at the second session in 1992. Among proposals made by the NGO Quaker Peace and Service was the appointment of a special rapporteur or working group to study and monitor the issues.[31]

In 1994, on the recommendation of the UN Commission on Human Rights, the UN Economic and Social Council established a working group to begin drafting an optional protocol on the involvement of children in armed conflict. Likewise in 1994, following calls from the 1993 World Conference on Human Rights and the Committee on Rights of the Child for the investigation of children and armed conflict,[32] UN secretary-general Boutros Boutros-Ghali appointed Graça Machel, former minister for education of Mozambique, to investigate a number of issues, including "participation of children in armed conflict; reinforcement of preventive measures; relevance and adequacy of existing standards; measures required to improve protection of children affected by armed conflict; and, actions needed to promote the physical and psychological recovery and social reintegration of children affected by armed conflict."[33] Her report, issued in 1996, provided "the first comprehensive assessment of the multiple ways in which children suffer in times of armed conflict."[34] Most important, according to Machel, the report "exposed a moral vacuum in which all taboos had been eroded and discarded and a world in which children were no longer considered precious."[35] It called for immediate action to ameliorate the situation and for the appointment of a special representative to the secretary-general on children and armed conflict.

Children suffer as victims, perpetrators, and bystanders of violent conflict and as refugees, displaced persons, and victims of rape. Between 1990 (when the CRC came into effect) and 2000, more than two million children were killed in armed conflicts, and over six million were injured or disabled.[36] Furthermore, an estimated three hundred thousand children participated in armed conflict, some of them as young as ten.[37] In West Africa alone, security analysts estimate that fifteen thousand children were used as combatants in Liberia's civil war and another ten thousand in Sierra Leone's brutal conflict.[38] UNICEF estimates that nearly half of the forty million people displaced by conflict or human rights violations are children.[39] Today, nearly seventy thousand children are estimated to be participating in violent conflict in Myanmar, one of several countries in which child soldiers are currently used. Children are even frequently used by militias and paramilitary groups.

Although the use of children in war is not new, several factors account for increased usage in the 1990s. These include the proliferation of civil and ethnic conflicts without clear war zones and distinction between combatants and civilians. Also, arms such as the M16 and AK-47 are light enough for a child to use and are widely available. Poverty and homelessness, compounded by large numbers of HIV/AIDS orphans, especially in Africa, provide not only incentives for children to join military and paramilitary forces but also opportunities for forcible abduction. Whether children come to be combatants through "conscription, abduction or coercion" or by volunteering, they often suffer brutal treatment.[40]

On May 25, 2000, the UN General Assembly adopted optional protocol 2, on children and armed conflict. The protocol seeks to protect children from the increasing threat and effects of armed conflict and prohibits governments and nongovernmental armed groups from using children under eighteen years of age as direct participants in combat. Additionally, it raises the age of voluntary enlistment to sixteen and strengthens international standards by requiring proof of age and informed consent by both parents and volunteers. The optional protocol had been signed by 111 countries and ratified by sixty-three countries as of 2004. Among ratifying parties is the United States, which insisted that the protocol stand alone from the CRC so that it could ratify the protocol without having ratified the convention itself.[41]

Three actors were important to achieving the protocol by raising the general awareness of the issues. They include the Special Representative for Children and Armed Conflict Olara Otunnu, former foreign minister of Uganda and president of the International Peace Academy, who was appointed by Secretary-General Kofi Annan in 1997; the group of NGOs that in 1998 formed the Coalition to Stop the Use of Child Soldiers; and the UN Security Council.

As special representative, Olara Otunnu has proven to be an effective spokesman for children around the world. His numerous initiatives have increased awareness of the issue throughout the world through his annual reports, media attention, website, and travels to various conflict areas, with particular attention on Africa, where the problems are greatest. Graça Machel describes Otunnu's work as having "raised the profile of this issue to the extent that is now placed firmly on the international peace and security agenda."[42] Indeed, at least within the UN system, nothing testifies to this more than the increased attention that children and armed conflict have received from the Security Council since 1998.

The NGO coalition's goal for children was "to prevent their recruitment and use, to secure their demobilization, and to ensure their rehabilitation and reintegration into society."[43] In addition to advocating the "straight 18 principle," the coalition sought to include nonstate groups as parties. Its activities were aimed not only at the negotiations in the working group on a draft protocol but also at public education, media campaigns, and regional conferences to raise awareness of the issue, stop the use of children in armed conflict, and build support for the proposed optional protocol. The NGO coalition was also active in efforts to get conscription, use, or enlistment of children under the age of fifteen included as a war crime in the statute of the International Criminal Court.[44]

The Security Council took up the issue of children and armed conflict as a result of "concern at the harmful and widespread impact of armed conflict on children and the long-term consequences this has for durable peace, security and development."[45] It has passed four resolutions dealing with the issue, and it now holds an annual open session on children and armed conflict in addition to considering how specific conflicts affect children.[46] The council also included child protection advisors in the mandates of the peacekeeping missions to Sierra Leone, the Democratic Republic of the Congo, and Angola, and it included the use of child soldiers among the war crimes to be prosecuted by the International War Crimes Tribunal for Sierra Leone.

The first legal application of the optional protocol has been underway in the International Criminal Court, which agreed in January 2004 to hear the Ugandan government's case against the Lord's Resistance Army and its use of child soldiers during the country's long civil war. A further extension of the norm against child soldiers is the provision in the African Charter on the Rights and Welfare of the Child banning recruitment of children under the age of eighteen. Ratified by thirty-one states, this is the first regional human rights treaty to incorporate the ban.

Although much of the implementation effort has focused on these issues of child labor, child prostitution, trafficking, and child soldiers—the so-called norms of prohibition—efforts have also been devoted to implementing some of the CRC's positive rights provisions. Here, there are even greater challenges to be met.

## POSITIVE RIGHTS: IMPROVING THE WELL-BEING OF THE WORLD'S CHILDREN

Unlike human rights conventions such as the Convention on Torture or the Genocide Convention, the CRC's broad scope calls for measurable, tangible improvements in the lives of children around the world that fit squarely within the realm of so-called positive rights. For this aspect of implementation, governmental and private resources must be redistributed to ensure greater efforts to promote children's material well-being. Governments, UNICEF, the World Bank, the WHO, the major children's rights organizations, and private foundations are all key actors. Also critical to this aspect of implementation, however, is the development of an agreed-on set of indicators and benchmarks for measuring changes in children's well-being.

Since the promulgation of the CRC, efforts have been made to improve measurements of children's well-being by developing better indicators. Such indicators are a tool for securing permanent change and shifts in thought. Along with regular reports, they serve to increase public awareness, record achievements, and provoke action.[47] Those commonly used include the infant mortality rate, gross primary school enrollment ratio (number of students enrolled in school compared to children of primary school age), percentage of children under five suffering from acute malnutrition, and the percentage of the population with access to safe water. The UN has sponsored seminars and conferences for exchanging ideas on effective methods, while Childwatch International of Norway sponsors the Child's Rights Indicators Project. These efforts seek ways to measure states' compliance with generalized treaty standards, such as the right to an education. Yet, when there are wide discrepancies between rich and poor countries, what constitutes a violation of the convention? The goal is "not [to] impose a set of universal guidelines but . . . [to establish] a framework . . . for data collection and indicator development that are relevant to regional, national and local situations" and that cover every article in the CRC.[48] The task is further complicated by the fact that existing data have often proven inconsistent and inadequate. UNICEF's *State of the World's Children* remains a primary source of data. In addition, the International Save the Children Alliance published its first annual *State of the World's Mothers Report: 2000,* linking mothers' well-being to that of their children and providing a new set of indicators.

Two primary areas of children's positive rights are health and education. To illustrate the challenge of implementing these aspects of the CRC in various parts of the world, we focus briefly on the efforts of UNICEF, NGOs, and other actors and on trends in children's well-being since the promulgation of the CRC in 1990. A clear pattern of partnerships among various actors and mixed results emerges. It is much more difficult to establish a clear relationship between the convention and those results.

## Improving Children's Health and Education

Although UNICEF has always promoted the well-being of the world's children, historically this occurred with minimal reference to the language of human rights.[49] It revised its mission statement in 1996 to reflect its rights-based focus in partnership with governments, civil society organizations, and communities. Its priorities include access to immunizations, routine health services, adequate nutrition, improved sanitation and safe water, and quality education. UNICEF is also one of the UN partner organizations in delivering humanitarian relief in natural disasters, armed conflicts, postconflict situations, and refugee camps. The very nature of its role makes UNICEF the coordinator and leader of CRC implementation.

Because healthy people are a prerequisite to further economic and social development within a country, UNICEF has made health initiatives a priority and has worked with several public and private partners. It spends $100 million annually for health efforts and focuses much of its attention on the estimated twelve million children under five years of age that die annually of preventable conditions such as diarrhea, respiratory infections, vaccine-preventable diseases, malaria, and perinatal conditions.

In 1992, UNICEF joined with the WHO to create the Integrated Management of Childhood Illness, targeting the leading killers of children. The program now works in sixty countries.[50] More recently, the two organizations have stepped up immunization efforts with the support of the World Bank, the Bill and Melinda Gates Children's Vaccine Program, and the Rockefeller Foundation by creating the Global Alliance for Vaccines and Immunization (GAVI). With a five-year mandate and $750 million from the Bill and

Melinda Gates Foundation, GAVI purchases vaccines and safe-injection materials. In March 2000, UNICEF secured availability of the polio vaccine with three international suppliers to meet its goal of global polio eradication by 2005. Working with WHO, Rotary International, and the U.S. Centers for Disease Control and Prevention, it planned to vaccinate 450 million children by the end of 2000.[51]

Immunizations have contributed significantly to the decrease of child deaths. Although polio has not yet been officially eradicated, due largely to problems of noncooperation in Nigeria, it along with measles, diphtheria, tetanus, and other common child killers has decreased significantly with the increased immunization efforts. Still, thirty million children have never been immunized against any sort of disease, according to the *State of the World's Children 2002.* Quantitative analysis of immunization trends is difficult, however, due to a lack of consistent time-series data. (A similar problem prevents progress evaluation regarding access to safe drinking water.) WHO has pledged to make 2000 a base year for various health indicators to facilitate future analyses.

Due in part to increased immunizations, infant mortality rates dropped in half between 1980 and 1998 in both middle- and high-income countries. In fact, sixty countries reduced child mortality by one-third, achieving a goal set by the World Summit in 1990.[52] A reduction of nearly thirty deaths per one thousand births over an eighteen-year period occurred in both middle- and low-income countries. The drops in the first eleven years, however, are significantly higher than those of the second decade, calling into question trends *since* the CRC's promulgation. The drops in deaths of children under five years of age are even more significant: sixty-one fewer deaths per thousand in low-income countries, and forty-one fewer deaths per thousand in middle-income countries over the nineteen-year period. The effects of HIV/AIDS are particularly evident, however, for sub-Saharan Africa, where AIDS has significantly set back children's health improvements. "Half of all new HIV infections in the world are among youngsters," and AIDS has orphaned over 13 million children.[53]

With respect to education, overall access has improved in the past two decades. Although a drop in the percentage of children attending school occurred as a result of population growth in the 1980s, the fact is that more children attend school today than ever before. Of the 130 million children that do not attend school, however, 60 percent are girls.[54] In part because of this problem, the 1994 UN Conference on Population, the 1995 Fourth World Conference on Women, and 2000 World Conference on Education all called for ending discrimination against girls. To address educational needs, states participating in the 2000 conference on education agreed to spend $8 billion to guarantee free education by 2015, and the World Bank pledged "multiples" of the $1.9 billion lent the previous year. Private foundations such as Ford, Rockefeller, and MacArthur also pledged more than $100 million over five years to support higher education in sub-Saharan Africa.[55]

It is difficult to make a direct causal connection between the CRC and these efforts to improve the education and health of children. Yet, it is hard not to see that the treaty was both a product of efforts to promote and protect children's rights and an impetus for further efforts to secure tangible improvements not only in legal protections but also in material conditions.

## CONCLUSION

The task of turning the CRC's vision of children's rights into reality has barely begun more than a decade after the convention came into effect. Yet the process of implementation shows the active efforts of many actors — including national governments, NGOs, UNICEF, and other international agencies — to turn the rhetoric of the CRC's principles into realities of greater respect for children as subjects of rights and increased well-being, demonstrated by improvements in key indicators such as education/literacy, health/immunizations, and poverty rates. In addition, the legal scope of the norms for children's rights has been expanded through the two optional protocols and ILO convention 182. The treaty-monitoring process, however, has become bogged down in the Committee on the Rights of the Child because of the sheer volume of reports to be reviewed. Many factors impede progress, among them the slow process of changing thought patterns and the finite resources available to improve the well-being of children in many parts of the world. In a decade that has seen rapidly escalating demands on those resources for unprecedented humanitarian disasters, questions have been raised about where the UN should intervene. Thomas Weiss notes, "Humanitarian practitioners estimate that 10 to 20 times more could be accomplished with the same limited resources by attacking what United Nations Children's Fund (UNICEF) has called poverty's 'silent' emergencies, rather than the 'loud' emergencies caused by warfare. Each day, for example, 35,000 to 40,000 children worldwide perish from poverty and preventable diseases."[56]

The "loud" emergencies do continue to receive the brunt of attention and resources. With the increasing poverty gap fostered by globalization, neither the "silent" nor the "loud" problems appear to be on the verge of solution. The vision of the Convention on the Rights of the Child remains tainted by poverty, abuse, neglect, and war — to name a few culprits. The CRC, however, strives not just to rescue children from terrible conditions but also to empower them *as children* to be competent participants in shaping the world they will inherit. "Tomorrow's challenges have to be met by today's children."[57] How well they meet those challenges will be the measure of the success of efforts today by governments, international organizations, and civil society to prepare children for leadership and collective responsibility.

One small indicator of success was evident in the participation of nearly two hundred children at the UN General Assembly Special Session on Children, May 8–10, 2002, and of ninety-four million people, including many children, in UNICEF's 2001 "Say Yes to Children" campaign to choose the three most important issues concerning children. In a statement before the General Assembly's opening session, children pledged their equal partnership in securing their rights. The special session itself reaffirmed the priority of the 1990 goals and set new ones for the year 2015, recognizing that the task of turning the CRC's vision into reality continues.

## NOTES

1. Paul Gordon Lauren, *The Evolution of International Human Rights* (Philadelphia: University of Pennsylvania Press, 1998), 282–83.

2. For a short history of Save the Children, see Michael Longford, "NGOs and the Rights of the Child," in *"The Conscience of the World": The Influence of Nongovernmental Organisations in the UN System*, ed. Peter Willetts (Washington, D.C.: Brookings Institution, 1996), 215–16.

3. Longford, "NGOs," 220–23.

4. Claire Breen, "The Role of NGOs in the Formulation of and Compliance with the Optional Protocol to the Convention on the Rights of the Child on Involvement of Children in Armed Conflict," *Human Rights Quarterly* 25 (2003): 453–81.

5. Glenn A. Mower Jr., *The Convention on the Rights of the Child: International Law Support for Children* (Westport, Conn.: Greenwood Press, 1997), 17. For extended treatment of NGOs' role in drafting the convention, see Per Miljeteig-Olssen, "Advocacy of Children's Rights—the Convention as More Than a Legal Document," *Human Rights Quarterly* 12, no. 1 (1990): 148–55; Longford, "NGOs," 218–30; and Cynthia Price Cohen, "The Role of Nongovernmental Organizations in the Drafting of the Convention on the Rights of the Child," *Human Rights Quarterly* 12, no. 1 (1990): 137–47.

6. Longford, "NGOs," 224–25.

7. See Richard Jolly, "Implementing Global Goals for Children: Lessons from UNICEF Experience," in *United Nations–Sponsored World Conferences: Focus on Impact and Follow-Up*, ed. Michael G. Schechter (Tokyo: United Nations University Press, 2001), 10–28; Maggie Black, *Children First: The Story of UNICEF, Past and Present* (New York: Oxford University Press, 1996); and Joel E. Oestreich, "UNICEF and the Implementation of the Convention on the Rights of the Child," *Global Governance* 4, no. 2 (April–June 1998): 185.

8. Longford, "NGOs," 220.

9. Oestreich, "UNICEF," 187.

10. Thomas Hammarberg, "The UN Convention on the Rights of the Child—and How to Make it Work," *Human Rights Quarterly* 12, no. 1 (1990): 99. See also, Mower, *Convention on the Rights*. Western states opposed the inclusion of economic and social rights as they had opposed "second generation" rights that are incorporated in the Covenant on Economic, Social, and Cultural Rights.

11. Breen, "Role of NGOs," 458.

12. For an overview of the first decade of implementation, see International Save the Children Alliance, *Children's Rights: Reality or Rhetoric? The UN Convention on the Rights of the Child: The First Ten Years* (London: International Save the Children Alliance, 1999). For a discussion of treaty reservations, see William A. Schabas, "Reservations to the Convention on the Rights of the Child," *Human Rights Quarterly* 18, no. 2 (1996): 472–91.

13. Mower, *Convention on the Rights*, 14–15. Mower has the most extensive treatment of the committee's work. Originally, ten experts composed the committee; a 2002 amendment to article 43.2 increased its size in an attempt to expedite the review process. See www.ohchr.org/english/bodies/crc/index.htm.

14. Cynthia P. Cohen, Stuart N. Hart, and Susan M. Kosloske, "Monitoring the United Nations Convention on the Rights of the Child: The Challenge of Information Management," *Human Rights Quarterly* 18, no. 2 (1996): 443–45. Four sections constitute the concluding observations: Introduction, Positive Factors, Principal Subjects of Concern, and Suggestions and Recommendations; an additional section may be added for any serious violations.

15. The data on reports are available online at www.unhchr.ch/tbs/doc.nsf.

16. Cohen, Hart, and Kosloske, "Monitoring the United Nations Convention," 445–46. See also, Oestreich, "UNICEF," 191.

17. Oestreich, "UNICEF," 191 and 195.

18. Two excellent studies of NGO networks are Margaret E. Keck and Kathryn Sikkink, *Activists beyond Borders* (Ithaca, N.Y.: Cornell University Press, 1998); and Ann M. Florini, ed., *The Third Force: The Rise of Transnational Civil Society* (Washington, D.C.: Carnegie Endowment for International Peace, 2000).

19. Sophie Beach, "Children and Youth," in *A Global Agenda: Issues before the 55th General Assembly of the UN*, ed. John Tessitore and Susan Woolfson (New York: Rowman & Littlefield, 2000), 209.

20. Save the Children, *Children's Rights*, 24.

21. The ten are India, Slovenia, Burkina Faso, Mali, Venezuela, Ecuador, Jordan, Lebanon, Bangladesh, and Uganda, at www.humanrights-usa.net/child.html.

22. At www.crin.org. See also, Cohen, Hart, and Kosloske, "Monitoring the United Nations Convention," 466. About 84 percent of CRIN's members are NGOs. Leading members include Save the Children (United Kingdom), Rädda Barnen (Save the Children, Sweden), the International Save the Children Alliance, the NGO Group for the Convention on the Rights of the Child, Defence for Children International, the International Children's Centre, and Human Rights Internet.

23. Arlene Bowers Andrews and Natalie Hevener Kaufman, "Confronting the Implementation Challenge," in *Implementing the UN Convention on the Rights of the*

*Child: A Standard of Living Adequate for Development*, ed. Andrews and Kaufman (Westport, Conn.: Praeger, 1999), 216.

24. Save the Children, *Children's Rights*, 287.

25. Beach, "Children and Youth," 210.

26. For statistics on child labor, see www.ilo.org.

27. Oestreich, "UNICEF," 189–90.

28. Information on End Child Prostitution in Asian Tourism is available at www.ilo.org.

29. Oestreich, "UNICEF," 189.

30. U.S. Congress, Senate Committee on Foreign Relations, 106th Cong., 2nd sess., Protocols to the Convention on the Rights of the Child: Message from the President of the United States Transmitting Two Optional Protocols to the Convention on the Rights of the Child, Treaty Doc. 106–37 (Washington, D.C.: GPO, 2000), viii.

31. Breen, "Role of NGOs," 461–65.

32. A/CONF.157/23 and General Assembly resolution 48/157.

33. "Report on Impact of Armed Conflict on Children Exposes Moral Vacuum, Secretary-General's Expert Tells Third Committee," press release GA/shc/3382, 8 November 1996.

34. A/55/442, 3.

35. A/shc/3382.

36. Beach, "Children and Youth," 211.

37. A/55/442. Olara Otunnu, *Protection of Children Affected by Armed Conflict*, report of the special representative of the secretary-general for children and armed conflict (New York: UN Department of Public Information, 2000).

38. "Voices of the Children: 'We Beat and Killed People,'" *Newsweek*, May 13, 2002, 29.

39. At www.unicef.org.

40. Graça Machel, *Impact of Armed Conflict on Children*, A/51/306 (New York: UNICEF/UN, 1996), available at www.unicef.org/graca. For further discussion of the factors, see Center for Defense Information, "America's Defense Monitor," *Child Soldiers: Invisible Combatants*, show transcript (June 29, 1997), available online at www.cdi.org/adm/1042; Ilene Cohn and Guy S. Goodwin-Gill, *Child Soldiers: The Role of Children in Armed Conflict* (Oxford: Clarendon Press, 1994); and "Kalashnikov Kids," *Economist*, July 10, 1999.

41. A/55/442, 5.

42. A/55/442.

43. At http://web.amnesty.org/ai.nsf/Index/IOR510052000?OpenDocument&of= THEMES\HUMAN+RIGHTS+INSTRUMENTS.

44. See Breen, "Role of NGOs," 466–81, for an extended discussion of the efforts by NGOs to influence the text of the Optional Protocol on Children in Armed Conflict.

45. S/RES/1261.

46. The four Security Council resolutions are S/1261 (1999), S/1314 (2000), S/1379 (2001), and S/1460 (2003).

47. Asher Ben-Arieh, "The International Effort to Measure and Monitor the State of Children," in Andrews and Kaufman, *Implementing the UN Convention*, 33–46.

48. Quoted in Cohen, Hart, and Kosloske, "Monitoring the United Nations Convention," 464. The conferences and seminars included a 1992 Seminar on Appropriate Indicators to Measure Achievements in the Progressive Realization of Economic, Social, and Culture Rights, held in Geneva; and the 1996 Measuring and Monitoring the State of Children Conference, in Jerusalem.

49. Thomas G. Weiss, David P. Forsythe, and Roger A. Coate, *The United Nations and Changing World Politics*, 3rd ed. (Boulder, Colo.: Westview Press, 2001), 194.

50. At www.unicef.org.

51. Beach, "Children and Youth," 213.

52. Dafna Linzer, "Despite Positives, Notable Failures Also Confront UN Children's Summit," *Dayton Daily News*, May 5, 2002, 16A.

53. Somini Sengupta, "Goals Set by UN Conference on Children Skirt Abortion," *New York Times*, May 11, 2002, A8; and Sengupta, "UN Session Begins to Tally the Perils of Being Young: Record Shows Some Gains, Much Suffering," *New York Times*, May 9, 2002, A8.

54. Kofi Annan, "Opening Statement," at www.un.org/ga/children/sgopening/htm.

55. Beach, "Children and Youth," 210.

56. Thomas A. Weiss, "Collective Spinelessness: UN Actions in the Former Yugoslavia," in *The World and Yugoslavia's Wars*, ed. Richard H. Ullman (New York: Council on Foreign Relations, 1998), available at www.cfr.org.

57. International Save the Children Alliance, *Children's Rights*, 294.

*Chapter Three*

# Strengthening the Framework for Enforcing Children's Rights: An Integrated Approach

Ursula Kilkelly

The Convention on the Rights of the Child is the most highly ratified instrument in international law.[1] But, it is regrettably true that in some states, the convention has had no real impact on the lives of children who endure poverty, exploitation, and abuse on a daily basis. Even in other states—where the convention has paralleled, if not been directly responsible for, some change in attitudes to children, a greater awareness about children's rights, and an increased visibility of children in society—complacency and children's-rights fatigue threaten the continued momentum of the children's rights movement. In both cases, vigilance is required to ensure that pressure is kept on governments to fulfill their commitment to guarantee convention rights to all children. Attention must be directed to mainstreaming children's rights and developing dynamic ways to measure and monitor implementation and compliance with children's rights standards. In this regard, the Committee on the Rights of the Child has prioritized the establishment of structures and systems for monitoring and coordinating implementation of the convention.[2] This process must include the development of benchmarks and indicators to assist in the process of children's rights proofing of law, policy, and budgetary matters; and the establishment of national bodies with statutory responsibility for overseeing the development and implementation of policies concerning children's rights, including an independent office of Ombudsman for Children.[3]

While these approaches have clear potential to bring about improvement in the lives of children in the long term, in isolation, their potential to remedy serious violations of children's rights or to provide an effective remedy in individual cases is limited. The search must thus continue for ways to secure greater legal protection for children's rights at the international and national levels. Continuing attention should be given to maximizing the potential of existing mechanisms for the enforcement of children's rights.[4] Such an approach should involve, inter alia, persuading national, regional, and international courts to be guided by the comprehensive range of children's rights standards that the Convention on the Rights of the Child offers in their determination of children's cases. This approach is already evident in the European Court of Human Rights, the Inter-American Court of Human Rights, and some national courts, including those in Canada and the United States. This chapter explains the varying legal bases for the approach, looks at its application in a number of areas and jurisdictions, and questions generally whether it can bring about greater legal protection of children's rights at the national and international levels.

## CONVENTION ON THE RIGHTS OF THE CHILD: A SOURCE OF STANDARDS

The Convention on the Rights of the Child (CRC) enjoys enormous consensus at the international level. Since its unanimous approval by the General Assembly of the United Nations in 1989, it has attracted the highest number of ratifications of any international treaty within an extremely short period of time.[5] It is clear that in addition to its legally binding nature, the CRC also enjoys a certain moral force.

The CRC's most outstanding feature is the comprehensive nature of its substantive provisions.[6] It has four principal provisions: the right to life, survival, and development (article 6); the right to enjoy convention rights without discrimination (article 2); the requirement that the best interests of the child is a primary consideration in all actions taken concerning children (article 3); and the right of children, in all matters concerning them and in accordance with their age and maturity, to express their views and have them given due weight (article 12). According to the Committee on the Rights of the Child, these principles must apply to how all of the convention's provisions are implemented. In addition to these guiding principles, the convention sets out the rights to be secured to children and young people in many aspects of their lives and in a variety of circumstances. Its provisions are numerous and detailed and combine widely recognized civil and political rights, such as the right to identity, freedom of expression, and the right to a fair trial;[7] and social, economic, and cultural rights, including the right to an adequate standard of living and the right to health care.[8] Many convention provisions reflect those of the UN's more general human rights instruments,[9] but the CRC also recognizes rights specific to children, such as the right to play; the right to maintain regular contact with both parents; and the right to protection from abuse, neglect, and ill-treatment.[10]

However effective the reporting mechanism is under the CRC, the Committee on the Rights of the Child has no power to hear individual complaints or to sanction states for noncompliance.[11] In the absence of an international mechanism for enforcing the convention's standards, it is only by putting the standards to use elsewhere that the convention can hope to play a truly effective role in the protection of the rights of children and young people. Invoking the standards in judicial hearings at the national and international levels in cases concerning children is an approach that has the potential to combine the enforcement potential of existing systems of individual petition—such as the European Court of Human Rights, the Inter-American Court of Human Rights, and higher courts at the national level—with the convention's comprehensive and detailed standards. The short-term result is to provide individual children with an effective remedy based on the convention, this approach may also promote greater respect for children's rights by encouraging greater legal reliance on and reference to widely accepted children's rights values throughout the domestic and international legal systems.

The legal basis for this approach will vary depending on the jurisdiction. In the regional or international context, it is possible to argue generally that the almost-universal ratification of the convention makes reliance on its provisions relatively uncontroversial. Stronger arguments may be made in relation to certain provisions such as nondiscrimination and best interests, which may be said to have acquired the standard of customary international law. In the domestic context, the approach will depend on the standing enjoyed by international treaties ratified by the state. Thus, while in many jurisdictions, ratification gives the convention the force of domestic law, ratification in itself is insufficient to give the convention such authority in dualist states, making the approach more problematic. Even where the convention falls short of the binding legal standard, there can be little legal objection to a court seeking mere guidance or support from the widely accepted, minimum standards that the convention represents. Indeed there is much to support in an integrated approach to the protection of the rights of children, which promotes the interactive effects in standards and mechanisms and aims to combine the benefits of both.

## THE EUROPEAN EXPERIENCE

### Suitability of the European Convention of Human Rights for This Approach

The European Convention of Human Rights (ECHR) is a uniquely successful system for enforcing human rights at the regional level. The convention has

been ratified by forty-five states and has now been given further effect or has
been incorporated in some form into the legal systems of all state parties. However, the ECHR's relevance to children is limited by the fact that the convention contains few specific references to the rights of the child.[12] Nevertheless,
the case law of the European Court of Human Rights has made a considerable
contribution to child law and policy across Europe.[13] Whether supplementary
or complementary, one feature of the European Court's dynamic approach to
the interpretation and application of the convention in children's cases has
been its practice of drawing on the provisions of the Convention on the Rights
of the Child and other international children's rights standards. It has made
such references with positive effect in a number of areas, which are detailed in
the following section. Although the ECHR is short on substantive rights for
children, a number of its features make use of the CRC as an interpretive guide
that is both possible and valuable in the ECHR context. First, many of the
ECHR's provisions are phrased in broad terms, allowing them to be interpreted
in an expansive and imaginative way. For example, article 8, which guarantees
the right to respect for private and family life, has been found to include the
right to maintain direct contact with both parents,[14] the right to identity,[15] and
the right to family support, such as parental leave allowance.[16] Thus, the broad
nature of convention provisions like article 8, which is obviously particularly
relevant to children, facilitates their interpretation in a way that takes into account the particular needs and rights of the child.

Second, article 1 of the ECHR guarantees convention rights and freedoms
to "everyone," and this provision has a central role in the way in which the
convention is interpreted and applied. The child's equal entitlement under the
convention is enforced further by article 14, which prohibits discrimination in
the enjoyment of convention rights on numerous grounds, including age.[17] In
theory, then, convention rights are guaranteed to all, and except for practical
difficulties, there is little to prevent their application to children. Moreover, in
practice, the court has not placed either express or general limits on the application of the convention in children's cases. References to the standards of
the CRC have encouraged this approach and generally raised the profile of
children's rights in ECHR proceedings, as well as at the domestic level,
where such cases necessarily originate.

Third, the court has frequently noted that the ECHR is a living instrument that
must continue to evolve to maintain relevance to current legal and social conditions.[18] This approach recognizes that the convention cannot operate in isolation
from surrounding legal and social influences, and indeed, the court has always
drawn on factors outside of the ECHR in applying the convention's standards.
This is evident from the court's application of the margin of appreciation according to which contracting states are allowed a certain degree of discretion
when they take legislative, administrative, or judicial action in the area of a con-

vention right.[19] The exercise of this discretion is subject to European supervision, and the European Court of Human Rights has applied it to mean that where issues in a particular case touch on areas where there is little common ground among member states, the respondent state must be afforded a wide margin of appreciation within which to guarantee convention rights.[20] Consequently, then, states will enjoy less discretion where their approach is out of line with commonly accepted standards and norms both within the Council of Europe and beyond. Moreover, in the court's judgment in *Goodwin v. UK*, in July 2002, the court went further by attaching less importance to the lack of evidence "of a common European approach" and more to the clear and uncontested evidence of a continuing international trend in the area (of recognizing the right of a postoperative transsexual to a new birth certificate).[21] There is thus clear evidence that the court is willing to look beyond the text of the ECHR when applying its standards to maintain the convention's relevance to modern law and society.

Among the sources upon which the court draws in applying the convention in new contexts are the various legal instruments and treaties that make up international human rights law. In children's cases, the European Court of Human Rights and the European Commission of Human Rights have referred to the Council of Europe's 1975 Convention on the Legal Status of Children Born Outside Wedlock[22] and the Convention on Adoption.[23] References have also been made to the UNESCO (United Nations Educational, Scientific, and Cultural Organization) Convention against Discrimination in Education, the 1959 Declaration on the Rights of the Child,[24] and more recently to the Convention on the Rights of the Child.[25] In 2002, the court referred in a judgment to the Charter of Fundamental Rights of the European Union.[26] This was not a children's case, but the charter contains a specific children's rights provision—article 24, which sets out the child's right to care and protection, the right to be heard, and the best interests principle—and thus makes the court's willingness to refer to it significant.[27] It is important also in the light of the tendency of the European Court of Justice and the European Court of Human Rights to share standards in the area of fundamental rights and freedoms generally.[28]

In terms of the legal basis for this approach, article 31.2 of the Vienna Convention provides that when interpreting a treaty, the agreements and instruments formally related to it should be taken into consideration along with the system within which it is inscribed. Moreover, article 53 of the ECHR itself provides that

> nothing in this Convention shall be construed as limiting or derogating from any of the human rights and fundamental freedoms which may be ensured under the laws of any High Contracting Party or under any other agreement to which it is a party.

Accordingly, all ECHR states are bound to give preference to treaties to which they are a party, such as the Convention on the Rights of the Child, to the extent that they set higher human rights standards of protection than the European Convention. Although article 53 does not expressly oblige or empower the European Court of Human Rights to police those higher standards, the court cannot be without a role in furthering this objective.

In any event, the fact that all contracting parties to the ECHR have ratified the Convention on the Rights of the Child means that all such states have, in principle, committed themselves to its implementation. This undoubtedly adds weight to the court's ability to use its provisions as a guide when interpreting ECHR provisions in cases in which children are involved. As long as it does not lead to an interpretation of its provisions that goes beyond the convention's spirit and purpose, use of the CRC in this way must be seen as a valuable and useful interpretive tool. This approach is particularly important in cases in which children are involved, where ECHR guidance is frequently absent and where, as a consequence, the detailed and specific provisions of the UN Convention on the Rights of the Child can be used to great effect as sign posts in the interpretive process.

## Reliance on the Children's Convention by the European Court of Human Rights

To date, the European Court of Human Rights has referred to the Convention on the Rights of the Child in a variety of areas, including juvenile justice, identity rights, and child protection. In doing so, its practice has varied from simply listing the relevant provisions in the section "Relevant International Texts," which precedes its judgment in the case, to making express references to CRC provisions as the basis for its reasoning in the case. There follows some illustrations of these approaches.

### *Juvenile Justice*

Article 6 of the ECHR guarantees the right to a fair trial in criminal and civil matters before an independent and impartial tribunal within a reasonable time. The second and third paragraphs set out the additional safeguards, which are to apply to criminal trials, such as the right to be considered innocent until proven guilty, the right to a lawyer, and the right to have witnesses cross-examined. With the exception of the reference in article 6.1 to the need to protect juveniles from adverse publicity, the provision offers no special protection for the rights of young people involved in criminal proceedings.

However, article 6 has been found to include other rights that are an inherent part of the fair-trial process, such as the right to access and participate effectively in such proceedings.[29] These have obvious significance for minors. In addition to reiterating these guarantees, article 40 of the CRC provides that children in conflict with the law must be treated in a way that promotes the child's sense of dignity and worth and takes the child's age into account.[30] In 1999, the European Court of Human Rights expressly recognized the importance of adapting the criminal justice system in children's cases. This it would have been unlikely to do without the guidance offered, directly or indirectly, by the Convention on the Rights of the Child and other child-specific international standards in this area.

Before the court's judgment in the *T* and *V* cases (in each case, a young boy was charged with murder and tried in an adult court), references to international standards in juvenile justice had been made only in concurring or dissenting judgments and opinions by members of the commission and court. In the *Nortier* case, for example, the applicant minor complained that he had not received a fair hearing by an independent tribunal, in contravention of article 6, because the same judge took decisions on his case both at the pretrial and the trial stages.[31] Although the lack of evidence of bias in the case meant that his claim failed, dissenting members of both the commission and the court found it relevant that the juvenile justice system in question was designed to take the particular needs and circumstances of the young accused into account.[32] Moreover, Judge Morenilla agreed with Trechsel and his like-minded colleagues on the commission that while minors are entitled to the same protection of their fundamental rights as adults, the application of article 6 to such cases should involve taking into account the developing state of the minor's personality and consequently his or her limited social responsibility. The judge quoted from the preamble of the CRC that states should afford young people the "necessary protection and assistance so that they can fully assume their responsibilities within the community" and to prepare them "to live an individual life in society."[33] He also referred to article 40.3 of the CRC, which requires states to promote the "establishment of laws, procedures, authorities and institutions applicable to children alleged as, accused of, or recognized as having infringed the penal law."[34]

Although this view was not shared by the majority of the court, it is encouraging that Judge Morenilla's opinion was expressed just three years after the CRC came into force and that it did not necessarily contradict the majority view but rather presented a more children's rights–friendly version of it. This awareness of children's rights is not always apparent among the judgments of the court, a point clearly illustrated by its treatment of the applicant in *DG v. Ireland*.[35] Here, the court held that the detention of a young man in a penal institution violated article 5.1.d because it did not serve the purpose of educational supervision. The court was otherwise unconcerned that the young man had not committed a criminal offense and that he was entrusted to the care of the state for his protection on account of his personality disorder rather than for punishment of any crime. Moreover, in measuring the damages at a mere £5,000, the Court noted the boy's detention was necessary on account of his behavior, even if it were not lawful and reduced the dispute to one concerning "disagreement about the place of detention and the presence of educational supervision, rather than the fact of secure detention itself."[36] Regardless of the outcome, reference to relevant international standards, including the Convention on the Rights of the Child, might have encouraged a judgment more in line with widely accepted children's rights standards in this area.

In contrast, the case of *T v. UK* illustrates the differing uses to which the court can put CRC and other international standards.[37] This case concerns the compatibility of articles 3, 5, and 6 of the ECHR with the trial of a ten-year-old boy charged with murder in an adult court in England and his subsequent indeterminate prison sentence. The court identified a number of relevant international texts before proceeding to judgment in the case. In particular, it detailed CRC article 3, which requires that the child's best interests be a primary consideration in all actions taken concerning the child; article 37, which prohibits torture and inhuman and degrading treatment and requires that children be detained only as a measure of last resort; and article 40, which requires the establishment of a minimum age of criminal responsibility and sets out the due process rights to which children in conflict with the criminal law are entitled.[38] Interestingly, in this case, the court listed among the relevant sources of law the recommendation of the Committee on the Rights of the Child that the United Kingdom pursue a child-oriented approach to the administration of juvenile justice and give serious consideration to raising the age of criminal responsibility. The court also cited article 14.4 of the International Covenant on Civil and Political Rights, which requires that criminal procedures take account of the age of young people and the desirability of promoting their rehabilitation, as well as excerpts from recommendation no. R.87.20 of the Committee of Ministers of the Council of Europe on the rights of children in the court process.[39]

Having recognized these standards' general relevance and importance, the court then went on to put them to use. It dealt first with the article 3 complaint, that the decision and process of trying the accused amounted to inhuman and degrading treatment principally due to the United Kingdom's low age of criminal responsibility (ten years). Having referred to the international standards, the court concluded, "At the present time there is not yet a commonly accepted minimum age for the imposition of criminal responsibility in Europe."[40] It went on to note that "no clear tendency can be ascertained from examination of the relevant international texts and instruments" and was particularly persuaded by the fact that neither the Beijing rules nor article 40.3.a of the CRC did more than encourage states not to set the age of criminal responsibility too low.[41] As to whether the boy's trial in an adult court in the full glare of media and public attention violated article 3, the court again referred to the international standards. It noted the relevance of both article 40.2.b of the UN convention, which provides that children accused of crimes should have their privacy fully respected at all stages of the proceedings, and rule 8 of the Beijing rules, which states that "the juvenile's privacy shall be respected at all stages" and that "in principle, no information that may lead to the identification of a juvenile offender shall be published." It then referred to the recommendation of the Committee of Ministers of the Council of Europe that member states should review their law and practice with a view to avoiding committing minors to adult courts where juvenile courts exist and to recognizing the right of juveniles to respect for their private lives.[42] The court went on to consider that these standards demonstrate an international tendency in favor of protecting the privacy of juvenile defendants and noted in particular that the UN convention is binding in international law on the United Kingdom in common with all the other member states of the Council of Europe. This protection, it noted, was also provided for in article 6.1 of the ECHR, which requires that "the press and public may be excluded from all or part of the trial . . . where the interests of juveniles . . . so require." Despite the overwhelming nature of international guidance available to the court in favor of protecting a child's right to privacy, the public nature of the trial was not in itself sufficient to bring the denial of that protection in the present case within the scope of inhuman and degrading treatment, something that arguably says more about the high threshold of article 3 than the persuasive character of the international standards.[43] Notably, the court did recognize that the existence of the international trend in favor of the protection of privacy was a factor to be taken into account when assessing whether the treatment of the applicant was acceptable under the other convention provisions.[44]

Accordingly, the international standards were deemed relevant also to the court's consideration of whether the young accused received a fair trial within the meaning of article 6 of the European convention, which essentially involves two factors: the fundamental question of the child's ability to participate in the proceedings and the inextricably related factor of publicity. Indeed, in its analysis, the court referred expressly to what it described as "the international tendency towards the protection of the privacy of child defendants." It went on to note that where a young child is charged with a grave offense attracting high levels of media and public interest, it is necessary to conduct the hearing in such a way as to reduce as far as possible his or her feelings of intimidation and inhibition. Given that the judge in his summation referred to the problems caused to witnesses by the blaze of publicity and that he asked the jury to take this into account when assessing the evidence, it was highly unlikely that the applicant would have felt sufficiently uninhibited to have consulted with his lawyers during the trial. The court observed that where it is considered appropriate in view of the age of the child and the surrounding circumstances, this need to protect the defendants' privacy could be balanced with the general interest in the open administration of justice by using a modified reporting procedure, including selected attendance rights and judicious reporting. As the trial in this case was conducted with heightened publicity, which led to the release of the defendant's name following the trial's conclusion, the case raised a clear issue of compatibility with article 6.[45] Moreover, given that "it is essential that a child charged with an offence is dealt with in a manner which takes full account of his age, level of maturity and intellectual and emotional capacities, and that steps are taken to promote his ability to understand and participate in the proceedings," this was found not to have occurred in this case, in violation of article 6.[46]

While the issue of the child's inability to participate effectively in the proceedings was the base of the violation of article 6, there is little doubt that the most offensive feature of the trial—and indeed the cause of the circumstances that gave rise to his inability to participate—was the failure not only to limit, if not exclude, public and press attendance and reporting but to otherwise protect his privacy. Although support for protection of the young accused's right to privacy can be found in the convention under article 6, it is notable that the court relied heavily on other international standards, including the Convention on the Rights of the Child, which it noted that the United Kingdom had ratified along with all other Council of Europe states. In this regard at least, the judgment is landmark in nature and provides valuable and necessary guidance to the compatibility of juvenile criminal proceedings and the sentencing of juveniles with article 6 and other ECHR provisions.[47] Even though the court failed to conclude either that the low age of criminal responsibility or the failure to fix the minimum part of an indeterminate sentence was severe enough to constitute inhuman punishment under article 3, the court nonetheless refers expressly in its conclusions to article 37 of the CRC, which provides that the detention of a child should only be used as a measure of last resort and prohibits life imprisonment of minors without the possibility of release.[48] In this context, the court noted that a continued failure to fix a minimum sentence, leaving a detainee in uncertainty as to his or her future over many years, may give rise to an issue under this provision.[49]

Moreover, while the court's conclusion that the United Kingdom was not out of line with state practice in setting its age of criminal responsibility at ten years is a clearly contestable interpretation of the international standards in this area—particularly when states such as Spain use a limit almost twice that age (eighteen years)—its use of the more decisive guidance available on the right to have privacy protected and to ensure that the criminal process be child oriented had a clear impact on its ruling. In this regard, the case stands as a positive example of how the child-specific human rights standards in the Convention on the Rights of the Child can be used to inform the application of a standard provision such as the right to a fair trial in children's cases. It is apparent from the judgment that many of the CRC's standards on juvenile justice have been accepted by the court, which, as an international tribunal, is in a position to enforce them.

## Physical Punishment and Abuse

The influence of the Convention on the Rights of the Child is also clearly evident in cases of physical punishment and abuse. In fact, one of the first references to the CRC was made by the court in the *Costello-Roberts* case, which concerns the physical punishment meted out to a seven-year-old boy in a private school in the United Kingdom.[50] The boy's counsel complained that his treatment violated both article 3 of the ECHR, which prohibits inhuman or degrading treatment, as well as article 8, which requires respect for private life including the right to physical integrity. Although the boy was unsuccessful before the court, the case established for the first time that the state could be held responsible for breaches of the ECHR that occur in the private sphere. In reaching this conclusion, the court gave particular regard to the educational context of the dispute and recalled the state's obligation to secure to children their right to education under article 2 of the first protocol. In this regard, the court noted that the provisions of the convention must be read as a whole. The court held that functions relating to the internal administration of school, such as discipline, cannot be said to be ancillary to the education process. Importantly, support for the court's proposition that the disciplinary system of a school falls within the ambit of the right to education was found in article 28 of the CRC. Thus, the court went on to cite paragraph 2 of that provision, which places an obligation on states to take all measures to ensure that school discipline is administered in a manner consistent with the child's human dignity and in conformity with the CRC. The court relied on this provision to conclude that the state cannot absolve itself from responsibility by delegating its obligations to private individuals or bodies.

The former European Commission of Human Rights has led the way in looking to the CRC for appropriate guidance when applying the European convention's provisions to children. Indeed, in the case of *A v. UK*, the commission was first to make express use of the concluding observations of the UN Committee on the Rights of the Child.[51] *A* was a nine-year-old boy whose representatives complained that the state had failed to protect him from being beaten by his stepfather with a garden cane causing him severe bruising and other injuries. The injuries were serious enough to warrant the prosecution of the boy's stepfather, who was acquitted by a jury that was persuaded by his defense that the punishment amounted to moderate and reasonable chastisement. The boy's complaint to the commission that this amounted to a breach of article 3 was successful, and in its opinion, the commission drew support both from the CRC and the UN committee's application of it. Having found that the treatment in question fell within the scope of article 3, the commission went on to consider whether responsibility could be imposed on the state for punishment inflicted by one private individual on another. While it recognized that a state cannot guarantee through its legal system that such ill-treatment can never be inflicted by one individual on another, the commission concluded that state responsibility will be incurred where it is shown that the domestic legal system, in particular the relevant criminal law, fails to provide practical and effective protection of the rights guaranteed by article 3. In determining whether such protection was provided in this case, the commission attached importance to the international recognition of the need to protect children from all forms of ill-treatment. Here it made particular reference to article 19 of the CRC, which requires states to take all appropriate measures to "protect the child from all forms of physical or mental violence, injury or abuse."[52] In terms of the protection available to the applicant, the commission then noted that criminal sanctions for assault were set out in English law. However, it went on to find that

> the protection afforded in this area by the law to children within the home is significantly reduced by the defense open to parents that the acts in question were lawful, as involving the reasonable and moderate physical punishment of the child.[53]

This defense caused the commission the most concern because in such cases the burden lies on the prosecution to satisfy a jury beyond a reasonable doubt that the punishment was not in all the circumstances reasonable or moderate. The defendant is thus not required to substantiate the reasonable and moderate value of the punishment. The fundamental problem in this case, however, was that the jury, which was required to consider this defense, was provided with little guidance as to the meaning of "reasonable and moderate chastisement." This is significant because, as the commission noted, "the imprecise nature of the expression" had led the UN Committee on the Rights of the Child, when considering the initial report of the United Kingdom under the convention in 1995, to express its concern about the possibility of its being interpreted in a "subjective and arbitrary manner."[54] The commission thus referred directly to the concluding observations of the Committee on the Rights of the Child, not simply to support its own position, but in pointing to further evidence of the problem that it identified. It then went on to add its own concern about the application of the defense of moderate and reasonable chastisement and its compatibility with the test under ECHR article 3 to that of the UN committee. In particular, it noted that the jury did not receive direction on the relevance of such factors as the age or state of health of the applicant, the appropriateness of the instrument used in his chastisement, the suffering experienced, or the relevance, if any, of the defense claim that the punishment was "necessary" and "justified." As a result, and unconvinced by the government's reliance on reported cases involving excessive physical punishment where convictions had been obtained, the commission concluded that domestic law had failed to provide the applicant with adequate and effective protection against corporal punishment that was, in the circumstances, degrading within the meaning of article 3.

While the court reached the same conclusion as the commission in the *A* case, its judgment is phrased in more general terms, not least because the government did not contest proceedings in the court.[55] The court confined its references to the CRC to the question of state responsibility, where it recalled that children are entitled to state protection against serious breaches of personal integrity apropos articles 19 and 37 of the CRC.[56] Thus, although the court failed to make the same specific reference to the UN committee's criticism of the defense of "moderate and reasonable chastisement," it nonetheless made the all-important link between the general prohibition in ECHR article 3 and the equivalent, but more detailed, child-specific provisions of the children's convention. This is evident from the court's conclusion, where it drew on the CRC to establish that

> children and other vulnerable individuals, in particular, are entitled to State protection, in the form of effective deterrence, against such serious breaches of personal integrity.[57]

The commission went on to refer to article 19 of the Convention on the Rights of the Child in *Z and Others v. UK*, including four adults who, as children, had been subjected to appalling neglect and abuse by their parents. The social authorities, aware of the situation, pursued a policy of home visits to monitor the situation rather than remove the children into state care. As a result, the children went on to suffer either long-term or permanent psychological harm. According to the commission, the authorities' failure to remove the children from the care of their abusive and neglecting parents amounted to a violation of the state's positive obligation under article 3 to protect everyone, especially children, from ill-treatment.[58] Thus, in addition to relying on previous case law of the European Court of Human Rights, the commission referred expressly to the international recognition of the principle that children at risk from another individual must be protected under article 19 of the CRC.

While it made no direct reference to the children's convention, the court continued to develop its specific application of the article 3 standard in children's cases in its judgment in Z.[59] The court largely agreed with the commission finding that there had been a violation of article 3, given that the children's ill-treatment constituted inhuman and degrading treatment and that the local authority, which was both aware of the ill-treatment and had the duty and the power to protect the children, failed to intervene.[60] Although the court did not refer expressly to the CRC, the court's judgment reflects a clear understanding of the rights of the child under articles 19 and 37, which can thus be said to have informed its judgment, particularly given the commission's conclusions. In general, it is arguable that the unequivocal nature of these CRC provisions has prompted the court to shape article 3 of the ECHR into an effective remedy for child victims of ill-treatment, even where the injury was not directly inflicted by anyone in a public capacity. Unfortunately, however, the high threshold necessary to attract the protection of article 3 means that it only offers a remedy against severe forms of ill-treatment.[61] Thus, the convention—including the protection of physical integrity as part of private life under article 8—does not yet offer children protection from all forms of abuse and neglect as required by article 19 of the CRC, although certain factors, including the increasing number of Council of Europe countries that have banned physical punishment, may eventually have an impact here.[62]

## Family Law and Identity

There is evidence of the influence of the Convention on the Rights of the Child in other areas of case law of the European Court of Human Rights. For example, there is a strong link between much of the case law on family life in relation to the alternative care of children and the principles and provisions of the CRC.[63] In particular, much of the ECHR case law mirrors the reliance on the best interests principle in article 3 of the CRC as well as the importance of contact between parents and children in care recognized in article 9.3

of the CRC.[64] Moreover, the importance of parental involvement in all aspects of alternative care proceedings, recognized in article 9.2 of the CRC, is put into practice by the European Court of Human Rights, which has found implicit with respect for family life the requirement that parents be involved in the decision-making process.[65] Cases with indirect relevance to the right of the child to be heard, such as the series of cases against Germany involving the rights of unmarried fathers to contact, have also made reference to the convention in this area.[66]

A further area in which the influence of the Convention on the Rights of the Child is apparent is in relation to the child's right to identity. This case law is inconsistent, however. In 1979, the European Court of Human Rights established the important principle that legal safeguards must enable the child born outside marriage to integrate into her or his family from the moment of birth.[67] Much later, in *Keegan*,[68] concerning the placement for adoption of the child of an unmarried father without his knowledge or consent, the court went on to refer expressly in that context to article 7 of the CRC, which recognizes the child's right to know and be cared for by his or her parents.[69] Yet, only two years later, in *X, Y, and Z v. UK,* the court appeared to sidestep dealing directly with the child's right to know his or her biological parents, in a case concerning the relationship between a child born by assisted human reproduction, her mother, and the mother's partner, who was a female-to-male transsexual.[70] While recognizing that the relationship between the three family members constituted family life within the meaning of article 8, the court failed to find that respect for this relationship required the father's name—that is, the name of the mother's partner—to be entered onto the child's birth certificate, given that he could not biologically be her father. While the court appeared to postpone the question of whether it is in the child's interests to have the name of a person who is not the biological father on her birth certificate, it would appear that the transsexual dimension of the case was more influential than any genuine regard by the court for the child's right to know the identity of her birth father.[71] The fact that the transsexual's right to identity has itself received a significant boost by the Strasbourg court's ruling in the *Goodwin* case may mean a future *X, Y, and Z* would be decided differently.[72] In addition to its clear recognition of the important practical significance of the right to identity in the *Goodwin* case, the court upheld the child's right to identity in two other important cases—the *Gaskin* judgment before and the *Mikulic* judgment since—in an approach very much in line with the article 7 of the CRC. In *Gaskin*, for example, the court acknowledged the importance that people can access information "necessary to know and understand . . . childhood and early development" and noted that persons who, like the applicant, have spent the majority of their lives in care, have a vital interest, protected by the convention, in receiving that information.[73] Moreover, according to the commission,

> an individual's entitlement to such information relating to his or her basic iden-
> tity and early life is not only of importance because of its formative implications
> for his or her personality. It is also, by virtue of the individual's age and condi-
> tion at the relevant time, information which relates to a period when the individ-
> ual was particularly vulnerable as a young child and in respect of which personal
> memories cannot provide a reliable or adequate source of information.[74]

The court made it clear that this right was not absolute, however, and that it must be balanced with the need for a reliable and objective system of record keeping, of which confidentiality is an important part. Ultimately, therefore, it was the lack of an independent authority with the power to determine whether access to information should be permitted where the contributor withholds consent that amounted to a violation of the applicant's respect for his private and family life under article 8.

The court showed further appreciation for the significance of the child's right to information relating to his or her identity in *Mikulic v. Croatia* in 2002.[75] Here, the five-year-old applicant and her mother instituted civil pro-ceedings to establish paternity. When the alleged father failed to attend for DNA testing on several occasions, the domestic court gave judgment that this corroborated the mother's testimony that he was the child's father. Concerned that this did not establish whether this man was in fact her father, the appli-cant complained to the European Court of Human Rights that the failure to resolve the situation decisively violated her right to respect for private and family life. The court agreed unanimously, noting that the procedure available to establish paternity, whereby no sanction compelled the alleged father to comply with the court's order, failed to strike a fair balance between the right of the child to have her uncertainty as to her personal identity eliminated without unnecessary delay and that of her supposed father not to undergo a DNA test. While the court did not refer expressly to article 7 of the Conven-tion on the Rights of the Child, it is clearly in line with this provision regard-ing the child's right to identity.

Yet the strength of this principle was largely ignored when the court con-sidered the issue of access to birth information following adoption in *Odievre v. France* in 2003.[76] The applicant in this case submitted that her inability to trace her birth mother, who had abandoned her at birth and expressly re-quested that information about the birth remain confidential, violated her rights under article 8. Rejecting her complaint, the Grand Chamber held that the French legislation, which entitled adopted children to certain nonidenti-fying information about their birth parents but prohibited contact where birth parents withheld consent, struck a proportionate balance between the competing interests, given the wide margin of appreciation enjoyed by the state in this complex and sensitive area. Quite apart from being out of line with the well-established precedent of *Gaskin*, which was followed in *Mikulic* in 2002, the decision can be criticized for the unjustifiably wide margin of appreciation given to France in relation to the concept of anonymous births. Such a policy is relatively rare throughout the rest of Europe—in fact, as the court noted, a far greater number of states actually *require* the names of both mother and father to be registered at birth. That fact should have therefore highlighted the exceptional nature of the French approach, thereby narrowing the discretion to which the state is entitled here. Moreover, the lack of consensus among the court members is clear from the fact that out of the majority (seven of ten dissented), four judges wrote separate opinions. Indeed, the view of the minority more accurately reflects international law and best practice on the issue of secrecy in adoption—that is, that the court had failed to give proper consideration to whether France had reached an appropriate balance between the parties in the light of the clearly established importance of birth information to adopted children. Rather than acknowledge, as the majority did, that contacting birth parents is a risky process for all parties, the minority view recognized in particular the suffering that lack of information about family origins can cause a child. The view thereby coincides more readily with the provisions of the Convention on the Rights of the Child, to which the dissenting opinion referred. While the particular circumstances of *Odievre* and the lack of agreement in the court over its judgment undermine its value, it is nonetheless of serious concern that the Grand Chamber of the court can produce a judgment so out of line with clear international standards on the child's right to identity and, indeed, with its own case law. It is a reminder of the need for vigilance among lawyers and the judiciary alike to ensure that attitudes and practices that are out of line with the Convention on the Rights of the Child are not justified in other terms and that widely accepted international principles should at least inform case law on children's rights before international tribunals.

## INTER-AMERICAN COURT OF HUMAN RIGHTS

While the American Convention on Human Rights (ACHR) offers greater express protection for children's rights than the ECHR, the Inter-American Commission of Human Rights and the Inter-American Court of Human Rights have not had many opportunities to apply their standards in children's cases. However, in the one case that did address the rights of children—the

*Street Children* case—the court made the bold step of making explicit use of the Convention on the Rights of the Child as an interpretive tool, and in its approach went clearly beyond the approach of the European Court of Human Rights illustrated earlier.[77] The case concerned the kidnapping, torture, and murder of five children who lived on the streets of Guatemala City and the failure to investigate and prosecute those responsible. The commission, who referred the case to the court, argued inter alia that there had been a violation of article 19 of the convention, which provides that "every minor child has the right to the measures of protection required by his condition as a minor on the part of his family, society and the State." In particular, it alleged that Guatemala had violated article 19 by omitting to take measures to "safeguard the development and life of the victims," to investigate and end the abuse, to punish those responsible, and to "train and impose adequate disciplinary measures and penalties on its agents."[78] The court noted in the strongest terms the particular gravity of the fact that a party to the ACHR can be charged with having applied or tolerated a systematic practice of violence against at-risk children in its territory. It noted that when states violate the rights of at-risk children such as "street children" in this way, it makes such children victims of a double aggression. First, the states do not prevent the children from living in misery, thus depriving them of the minimum conditions for a dignified life and harmonious development as required by the CRC; second, they violate their physical, mental, and moral integrity, and even their lives.[79]

Regarding the interpretation of article 19 of the ACHR, the court reiterated its case laws that when interpreting a treaty, the agreements formally related to it should be taken into consideration (article 31.2, Vienna Convention) as should the system within which it is inscribed. The court noted that it had indicated that this focus is "particularly important for international human rights law, which has advanced substantially by the evolutive interpretation of international protection instruments" to which it has itself subscribed. The court went on to say that

> both the American Convention and the Convention on the Rights of the Child form part of a very comprehensive international *corpus juris* for the protection of the child that should help this Court establish the content and scope of the general provision established in Article 19 of the American Convention.[80]

The court noted that the CRC contains various provisions that relate to the situation of "street children," and "in relation to Article 19 of the American Convention, it throws light on the behavior that the State should have observed towards them."[81] According to the court, these provisions "allow us to define the scope of the measures of protection referred to in Article 19 of the

American Convention, from different angles." Among them, the court continued, "we should emphasize those that refer to non-discrimination, special assistance for children deprived of their family environment, the guarantee of survival and development (art 6), the right to an adequate standard of living and the social rehabilitation of all children who are abandoned or exploited." It concluded, accordingly, that it was clear that "the acts perpetrated against the victims in this case, in which state agents were involved, violate these provisions" and that, accordingly, article 19 of the American convention had been violated as well.[82]

The Inter-American Court of Human Rights clearly took the opportunity in this case to make explicit use of the Convention on the Rights of the Child to elucidate the obligations that article 19 of the American Convention on Human Rights places on state parties. Of relevance here is the fact that all parties to the American convention have also ratified the CRC and that the court was clearly persuaded that this gave the convention additional force that supported its approach.

## DOMESTIC COURTS

### The United States of America

The possibility of relying on the Convention on the Rights of the Child may be regarded as more problematic in the United States, given that it is the only country that has signed but not ratified the convention. However, the U.S. Supreme Court is not completely adverse to considering laws of other jurisdictions, which clearly do not bind it, as a way of referring to standards in use elsewhere. For example, it made effective use of the case law of the European Court of Human Rights in a recent case concerning the criminalization of homosexuality. In *Lawrence v. Texas*, the Court relied on the case of *Dudgeon v. UK* and other judgments to support its position that allowed it to overrule the famous *Bowers* decision and conclude that a Texas statute criminalizing homosexuality was incompatible with the due process clause of the U.S. Constitution.[83] According to the Court

> to the extent *Bowers* (the decision upholding homosexuality as criminal behavior) relied on values we share with a wider civilization, it should be noted that the reasoning and holding in *Bowers* have been rejected elsewhere. The European Court of Human Rights has followed not *Bowers* but its own decision in *Dudgeon v. United Kingdom.* . . . Other nations, too, have taken action consistent with an affirmation of the protected right of homosexual adults to engage in intimate, consensual conduct. . . . The right the petitioners seek in this case has been accepted as an integral part of human freedom in many other countries.

There has been no showing that in this country the governmental interest in circumscribing personal choice is somehow more legitimate or urgent.[84]

It is clear from this passage that the Supreme Court was persuaded by the norm established in ECHR jurisprudence on the right to privacy of homosexuals and that the Court saw no justification for the U.S. position to be out of line with this well-established, albeit European, standard. This approach is clear precedent for petitioners to raise law of the European Court of Human Rights in other areas before the U.S. Supreme Court, and the potential for interactive effects of human rights standards is obvious. Political intentions aside, the fact that the United States has not ratified the Convention on the Rights of the Child may not necessarily prevent the U.S. courts from referring to its provisions, given the almost-universal support that the convention enjoys outside the United States. One of the areas in which this approach has already been tested is immigration law, and the judgment of note here is that handed down by the Court of Appeals for the Second Circuit in *Beharry v. Ashcroft*.[85] The petitioner in this case was a native of Trinidad who entered the United States as a lawful permanent resident at the age of seven and who had a daughter who was an American citizen. Following his conviction for robbery, the Immigration and Naturalization Service (INS) declared him to be deportable, and Beharry sought to challenge his treatment in the district court under section 212.h of the Immigration and Naturalization Act. Section 212, together with relevant case law, grants the attorney general discretion inter alia to waive the deportation of an immigrant who is the parent of a citizen of the United States if it is established that the alien's deportation would result in extreme hardship to the child. Although this relief was prima facie inapplicable to Beharry as a convicted felon, the district court held that precluding relief to him would contravene American obligations under international law, among which the court considered the International Covenant on Civil and Political Rights, the Convention on the Rights of the Child, the Universal Declaration of Human Rights, and customary international law. According to the court, these sources of law might be violated by deporting Beharry without considering the impact such deportation would have on his daughter as a U.S. citizen and that section 212.h should be construed in conformity with international law to avoid a constitutional issue if "fairly possible." Accordingly, the district court attempted a reading that sought to avoid the perceived constitutional issue by holding that "aggravated felons" as referred to in the U.S. legislation were only those aliens whose crimes qualified as aggravated felonies at the time they were committed. Because this was not the case for the petitioner, the district court held that Beharry was entitled to the relief sought and ordered the INS to conduct a hearing under section 212.h. While the decision was reversed on appeal, on the grounds that the petitioner had failed to exhaust administrative remedies, the court of appeals did not find it necessary to discuss the merits of the district court's analysis of the interaction between international law, the supremacy clause, and section 212.h. While it did not expressly disagree with the district court, it did indicate that

> nothing in our decision to revise on other grounds the judgment of the district court should be seen as an endorsement of the district court's holding that interpretation of the Immigration and Naturalization Act in this case is influenced or controlled by international law.

Appeals in other cases have not been successful where the petitioners have attempted to challenge their deportations on the grounds that the rulings are incompatible with international law, including the CRC. The individual courts' responses to them have varied. For example, in *Naoum et al v. Attorney General*, a district court in Ohio held that even assuming that the International Covenant on Civil and Political Rights and the CRC incorporate norms of customary international law as proposed by the petitioner, these provisions—including the best interest principle under CRC article 3 and the right to know and be cared for by his or her parents under CRC article 7—do not prohibit the deportation of alien parents of citizen children.[86] Similarly, in the *Ayala-Caballero* case, the U.S. Court of Appeals for the Ninth Circuit held that it did not have to decide whether article 3 of the CRC was enforceable as federal law.[87] What was important was that the authorities gave significant consideration to the challenges and disadvantages that his children might face if they were forced to return to Mexico with their father. Moreover, it noted, article 3 of the Convention on the Rights of the Child merely requires that "the best interests of the child shall be a primary consideration"; it does not require that those interests will always prevail.

While negative in outcome, these cases are nonetheless important insofar as they affirm an approach entirely in line with article 3 of the Convention on the Rights of the Child, which requires the authorities to undertake an analysis of the impact of the deportation order of a parent whose child is a U.S. citizen.[88]

## Canada

These arguments have enjoyed greater favor in the Canadian courts. In the case of *Baker v. Canada (Minister of Citizenship and Immigration)*, the applicant tried to challenge his deportation by relying on the CRC and, in particular, by arguing that the best interest of the child should be a primary consideration in the determination of the immigration matter.[89] When the case was heard by the Supreme Court, it held that the immigration officer did not adequately consider the best interests of the children, and the appeal was allowed. The Court considered the status of the convention in Canadian law and before the Court in some detail. According to L'Heureux-Dube J., speaking on behalf of the majority, although Canada had ratified the convention, this did not give rise to a legitimate expectation that the immigration authorities would apply particular criteria or reach certain conclusions. As it had not been implemented by the Canadian parliament, the convention's provisions had no direct application within Canadian law.[90] That said, however, L'Heureux-Dube J. went on to find that the values reflected in international human rights law might help inform the contextual approach to statutory interpretation and judicial review. More specifically, she noted that a reasonable exercise of the statutory power to allow a person to remain on humanitarian and compassionate grounds requires close consideration to the needs and interests of children, as children's rights are important values in Canadian society. It was implicit in the judgment that the provisions of the Convention on the Rights of the Child would help inform whether the immigration officer had exercised his or her power reasonably.[91] There was some disagreement in the Court regarding the status of international law within the domestic legal system and the approach of applying the underlying values of an unimplemented international treaty consistently. However, the overall conclusion was that the best interest of the child was required to be taken into account as a primary consideration in the immigration decision-making process.

While the Canadian court was more explicit here about the relevance of the Convention on the Rights of the Child, the result of the judgment in *Baker* was the same as that of the U.S. cases—that is, the incorporation into the immigration decision-making process of a requirement to consider the child's best interests. Interestingly, this conclusion is not one that the European Court of Human Rights has been willing to reach so far, and it highlights just one area where the sharing of jurisprudence could work the other way.[92]

## CONCLUSION

It is clear from the small sample of jurisprudence presented here that the interactive effects of international and national standards have the potential to provide enhanced protection of the rights of all children. While the standards used are derived mainly from the Convention on the Rights of the Child, issues regarding how they are implemented in practice emerge both from the conclusions of the Committee on the Rights of the Child and from international and domestic courts. Lawyers and NGOs presenting amicus briefs before such courts should make reference to the convention a consistent part of their petitions to ensure that children's rights are always kept in frame in children's cases. Reference should also be made, where possible, to the concluding observations of the Committee on the Rights of the Child, which are otherwise unenforceable, as this approach could strengthen further the impact of the committee's conclusions on state implementation of the convention. It is further recommended that the committee itself be made aware of other, higher international standards, where they exist, in order to remind states of their wider obligations in the area of children's rights.[93]

In terms of subject area, major advances have been made in relation to family, juvenile justice, identity, and immigration issues. One important challenge that has not yet been tackled is the article 12 principle that children have the right to be heard. It is important that the failure to consult with or involve children directly or indirectly, particularly in legal proceedings, be worthy of test litigation in the European Court of Human Rights and elsewhere.

The importance of using the CRC as an interpretive tool in international and domestic courts cannot be underestimated, particularly given the unprecedented number of states that have ratified the convention. Courts will, by their nature, exercise caution in this area, so it is vital that lawyers and third parties who are submitting amicus briefs remind the courts of the status that the convention enjoys in international law and the significant children's rights perspective that references to its standards can bring. This approach, if used to its full potential in all courts, holds real promise for the enforcement of children's rights values that have been accepted in some form worldwide. It is now time to ensure that the potential is realized.

## NOTES

1. Convention on the Rights of the Child, adopted 20 November 1989, General Assembly Resolution 44/25, UN GAOR, Forty-fourth Session, Supplement 49, UN Document A/44/49 (1989) (entered into force 2 September 1990), reprinted in 28 ILM 1448 (1989).

2. See CRC/GC/2003/5 General Comment No. 5 on general measures of implementation for the Convention on the Rights of the Child.

3. While Australia, New Zealand, and some Scandinavian countries have a longer tradition of establishing offices of ombudsman for children, recent offices have been established in France and Poland (2000); Wales, Slovenia, and Georgia (2001); and Scotland, Northern Ireland, and Ireland (2003).

4. See Ursula Kilkelly, "The Best of Both Worlds for Children's Rights: Interpreting the European Convention on Human Rights in the Light of the UN Convention on

the Rights of the Child," *Human Rights Quarterly* 23, no. 2 (2001): 308–26; and Kilkelly, "Effective Protection of Children's Rights in Family Cases: An International Approach," *Transnational Law & Contemporary Problems* 12, no. 2 (2002): 336–54.

5. The convention was adopted on 20 November 1989 and came into force on 2 September 1990. In sum, 197 states have ratified it. The United States of America signed the convention in 1995, but neither it nor Somalia has ratified it.

6. See, for example, Dominic McGoldrick, "The UN Convention on the Rights of the Child," *International Journal of Law & Family* 5 (1991): 132.

7. See UN Convention on the Rights of the Child, articles 7 and 8, 13 and 40, respectively.

8. UN Convention on the Rights of the Child, articles 27 and 24, respectively.

9. Note, for example, the similarity between article 40 of the CRC and article 14 of the International Covenant on Civil and Political Rights, adopted 16 December 1966, General Assembly Resolution 2200 (XXI), UN GAOR, Twenty-first Session, Supplement 16, article 14, UN Document A/6316 (1966), 999 UNTS 171 (entered into force 23 March 1976). There are also similarities between article 28 of the CRC and article 13 of the International Covenant on Economic, Social, and Cultural Rights, adopted 16 December 1966, General Assembly Resolution 2200 (XXI), UN GAOR, Twenty-first Session, Supplement 16, article 13, UN Document A/6316 (1966), 993 UNTS 3 (entered into force 3 January 1976).

10. See CRC, article 19, which protects all children from abuse, neglect, and ill-treatment; article 20, concerning children deprived of a family environment; article 22, concerning refugee children; and article 23, concerning children with disabilities. Article 9 recognizes the child's right to maintain contact with both parents unless it is contrary to the child's best interests, and article 30 guarantees the child's right to play and leisure.

11. See, for example, Ursula Kilkelly, "The UN Committee on the Rights of the Child: An Evaluation in the Light of Recent UK Experience," *Child and Family Law Quarterly* 8 (1996): 105; Ursula Kilkelly, "In the Best Interests of the Child? An Evaluation of Ireland's Performance before the UN Committee on the Rights of the Child," *Irish Law Times* 19 (1998): 293.

12. Children appear only twice in the convention: in article 5 (detention of minors) and article 6 (exclusion of public from a trial where it is in the interests of juveniles).

13. See Ursula Kilkelly, *The Child and the European Convention on Human Rights* (Brookfield, VT: Ashgate/Dartmouth, 1999).

14. See, for example, *Sahin v. Germany* (GC) no. 30943/96, judgment of 8 July 2003. See also, Kilkelly, *Child and the European Convention*, 251–57.

15. *Mikulic v. Croatia*, 7 February 2002, unreported.

16. *Petrovic v. Austria*, 67 Reports Eur. Ct. HR (1998–II).

17. See Kilkelly, *Child and the European Convention*, 2–6.

18. The court established this approach at an early stage. See *Tyrer v. UK*, 26 Eur. Ct. HR (ser. A) (1978). See also, *Goodwin v. UK*, judgment of 11 July 2002, para. 75, where the court makes it clear that its role was "to assess in the light of present-day conditions what is now the appropriate interpretation and application of the Convention."

19. See also, Nicholas Lavender, "The Problem of the Margin of Appreciation," *European Human Rights Law Review* 4 (1997): 380.

20. *X, Y, and Z v. UK*, 35 Eur. Ct. HR (1997–II).

21. *Goodwin v. United Kingdom*, Eur. Ct. HR, para. 85 (2002). The case concerned legal recognition of the postoperative gender status of a transsexual. Heretofore the court had allowed states a margin of appreciation in this area in the absence of a common European approach. In *Goodwin*, however, the court relied, inter alia, on the evidence of a continuing international trend in favor of legal recognition of the new sexual identity of postoperative transsexuals in order to reduce the margin of appreciation enjoyed by the United Kingdom and found that the failure to allow the applicant to change her birth certificate constituted a violation of article 8 of the convention.

22. ETS No. 85; *Marckx v. Belgium*, 31 Eur. Ct. HR (ser. A), 2 Eur. HR Rep 330, para. 41. This reference was made notwithstanding that only four members of the Council of Europe had ratified it and that it was not yet in force. See Davidson, "The European Convention on Human Rights and the 'Illegitimate' Child," in *Children and the Law: Essays in Honor of Professor HK Bevan*, ed. D. Freestone (Hull, Eng.: Hull University Press, 1990), 75, 94–97, for a criticism of this approach. See also, *Inze v. Austria*, 126 Eur. Ct. HR (ser. A), 10 Eur. HR Rep 394, para. 41 (1987).

23. ETS No. 58. See *X v. UK*, App. No. 7626/76, Eur. Comm. HR DR 11, p. 160 (1977).

24. *Kjeldsen, Busk Madsen & Pedersen v. Denmark*, App. Nos. 5095/71, 5920/72, 5926/72, Eur. Comm. HR 23, Eur. Ct. HR (ser. A) (1975), para. 153. Here, the commission refers to the UNESCO Convention against Discrimination, 1960, 429 UNTS 93, and also the Declaration on the Rights of the Child, 1959.

25. See *A v. UK*, Eur. Ct. HR (1998), para. 22; *T v. UK*, Eur. Ct. HR (1999), para. 71.

26. See also, *Goodwin v. UK*, judgment of 11 July 2002, at 100. See, de Burca, "The Drafting of the European Union Charter of Fundamental Rights," *European Law Review* 26 (2001): 126.

27. Clare McGlynn, "Rights for Children? The Potential Impact of the European Union Charter of Fundamental Rights," *European Public Law* 8, no. 3 (2002): 387–400.

28. See Costello, "EU Law," in *ECHR and Irish Law*, ed. Ursula Kilkelly (Bristol, Eng.: Jordans, 2004).

29. *Airey v. Ireland*, 32 Eur. Ct. HR (ser. A) (1979). See also, P. Van Dijk and G. J. H. Van Hoof, *Theory and Practice of the European Convention on Human Rights*, 3rd ed. (Boston: Kluwer Law International, 1998), 418–28.

30. UN Convention on the Rights of the Child, article 40.1.

31. *Nortier v. the Netherlands*, App. No. 13924/88, Comm. Rep., 9.7.92, unpublished; *Nortier v. the Netherlands*, 267 Eur. Ct. HR (ser. A) (1993).

32. See the dissenting opinion of Trechsel, joined by Schermers, Frowein, and Sir Basil Hall, report of the Commission of Human Rights, and the dissenting opinion of Judge Morenilla, in *Nortier v. the Netherlands*, 267 Eur. Ct. HR (ser. A) (1993).

33. See note 32, p. 18.

34. See note 32, para. 2.

35. *DG v. Ireland*, E. Ct. HR, 16 May 2002.

36. See also, Ursula Kilkelly, "*DG v. Ireland*: Protecting the Rights of Children at Risk—Lazy Government and Unruly Courts," *Dublin University Law Journal* 24 (2002): 268–90.

37. Judgment in two almost-identical cases was handed down on the same day: *T v. UK* and *V v. UK*. Reference here is made only to *T v. UK*.

38. *T v. UK*, E. Ct. HR, 16 December 1999, paras. 44–47.

39. There can be little doubt that the court was following the lead of Sir Nick Bratza, member of the commission, whose concurring opinion in support of the commission's findings of a similar violation of article 6 also made express reference to the best interests principle in article 40 of the CRC, article 14.4 of the International Covenant on Civil and Political Rights, as well as the Beijing rules (UN Standard Minimum Rules for the Administration of Juvenile Justice).

40. See note 39, para. 71.

41. See note 39, para. 72.

42. See note 39, para. 74.

43. The court said that the suffering endured by the applicant also related to the nature of the crime he had committed. See note 39, para. 74.

44. See note 39, para. 75.

45. See note 39, para. 86.

46. *T v. UK*, para. 86.

47. The court also concluded that the failure to reset the applicant's tariff violated article 5.4 of the convention. *T v. UK*, paras. 114–21.

48. *T v. UK*, paras. 93–101.

49. *T* judgment, see note 38, para. 100.

50. *Costello-Roberts v. UK*, 247 Eur. Ct. HR (ser. A) (1993). See also, Kilkelly, *Child and the European Convention*, 160–70.

51. *A v. UK*, App. No. 25599/94, Comm. Rep., 18.9.97, Eur. Ct. HR Reports 1998–VI no. 90, 2703. See also, *T v. UK*, App. No. 24724/94, Comm. Rep.; *V v. UK*, App. No. 24888/94, Comm. Rep., 4.12.98 (unreported); and the aforementioned discussion of the judgment of the court.

52. *A v. UK*.

53. *A v. UK*, para. 50.

54. *Concluding Observations of the Committee on the Rights of the Child: United Kingdom of Great Britain and Northern Ireland*, UN Comm. on the Rts. of the Child, Eighth Session, 208th Meeting, UN Document CRC/C/15/Add. 34, sec. 16 (1995). See also, Kilkelly, *Child and the European Convention*, 114–15.

55. *A v. UK*, Eur. Ct. HR Reports 1998–VI no. 90, 2703 (judgment of 23 September 1998).

56. *A v. UK*, para. 21.

57. *A v. UK*, para. 22.

58. *Z and Others v. UK*, App. No. 29392/95, Comm. Rep. of 10 September 1999.

59. *Z and Others v. UK*, Eur. Ct. HR, 34 Eur. HR Rep 3 (2001).

60. See note 59, paras. 69–75.

61. See Kilkelly, *Child and the European Convention*, 160–83.

62. "The Street Children Case," judgment of May 26, 2001, Inter-Am. Ct. HR (ser. C) No. 77 (2001), paras. 185–96.

63. See, for example, *Olsson v. Sweden*, 130 Eur. Ct. HR (ser. A) (1988); *Andersson v. Sweden*, 226 Eur. Ct. HR (ser. A) (1992); and *Johansen v. Norway* 1996 Eur. Ct. HR, Reports 1996–III no. 12, 979; and see also, Kilkelly, "Effective Protection of Children's Rights."

64. See Kilkelly, "Effective Protection of Children's Rights."

65. See *W. v. UK*, 121 Eur. Ct. HR (ser. A) (1987), and *McMichael v. UK*, 308 Eur. Ct. HR (ser. A) (1995).

66. For example, in *Sahin v. Germany*, the court refers in the text of its judgment to articles 3 and 9 of the Convention on the Rights of the Child, set out in the section "Relevant Domestic and International Law." See *Sahin v. Germany*, [GC] E. Ct. HR, 8 July 2003, para. 64, referring to paras. 39–41.

67. *Marckx v. Belgium* (see note 22).

68. *Keegan v. Ireland*, 290 Eur. Ct. HR (ser. A) (1994).

69. *Keegan v. Ireland*, para. 50.

70. *X, Y, and Z v. UK*, Eur. Ct. HR Reports 1997–II no. 35, 619 (judgment of 22 April 1997).

71. For example, the court made no reference to the fact it is common practice where donor sperm is used for the social father to be placed on the child's birth certificate.

72. In *Goodwin*, the court held that it was no longer sustainable for the United Kingdom to allow those suffering from gender dysphoria to undergo a sex-change operation while refusing them full legal recognition of that change.

73. *Gaskin v. UK*, E. Ct. HR, Series A, no. 160, 12 EHRR 36, sec. 49.

74. No. 10454/ 85, *Gaskin v. UK*, Comm. Rep, 13.11.87, Series A, no. 160, 11 EHRR 402, para. 90.

75. *Mikulic v. Croatia* (see note 15).

76. *Odievre v. France*, E. Ct. HR, 13 February 2003. See also, Ursula Kilkelly, "Reform of Irish Adoption Law—Compliance with International Obligations," *Irish Journal of Family Law* 1 (2004): 10–14.

77. "The Street Children Case," judgment of 26 May 2001, Inter-Am. Ct. HR (ser. C) No. 77 (2001).

78. "The Street Children Case," para 181.

79. "The Street Children Case," para 191.

80. "The Street Children Case," para 194.

81. "The Street Children Case," para 195

82. "The Street Children Case," para 198. The court also found that articles 7 (right to liberty), 4 (right to life), 5 (right to humane treatment) had been violated, as well as articles 25 (right to judicial protection) and 8 (right to a fair trial), with respect to article 1.1 (duty to protect convention rights).

83. *Lawrence v. Texas*, 539 U.S. 558 (2003). See also, *Bowers v. Hardwick* 478 US 186 (1986).

84. *Lawrence v. Texas*.

85. *Beharry v. Ashcroft*, 329 F.3d 51 (2003), US App. Lexis 8279.

86. *Naoum et al. v. Attorney General of the US*, 300 F. Supp. 2n 521 (2004), US Dist. Lexis 1097.

87. *Ruben Ayala-Caballero v. Robert Coleman*, U.S. Immigration and Naturalization Service, U.S. Court of Appeals for the Ninth Circuit, 58 Fed Appx 669.

88. In contrast, see the case of *Lobe & Osayande v. Minister for Justice, Equality, and Law Reform,* Irish Supreme Court, unrep., 23 Jan 2003, which did not consider that the Irish-born child had any right to remain independent of his or her nonnational parents.

89. *Baker v. Canada*, 2 SCR 817 (1999).

90. *Baker v. Canada*, para. 69.

91. *Baker v. Canada*, para. 70.

92. Kilkelly, *Child and the European Convention*, 218–21.

93. For example, when considering the initial report of Ireland, the committee questioned the delegation as to whether the European Court of Human Rights had found Ireland in breach of its obligations with respect to the rights of children. Committee on the Rights of the Child, *Summary Record: Ireland*, 03/03/98, UN Doc CRC/C/SR.437. This approach is to be encouraged.

*Part II*

# CHILDREN IN A
# DANGEROUS WORLD

A global commitment to children's human rights raises moral and practical questions about the distribution of resources among groups within developed countries such as the United States and between rich and poor nations. The opportunity to experience the rights of the child depends on the social and economic resources of laws, policies, and institutions with staff and budgets to commit to protecting children. The authors in this part examine serious social problems that affect children's life chances. They articulate explanations of the social forces and structural conditions involved and consider proposals for changes to address child maltreatment and marginalization.

The chapter titled "The Problem of Sexual Trafficking in Postcommunist Europe," treats the sexual exploitation of children for profit as an aspect of the more general problem of human trafficking. Child prostitution, child pornography, and the sale of children for forced and exploitive labor, including sex, are among the fastest-growing profit sectors for international organized crime. The author analyzes the difficulty of coordinating effective public policy responses across national borders due to conflicting definitions and to the association of child sexual trafficking with the generalized problem of illegal labor migration.

The chapter describes the recruitment of children and minor teens through deception, enticement, and physical abduction. Illegal businesses then keep their coercive control of the victims by physical violence, social isolation as foreigners with no language skills and documents, and the use of threats and even murder. If the victims should escape and be repatriated, they risk rejection by their families, resale, and forced return to sexual exploitation.

The chapter also examines the supply-side factors that have caused the problems to escalate in Eastern Europe, where there had been a great expansion of the sexual trafficking of girls and women to the more prosperous countries in Europe and Asia. The transition to market economies caused massive economic instability and social dislocations that are far from complete. Declines in governmental social spending (including that for education), the fall of the social safety net, and the feminization of poverty have weakened families and communities. In the case of gender-specific exploitation and violence, there is a special link involved in protecting the rights of children and protecting the rights of women. The author considers an array of responses at the national, regional, and international level that are required to prevent the abduction, sale, and sexual traffic of children and further address the gender dimension of children's rights. The author also surveys a set of treaties and the efforts of the Council of Europe to draft a convention with a human rights basis. The unfinished agenda is a daunting enterprise of reducing the economic and social hardships that cause youth displacement, reducing the demand for child sexual services, and removing the promotion of child trafficking that takes place through the Internet.

Empirical information about violations of the CRC in particular societies is a key ingredient in promoting awareness, informed criticism, and compliance with the treaty. The chapter titled "Three Prints in the Dirt: Child Soldiers and Human Rights" surveys contemporary changes in societies and institutional responses to the phenomenon of child soldiers, by which children become an increasing proportion of combatants and victims of modern warfare as it increasingly envelops civilian populations. The author discusses the military roles that children play as combatants, messengers, forced wives, sex workers, porters, and cooks. Countries throughout Africa, Asia, and Latin America have experience with children as young as six to eight years old being conscripted as soldiers. A child soldier is any child under the age of eighteen who is utilized in hostilities by armed forces, paramilitary units, civil defense forces, or other armed groups. The author bases her analysis on interviews she conducted with members of NGO committees and staff members of congressional committees in the United States. She gives particular emphasis to the actions of the UN Office of the Special Representative as it interacts with the Security Council and social movement organizations. She considers the organizations' influence in alleviating the problem of child soldiers by their functions in mediating internal conflicts, stemming the cross-border flows in small arms, and preventing the abductions of children as a resource in warfare. The author emphasizes the role that can be played by transnational advocacy networks. She sees the cultivation of linkages of intergovernmental organizations with NGOs as a unique means to affect state policy and set the global agenda.

The principles of children's human rights present particular challenges in developing countries for transforming a global consensus into significant reforms on behalf of the classes of children who are most at risk in these societies. The chapter "Children's Rights and the Tenuousness of Local Coalitions: A Case Study in Nicaragua" analyzes three community initiatives that seek to address problems of youth alienation and violence in a densely populated poor district of Managua. The authors show the paradoxical qualities of NGOs and their participation in Nicaragua as they attempt to realize the goals of the CRC, which the Nicaraguan government signed and ratified in 1990 and then passed legislation called the Code of Childhood and Adolescence. Children's circumstances in the city of Managua are described in the context of extensive urban poverty, high rates of unemployment, and few state-funded programs of social assistance. These conditions in turn reflect a weak central state operating under transnational political and economic forces that produce high international debt and economic stagnation. The authors examine three projects funded by international aid agencies in Managua over a ten-year period.

The authors find that NGO projects succeed in providing neighborhoods a legitimate forum for authorities and other adults and youth to negotiate differences, but the NGOs prove to be vulnerable to changing loose coalitions and shifts in institutional interests. Also, the NGOs must respond to external demands as they compete for foreign funding, especially when they are dependent on single donors. The authors show that NGOs are unable to sustain advocacy and that they lack the capacity to foster social transformation. They simply cannot depend on municipalities that lack solid tax bases and resource transfers from the central government.

The weak central state acknowledges the injustices of child poverty and its obligation to give children's human rights priority in public policy. It nevertheless remains unable to enforce its own Code of Childhood and Adolescence. The authors demonstrate the need for interconnected and sustained social action and a critical awareness of the political and economic dimensions of child poverty. Improvements in the life chances of the poorest children will depend on solidarity and consolidation of the coalitions working to realize children's well-being in Nicaragua.

The chapter "Protecting Children on the Margins: Social Justice and Community Building" considers actions promoting the fair distribution of the benefits of development on both sides of the U.S.–Mexican border. The authors describe private–public partnerships for children in two communities across national borders that are linked by the unintended consequences of globalization.

The well-being of children and families in both Dayton, Ohio, and Nogales, Sonora, Mexico, are at risk because of economic distress and the insufficiency of local resources to meet the citizens' basic needs. Both cities endure class segregation and failure of corporate investment in the social infrastructure. These limitations are reflected in concentrated poverty, low social cohesion, and problems experienced at the family level on both sides of the border. Also, both cities face serious environmental problems that threaten the livability of the communities, although for different reasons. Dayton is a site of deindustrialization, corporate disinvestment, and job loss that left a legacy of industrial waste sites and the weakening of established city institutions. Nogales is a city stressed by rapid population expansion due to the buildup of *maquiladoras* and the location of "invasion communities" as the demand for housing, sanitation, and human services vastly exceeds the financial ability of the city's tax base to supply them. In both cities, poverty isolates families and leads to children in crisis.

While children's human rights are recognized as a matter of international agreement, the realities of local conditions and negligent or discriminatory practices inhibit the survival and development of children. The role of grassroots approaches to advocacy, awareness, and reforms can be crucial to the protection of children. The insights in this chapter were developed as a result of the University of Dayton's efforts to form partnerships between the academy and the communities on both sides of the border. The authors base their analysis on direct observation in the communities and on participation in efforts to create private–public partnerships to protect children and work for social justice. In both cities, the challenge was to discover ways that the university might use its resources to create local, regional, and even binational partnerships to strengthen families' ability to provide for children. The Dayton case discusses the process that led to discovery of common ground and shared vision among city agencies, professionals, members of the academy, and clients. The purpose was to advocate for the kinds of institutional changes that would better create social justice and child development. The Nogales case discusses community-based solutions and binational efforts to reduce child abandonment and homelessness and find ways for children and their advocates to access political power and economic resources. Both cases involve the search for effective ways to strengthen the bond between the academy and community and to build communities for social justice. The authors conclude that children on the margins need partnerships and the best efforts of social services, neighborhoods, business and government, and academics to support families and create and sustain environments free of neglect, abuse, and exploitation. This chapter illustrates how community building becomes a strategy to alleviate children's distress as disadvantaged persons and a base of action to fulfill the moral obligation to satisfy children's human needs.

*Chapter Four*

# The Problem of Sexual Trafficking in Postcommunist Europe

Jaro Bilocerkowycz

Human trafficking treats people as commodities to be bought and sold, used and reused, and eventually discarded. It has been called an "insidious form of violence" and a pernicious and degrading phenomenon.[1] Women and girls are especially vulnerable to trafficking for prostitution. Estimates of the number of people trafficked globally range from around one million to four million.[2] The International Organization of Migration estimates that some five hundred thousand women and girls, primarily from Central and Eastern Europe, are trafficked into the European Union states annually.[3] An estimated eighteen thousand to fifty thousand persons are trafficked into the United States each year as well.[4] Abundant evidence indicates that Central and Eastern Europe—which as a whole is undergoing major economic, social, and political transitions—have become key suppliers for the European and global sex-trafficking industries.

Traffickers and organized crime make huge profits in this lucrative enterprise. Human trafficking generates some $9 billion a year for organized crime.[5] It is, in fact, the fastest-growing segment of illegal profits for organized crime and ranks third as an overall source of profits, after illegal drugs and guns.[6] Organized crime staffs the sex industry around the world with trafficked women and girls from the Central and East European (CEE) states throughout Europe, Asia, the Middle East, and North America.[7] The human rights of trafficking victims, including child-age girls, are systematically violated as they are subjected to physical and mental degradation. Kofi Annan, secretary-general of the United Nations, states that the trafficking of women and children "for forced and exploitative labour, including for sexual exploitation, is one of the most egregious violations of human rights which the United Nations now confronts. It is widespread and growing."[8] This chapter examines three basic questions: What is human trafficking, and how does it violate the human rights of children and women? What are the supply-side and demand-side factors that explain the growth of sexual trafficking of persons from the CEE states? And, what has been the response of European states and the international community to human trafficking? This study focuses on human trafficking for purposes of sexual exploitation—namely prostitution—rather than for other forms of labor exploitation.

## HUMAN TRAFFICKING

Until recently, there was much confusion and ambiguity about the concept of human trafficking.[9] The conceptual confusion fueled a policy-based confusion over whether trafficking was primarily an issue of illegal labor migration, illegal immigration, organized crime, or human rights. The passage of the Optional Protocol to Prevent, Suppress, and Punish Trafficking in Persons, Especially Women and Children, as a supplement to the United Nations Convention against Transnational Organized Crime, establishes an internationally recognized definition in article 3.a:

> "Trafficking in persons" shall mean the recruitment, transportation, transfer, harbouring or receipt of persons, by means of the threat or use of force or other forms of coercion, of abduction, of fraud, of deception, of the abuse of power or of a position of vulnerability or of the giving or receiving of payments or benefits to achieve the consent of a person having control over another person, for the purpose of exploitation. Exploitation shall include, at a minimum, the exploitation of the prostitution of others or other forms of sexual exploitation, forced labour or services, slavery or practices similar to slavery, servitude or the removal of organs;[10]

The article also notes that "the consent of a victim of trafficking in persons to the intended exploitation . . . shall be irrelevant where any of the means set forth . . . have been used." In the case of trafficked children, those under eighteen years of age,

> The recruitment, transportation, transfer, harbouring or receipt of a child for the purpose of exploitation shall be considered "trafficking in persons" even if this does not involve any of the means set forth in subparagraph (a) of this article.[11]

The United Nations passed a separate Optional Protocol against Smuggling of Migrants by Land, Sea, and Air as a further supplement to the United Nations Convention against Transnational Organized Crime. Thus the issue of smuggling of migrants and aliens for a fee, without an element of forced labor or prostitution or slavery, has been disentangled from human trafficking.[12]

Deemed irrelevant was the contentious issue of whether a victim is one who willingly "consents" to being trafficked abroad for purposes of prostitution. Adult consent might have been given due to coercion, fraud, or deception. So long as there existed sexual exploitation of an individual, then the recruitment, transportation, transfer, and harboring of that person qualified as trafficking. Children under eighteen were treated as a distinct category of trafficked person in article 3 because their age disqualifies them from giving informed consent. Therefore, the issue was deemed not legally germane regarding whether coercion, fraud, deception, or other means were used to gain the consent of a child to be trafficked for prostitution. The recruitment, transfer, transportation, or harboring of a child for prostitution was deemed ipso facto sexual exploitation.

## HUMAN RIGHTS

Human trafficking is flourishing in this era of globalization, with greater freedom for travel for citizens of the CEE states and with more open borders within the European Union among the Schengen states. While the European Union seeks to create a single economic market and space, there also exists a regional and transnational market in trafficking and organized crime. Indeed, the European Union's Romano Prodi has identified organized crime as the major problem facing Europe since the end of communism. And human trafficking for prostitution is a key activity of organized crime in Europe and one that entails systematically violating the human rights of children and women.

Various provisions of the Convention on the Rights of the Child speak to the issue of sexual and economic exploitation of children, most prominently articles 32, 34, and 35.[13] Article 32 recognizes "the right of the child to be protected from economic exploitation and from performing any work that is likely to be hazardous or . . . be harmful to the child's health or physical, mental, spiritual, moral or social development." Article 34 enjoins signatories "to protect the child from all forms of sexual exploitation and sexual abuse." Furthermore, states are to take measures "to prevent: the inducement or coercion of a child to engage in any unlawful sexual activity; the exploitative use of children in prostitution or other unlawful sexual practices; the exploitative use of children in pornographic performances and materials." Finally, article 35 requires that "States Parties shall take all appropriate national, bilateral, and multilateral measures to prevent the abduction of, the sale of or traffic in children for any purpose or in any form." Thus by 1990, when the Convention on the Rights of the Child entered into force, there existed a newly approved international instrument to promote and protect children's rights.

The optional protocol on trafficking identifies "recruitment" as a key dimension of the trafficking phenomenon. So how do traffickers and organized crime "recruit" children (primarily girls under eighteen) and women into international prostitution, where they experience various human rights violations? Three methods of recruitment are most prevalent: deception, enticement, and physical abduction. Whatever the method of recruitment, trafficked persons from the CEE states are often subjected to forced labor and conditions of sexual servitude. Many of the girls and women are deceived by promises of well-paid jobs as dancers, models, waitresses, babysitters, or maids.[14] They have no idea that they were being recruited into forced prostitution. Many of these children and women, trying to escape the economic hardships at home by pursuing a well-paid job abroad, are naïve about the risks and dangers of trusting various employment agencies, newspaper advertisements, or acquaintances. The Russian mafia has even had a recruiting booth at universities and institutes to secure young women for trafficking purposes.[15] A high-level Ukrainian human rights official estimates that about 85 percent of Ukrainian women and girls in international prostitution were duped into the business.[16]

Other CEE girls are enticed to travel abroad to work as prostitutes. These trafficked persons—some of whom had been child prostitutes in their home countries—are aware that they are going abroad to work in the sex industry. Others feel desperate enough to enter or are naïve about the realities of the "oldest profession." Their expectations are that working conditions and pay in international prostitution are much better than the alternatives in their home countries and thus they see it as an opportunity. Physical abduction represents a third method of recruitment.[17] Young girls from Albanian villages, particularly orphans or those from large families, are kidnapped into international prostitution and then trafficked into Italy. Girls in Poland have been drugged in discotheques and bars and then abducted into international prostitution. Runaways or street children in the urban areas are also vulnerable to physical abduction. All three categories of girls and women—the duped, the enticed, and the abducted—face major and systematic violations of their human rights. From a human rights perspective, child prostitution, whether forced or with initial "consent," is inherently a violation of a child's human rights.

Trafficked persons face harsh conditions in brothels, bars, apartments, and other places of confinement. They are physically isolated from the local society and have their passports and personal documents confiscated. These girls and women are subject to physical violence and threats. Beatings, rapes, and even murder are used to impose discipline on the demoralized and traumatized victims. According to the *Economist*, the corpses of several hundred trafficked women are found every year in Europe.[18] Threats are also made against the victim's family members back in the country of origin to discourage efforts to escape, resist, or testify against traffickers. Among the violated human rights of these child victims are the "right to personal liberty, physical integrity of their person, health, the right not to be subjected to torture or cruel, inhuman or degrading treatment, and slavery or forced labour."[19] Victims of trafficking experience substantial damage to their physical health and psychological well-being due to this forced labor and sexual exploitation.

## CHILD PROSTITUTION AND SEXUAL TOURISM

Kofi Annan describes the commercial sexual exploitation of children as invisible, mobile, global, escalating, and highly profitable.[20] One region where child prostitution and trafficking has grown sharply is Central and Eastern Europe. According to UNICEF, there has been "an enormous increase in child prostitution in Eastern Europe—Russia, Poland, Romania, Hungary, and the Czech Republic."[21] Data from the Baltic states indicate that in Estonia between 1994 and 1996, as many as half the women in prostitution (most ethnic Russians) were under eighteen; in Lithuania as many as 20 percent to 50 percent of the prostitutes were minors; and in Latvia 50 percent of street prostitutes were under eighteen.[22] The sharp growth in domestic child prostitution in CEE states during the last decade overlaps with the problem of international child trafficking. This explosion in domestic child prostitution provides abundant resources for organized crime to traffic these girls across Europe and the world. Among the effects on children of trafficking for prostitution are

> injury, disease, and trauma associated with multiple sexual encounters. Child victims of trafficking are usually sent to another country, away from their families and familiar environment, they often do not speak the language, they have absolutely no idea what will be done with them, and they are completely vulnerable to all kinds of abuses. . . . They may become dependent and dangerously attached to pimps and brothel operators. . . . They may be jailed or deported and, on their return home, are at risk of being rejected by families and communities, resold, or forced to return to prostitution.[23]

The trafficking of children and women from the CEE states manifests in several geographical patterns: from East to West (Europe to North America), East to East (from less-prosperous Eastern European states to more-prosperous Central European states), or East to South (Asian states to developing states). The CEE states are variously countries of origin, transit, and destination for trafficked persons. Among the key destination states for trafficked children and women from Central and Eastern Europe are Germany, Italy, the Netherlands, Belgium, Austria, Turkey, Greece, Yugoslavia, Israel, the United Arab Emirates, Japan, and the United States.

While the trafficking of children and women abroad for prostitution involves the transportation of sexual providers across state borders to foreign consumers, sexual tourism involves sexual consumers traveling abroad to foreign sexual providers. Citizens from the more prosperous European countries visit Russia, Romania, or the Czech Republic to be able to engage the services of child prostitutes. Knowing that thousands of street children and runaways are available and have entered a life of prostitution, these tourists come to take advantage. Finnish tourists travel to have sex with twelve- and thirteen-year-old Russian girls (or boys) in Vyborg, Russia, near the Finnish border.[24] Sex tourists from Germany may visit Romania or the Czech Republic to engage in sex with child prostitutes.[25] Children are especially vulnerable to the phenomenon of sex tourism, where the customers seek sexual services from underage minors in an anonymous foreign setting.

The continued growth and traffic in child prostitution, child pornography, and the sale of children globally as well as in Central and Eastern Europe caused the United Nations to adopt the Optional Protocol to the Convention on the Rights of the Child on the Sale of Children, Child Prostitution and Child Pornography in May 2000.[26] This protocol represents an effort to better protect children from sexual exploitation, employs a "holistic approach" to address contributing factors, promotes the child victims' "full social reintegration" and "full physical and psychological recovery," and facilitates international cooperation.


## SOCIAL IMPACT OF ECONOMIC TRANSITION

Most of the states of Central and Eastern Europe are experiencing a significant level of social dislocation and hardship as they make the transition from state socialism to a market-based economy. During the communist era, most of these states had an extensive system of social programs and protections, including inexpensive health care, free education, and near-full employment.[27] As the communist economies struggled, the quality of these social programs and services deteriorated. In the transition to a market economy, governmental support for social spending and services has declined with the move toward establishing private health care, private educational institutions, and private-sector jobs.[28] Postcommunist governments also cut government subsidies for housing, transportation, utilities, and food. As a consequence, the social safety net that the population relied on has eroded, leaving much of the population to struggle to survive in the new economy.[29]

The cuts in social spending and downsizing of social programs have weakened families and communities and have undermined their sense of social well-being and security. Children and girls of the region are particularly vulnerable and socially at risk during this period of economic instability, social dislocation, and psychological stress. It is a period characterized by a feminization of poverty. The economic transition that is taking place in Central and Eastern Europe has caused some seventy-five million people in the region to fall into poverty, with an average decline in income of 50 percent.[30] Other estimates suggest than more than one hundred million people now live in poverty in the area.[31] For every 1 percent increase in poverty rate, there is an estimated 1.4–1.6 percent increase in the poverty rate for children.[32] In 1995, between 50 percent and 66 percent of the populations of Russia, Romania, Ukraine, and Moldova lived below the poverty line.[33] The rising gap between wealthy "haves" and the impoverished "have-nots" characterizes most CEE states and places their youth and children at risk. The gross national product per capita for most CEE states have significantly contracted during the past decade, with few exceptions. As of 1995, nine of twenty CEE states had a gross national product per capita under $1,420 (Ukraine, Macedonia, Bulgaria, Romania), and five scored at or below $760 (Moldova, Azerbaijan, Armenia, Albania, and Georgia).[34]

Rising unemployment is a major consequence of the shift to a market economy. Unemployment among parents adversely affects children's standard of living, contributes to nutritional deficiencies, and places deep strains on marriages and families. The added psychological stress of unemployment, hidden unemployment, or unpaid wages undermines the health and security of those affected and contributes to the premature death of parents in the region.[35] Women are often the first fired and last rehired in Central and Eastern Europe. Their employment rates have declined sharply during the past decade of transition. For example, the level of women's employment from 1985 to 1997 decreased by "40 percent in Hungary, 33 percent in Latvia, 31 percent in Estonia, 24 percent in Lithuania, and 21 percent in the Russian Federation."[36] Young women from fifteen to twenty-four years of age faced more unemployment than did young men.[37] In 1993, women represented 70 percent of the registered unemployed in Russia.[38]

The women in CEE states are also paid less than men for similar work. In addition, they are often subjected to sexual harassment on the job, and legal and cultural protections against sexual harassment are often lacking.[39] Domestic violence is a notable problem as well. Various manifestations of gender inequality promote feelings of low self-esteem and low social status.

Young girls who lack social status and self-esteem are significantly more vulnerable to exploitation.

Another indicator of economic stress in the region is the inflation rate. Inflation can significantly reduce personal savings, purchasing power, and economic security. Nine of the fifteen CEE states for which data were available had inflation rates above 20 percent in 1996.[40] The inflation rates for some various states were substantially higher: Bulgaria (121 percent), Ukraine (66.2 percent), Belarus (49.4 percent), Russia (47.8 percent), Romania (30.3 percent), Lithuania (26.5 percent), Estonia (24.6 percent), Hungary (21.2 percent), and Azerbaijan (20.4 percent). Rising poverty, increased unemployment, and high inflation have been major consequences of the shift to a market economy that have adversely affected the children of Central and Eastern Europe.

An important indicator of social and family stability is the divorce rate for a society. About one million children in the region are affected by divorce annually.[41] This represents a significant increase of 150,000 more divorces per year than that seen during the 1980s. The high divorce rates for numerous CEE states have major consequences for children. While a 40 percent divorce rate is the average in the most developed states, with some European rates as low as 12 percent (Italy) and 17 percent (Spain), five CEE states—including Belarus, Russia, and Ukraine—have divorce rates over 60 percent.[42] Trafficking in girls and women is a problem in each of the five states with high divorce rates. Broken families and one-parent households coupled with alcohol abuse, which is common in the region, place many children and girls in a difficult and stressful home environment. Moreover, if job prospects are not promising and home life is problematic, girls may turn to desperate measures to survive or pursue happiness.

While alcohol abuse has been a historic problem for much of Central and Eastern Europe, drug abuse among the young is a growing problem. The levels of drug abuse do not compare with the high levels of abuse in the more prosperous Western Europe. Still, a drug problem, which accelerates the rise in HIV/AIDS in the region, is a concern and makes the youth more vulnerable. Ukraine, Russia, Azerbaijan, Georgia, and Belarus, as well as the more prosperous states of Slovenia and Croatia, registered the highest numbers of drug offenses.[43] President Yeltsin underscored that drug abuse was a major problem facing Russian youth. One report estimates that 9 percent of Russians between ten and eighteen years of age are drug addicts, including three hundred thousand young people in Moscow alone.[44] Young girls who are addicted to drugs are vulnerable to becoming prostitutes to pay for their habit.

Another growing social problem in CEE states is that of street children and runaways. There are one million to three million street children in Russia, with as many as four million in the summer.[45] Half of them are orphaned or abandoned youth. It is estimated that there are 150,000 homeless street children in Moscow and another 50,000 to 80,000 in St. Petersburg. There are also some thirty thousand runaways each year in Russia, some of whom have escaped public care institutions such as orphanages and children's centers, which are beset by problems. These street children in Russia and other CEE states, such as Romania (which has two thousand street children, primarily in Bucharest), are particularly vulnerable to child prostitution as a means of survival.

The cutbacks in educational spending for state schools has also meant that fewer student-age youth are attending school, since they must pay various fees.[46] Five percent of Russian youth, one hundred thousand per grade, are also not attending school. In addition, the schools of the region have fewer extracurricular events to occupy the youth. In an environment of social dislocation, rising unemployment, and unpaid wages for teachers, many youth may not see the point of gaining an education. Quitting school and engaging in truancy provide children of the area unsupervised time to get into trouble with drugs, sex, and crime, particularly in one-parent households where the breadwinner may be struggling to make ends meet.

The crime rates have risen sharply in most CEE states during the past decade. The total numbers of reported crimes increased by 420 percent in Romania, 258 percent in Bulgaria, 212 percent in Lithuania, and 197 percent in the Czech Republic from 1990 to 1998.[47] The greater freedom for citizens, the economic and social hardships, the lack of rule of law, and the rise of organized crime are broad factors that explain this development. Youth crime is also growing exponentially. The number of juveniles sentenced for criminal activity rose 564 percent in Romania, 263 percent in Bulgaria, 213 percent in Slovakia, and 204 percent in the Czech Republic.[48] The breakdown of families, the moral vacuum, and the depiction of violence in the media, combined with rising economic and social inequalities, explain the explosion in youth crime. As of 1994, in four of the CEE states—Estonia, the Czech Republic, Belarus, and Ukraine—juveniles formed nearly 6 percent or more of the total prison population.[49] By contrast, juveniles' share of the total prison population was 0.23 percent in Sweden, 1.46 percent in Italy, and 3.60 percent for Belgium.

In sum, the social impact of economic transition in Central and Eastern Europe has led to sharply rising rates of poverty, unemployment, and higher inflation. These economic variables have fueled social distress in the form of higher rates of divorce, drug abuse, runaways, and crime (including youth crime). Children and women of the region have been particularly vulnerable to the social upheavals of transition and gender inequality. As young girls become deeply pessimistic about their economic prospects in their home countries and desperate to escape the feminization of poverty, many seek refuge in work abroad and in dreams of prosperity.

## WARS AND REFUGEES

Numerous ethnic conflicts during the late 1980s and 1990s in the region have created a huge number of refugees. The wars in Bosnia, Kosovo, Moldova, Georgia, Azerbaijan/Armenia, and Russia, among others, have produced some seven million refugees.[50] One-third of the refugees are under eighteen years of age. The CEE region accounted for 30 percent of the world's refugees. These wars have produced social and familial breakdown and have created severe hardships for children. As part of a campaign of "ethnic cleansing" in the Balkans, young girls and women were subjected to sexual violence and rape on a large and systematic basis.[51] An estimated twenty thousand Bosnian Muslim women and girls were raped, including those as young as twelve years of age. The young survivors of these wars have been scarred by the war and the sexual attacks, and some have been considered "dishonored" because they had sexual relations with the enemy, regardless of the circumstances. Other youth were orphaned by these wars or separated from their families. During this time of social chaos, young girls and refugees traumatized by the destruction and upheaval of warfare became vulnerable to abduction or deceit by traffickers.[52] The ethnic wars also strengthened the position of organized crime as they created strong demand for licit and illicit products and required covert methods of transportation and sale.

## SEXUAL FREEDOM

During the communist era, a degree of sexual repression reigned in the CEE states.[53] Overt sexual images were not common in the media, and pornography was not prevalent in the kiosks. Prostitution was hidden in hotels or bars. In addition, homosexuality was legally banned in numerous CEE states. With the transition to democracy and a market economy, one of the newfound freedoms was sexual freedom. Youth in the region felt free to express their sexuality more openly but not always more responsibly. As a result, there has been a rampant increase in sexually transmitted diseases in numerous CEE states. In the case of Latvia, the rate of sexually transmitted diseases among fourteen- to eighteen-year-olds tripled between 1991 and 1995.[54] Births to teenage mothers and to unmarried mothers have also increased significantly in the region.[55]

In this more open environment, the sex industry has flourished. There has been a sharp increase in prostitution, strip clubs, sex shops, and pornography. In addition, Western publications such as *Playboy* and *Cosmopolitan* and Western movies such as Julia Roberts's *Pretty Woman* became popular with the youth. Western advertising for clothes and cosmetics, often involving teenage models in sexy attire or poses, also filled the media airwaves. In this context, many girls and boys obtained a distorted image of youth sexuality, a glamorized view of prostitution, and felt less inhibited to experiment sexually. The UN special rapporteur noted that sexual freedom is considered one of the new attractions of the postcommunist era. "Thus, girls and boys become more easily involved in prostitution and/or pornography, most of the time without really knowing what it is all about."[56] Many young girls began to see prostitution as a way to become wealthy; prostitution abroad was seen as sharing drinks with handsome foreigners (à la Richard Gere) in fancy restaurants and hotels.[57] The economic and social desperation of young girls, combined with the materialism of the market economy and the moral vacuum of a society in transition, significantly eroded the stigma against prostitution and other sexual taboos. Thus, some of the girls caught up in child prostitution and trafficking were willing participants who were unaware of the harsh realities of the business and the conditions they would live under.

## ORGANIZED CRIME AND TRAFFICKERS

During the postcommunist transition, organized crime has grown much stronger while the states of the region have grown much weaker. Regional mafias have taken advantage of the lack of rule of law, the economic and social disarray, and the corruption. Organized crime plays a substantial role in the international trafficking of girls from the CEE states.[58] Organized crime and professional cliques of traffickers represent a major supply-side factor in the sex industry. They are able to exploit the economically and socially desperate girls and women of the region during an era of sexual freedom. Russian, Ukrainian, Polish, Yugoslav, Albanian, and Georgian organized crime groups, among others, are involved in trafficking girls and women for prostitution.[59] Compared with drug or gun trafficking, human trafficking for prostitution is a lucrative business characterized by high profits and low risks. While organized crime generates huge profits, as the girls can be reused and resold, criminal enforcement in the areas of trafficking and prostitution is more problematic, and it is difficult to obtain lengthy convictions.

Human trafficking is the fastest sector of profit growth for organized crime. Russian organized crime groups control over two hundred illegal sex businesses in Moscow alone, and they own nightclubs in Prague, Riga, and Kiev.[60] Russian organized crime groups control prostitution in Germany, Poland, and Israel.[61] Ukrainian criminal groups control prostitution in Austria and Hungary. Albanian criminal groups play a significant role in prostitution in Italy and Belgium. There appears to be much cooperation between criminal groups and traffickers from different countries as they transport their human cargo across borders and continents, although at times, turf wars or stealing from one another occurs. Clearly, in this era of globalization, organized crime and traffickers from the CEE states have become transnational in their operations as suppliers for the commercial sex industry.

## CORRUPTION

Corruption plays a key role in facilitating human-trafficking operations. Bribes given to police, border guards, government officials (in the visa and documentation departments), travel agencies, and transportation carriers allow human trafficking to thrive. Corruption in the governmental and private sectors occurs in the countries of origin, transit, and destination. These corrupted sectors may be direct participants in the trafficking operation or may acquiesce to trafficking and prostitution of children. Local police or government officials in charge of monitoring prostitution, such as that in the case of a German special commissioner on organized crime near the German–Polish border, may be customers themselves or demand sexual favors from the trafficked girls and women.[62]

Corruption in the CEE states is high in both regional and global contexts. Based on Transparency International's 1998 ranking of perceived international corruption in the business sector (which often correlates with governmental corruption), 50 percent of the CEE states ranked in the bottom one-third: out of eighty-five states rated, Russia rated seventy-sixth, Latvia seventy-first, Ukraine sixty-ninth, Bulgaria sixty-sixth, Yugoslavia and Romania sixty-first (tied).[63] By contrast, 85 percent of the Western European states ranked in the top one-third in corruption globally, and none ranked in the lower one-third. Corruption at the top of the political and economic power structures in these states also allows organized crime and traffickers to avoid detection or vigorous criminal prosecution.

## DEMAND-SIDE FACTORS

Girls and young women from the CEE states are in high demand for the sex industry throughout Europe as well as in parts of Asia and the Middle East.

In the postcommunist era, they are seen in the sex industry as being exotic or a novelty.[64] By various accounts, females from the CEE states are displacing females from Asia, Latin America, and Africa in the sex trade in Europe. Lower transportation costs and their status as fellow Europeans, although Europeans from the "bad side" of Europe, might explain this trend. The demand for younger prostitutes, those in their early teens, owes to the spread of HIV/AIDS and other sexually transmitted diseases and the fear it generates.[65] Prostitution clients assume that because child prostitutes (under eighteen) are young, they are less likely to have contracted AIDS and therefore pose fewer risks, although the evidence suggests that child prostitutes are just as likely, if not more likely, to have HIV/AIDS.[66] They are less experienced with safe-sex methods and more compliant to the sexual preferences of their older clients, who often demand unprotected sex. While child prostitutes had been a substitute for adult prostitutes, they are now becoming the preference.[67] The increased demand for child prostitutes has pushed the price of their services to a premium and has thus made them even more valuable to traffickers, brothel owners, and pimps. In Poland, for example, there is rising demand for twelve- and thirteen-year-old prostitutes often trafficked from Romania, Bulgaria, and Albania.[68] Most of the focus on the sex trade centers on the supply-side of the equation rather than on the demand side. As Kofi Annan, secretary-general of the United Nations, observes,

> Eliminating the demand is an often-forgotten facet of child protection. Attention is usually lopsided, focusing on the used rather than the user, seeking solutions addressing the source of supply without controlling measures to eliminate the demand for children.[69]

## INTERNET TECHNOLOGY

As a prominent antitrafficking NGO notes, "The scope, volume, and content of the material on the Internet promoting or enacting the trafficking, prostitution and sexual exploitation of women and children is unprecedented."[70] The Internet and World Wide Web revolution has increased demand for girls and young women from the CEE states. Numerous websites post images of young and attractive girls from Russia, Ukraine, and other CEE states as potential mail-order brides or for dating services. While some of these are legitimate businesses, others may be fronts for prostitution and are indirectly promoting sexual tourism. Advertisements for these girls portray them as more traditional and compliant than their female counterparts in the West. Organized crime in Russia often extorts these mail-order bride or dating services and may use their files on girls seeking foreign husbands for recruitment purposes.[71]

Electronic mail and chat rooms also facilitate more interaction and communication between girls from the CEE and global consumers, which also heightens sexual demand. The growth of pornography on the web, including child pornography, raises demand for girls (and boys) from the CEE. Hungary has become the pornography capital of Europe, and girls and women from CEE states are in demand in the global pornography industry because they work for less and are willing to do more.[72] The growth of online and offline pornography involving CEE girls and women, combined with e-mail, chat rooms, mail-order brides, and dating services on the web, has significantly raised demand for girls from the CEE states for prostitution and the commercial sex industry.


## MILITARY AND INTERNATIONAL PRESENCE

Since the end of the Bosnian (1995) and Kosovo wars (1999), large contingents of NATO/UN peacekeepers, UN officials, and nongovernmental organizations have been stationed in the Balkans. As a result, prostitution is reportedly booming in Bosnia and Kosovo.[73] Many trafficked girls and women from CEE states end up in Balkan brothels. The stationing of large numbers of military personnel nearby often aggravates the problem of prostitution and child prostitution, as was the case in Asia. Military personnel and other representatives of the international community have become customers at these brothels. Given the challenges of restoring ethnic stability, civil institutions, and economic viability, officials of the United Nations often believe that they lack the resources or personnel to effectively monitor and control the problem of prostitution and trafficking. While the ethnic wars in the Balkans contributed to the supply side by disrupting families, creating vulnerable refugees, and through the use of rape as a military strategy, the postwar stationing of tens of thousands of foreigners in the area has notably increased demand for prostitution and the sex industry in the region.


## GOVERNMENTAL AND SOCIETAL RESPONSES

### Phase One: 1990–1995

From the early to mid-1990s, most European governments in both the East and the West were not prepared to handle the growing problem of human trafficking of girls and women. Three key shortcomings were evident in the response to human trafficking: inadequate legislation, insufficient resources to combat it (particularly among the CEE states), and the lack of sufficient bilateral and multilateral cooperation.[74] Many European states did not have specific antitrafficking laws in place. While traffickers could be tried for breaking other laws, such as kidnapping or assault, this often raised problems of jurisdiction among law enforcement agencies and posed sentencing difficulties for courts. Because human trafficking was seen as occupying a gray legal area, some governmental bodies did not treat it as a priority concern or view it as their problem or responsibility. Human trafficking was often treated as an illegal immigration issue, leading to the swift deportation or imprisonment of the young victims. The well-entrenched organized crime groups and traffickers frequently avoided prosecution because witnesses feared testifying against them.

Insufficient allocation of resources to combat human trafficking also posed a major problem. Facing economic and social hardships, most CEE states lacked adequate funding for special police units, more border guards, and more electronic equipment and technology to battle the problem of human trafficking. It may well be that the transnational crime groups enjoyed advantages in organization, funding, and technology over the demoralized and often corrupt police in various transition states of the region. Also, while Western European states had sufficient resources to draw on, politicians often railed against organized crime but still cut police budgets.[75] As a result, during the early 1990s, insufficient resources were being allocated to fight this particular human rights problem in Western Europe as well.

Inadequate European-wide cooperation to combat human trafficking was another problem into the mid-1990s. Traffickers were able to cross borders and escape prosecution and extradition because of the lack of national antitrafficking laws and an international convention against human trafficking. While the trafficking of girls and women was a global and regional phenomenon, the governmental response was too-often fragmented and focused at the national level. Cross-border cooperation by police agencies and prosecutors was minimal, particularly among the CEE states. Traffickers and organized crime moved quickly and nimbly while the states of Europe trudged along slowly, lacking antitrafficking legislation, sufficient funding, and a framework for multilateral cooperation. Consequently, too little was being done to disrupt the supply-side factors of organized crime and corruption while demand-side factors were not even being addressed.

## Phase Two: 1996–2000

By the late 1990s, the media and various human rights nongovernmental organizations (NGOs) began to publicize the trafficking of girls and women.

LTAS LIBRARY LIS

Media exposés in the *New York Times* and the *Economist* and other newspapers highlighted the problem of sex slaves and caused public outrage. Antitrafficking NGOs such as the Foundation Against Trafficking in Women (STV), based in the Netherlands, have played a huge role in educating the media, the public, and governments about this human rights problem.[76] The STV also established the La Strada program in Central and East Europe—a network of affiliated NGOs in Poland, the Czech Republic, Ukraine, and Bulgaria—to combat trafficking. These NGOs have collected data about trafficking, sponsored conferences, published reports, lobbied governmental and intergovernmental bodies, provided assistance and counseling to the young victims of trafficking, and served as a valuable resource to European governments.[77]

The European Union established the STOP program (Stop Trafficking of Persons) in late 1996. This program "is intended to promote measures to combat trafficking in persons, the sexual exploitation of children, the production of and traffic in audiovisual material in any form and the disappearance of minors."[78] It includes exchange programs for governmental officials and NGOs working on the problem of human trafficking. Also in 1996, Europol extended its jurisdiction from drug trafficking and organized crime to include "the suppression of trafficking in human beings and exploitation of any kind, and particularly that of minors."[79] In the late 1990s, the European Union (EU) also established the DAPHNE initiative, which provides financial support for NGOs that seek to prevent violence against women and children. The EU commissioner for justice and home affairs, Anita Gradin, has played a large role in mobilizing the European Union to address the issue of trafficking in girls and women.[80] Meanwhile, the EU's commission sought to pass a uniform EU law against human trafficking. While more and more CEE and EU states began passing specific antitrafficking laws, a number of CEE states with serious trafficking problems had not.

The Trafficking Victims Protection Act of 2000, passed by the U.S. Congress and signed by President Clinton, also represents a significant milestone in the global campaign against trafficking of girls and women.[81] This law seeks to promote measures to prevent trafficking, protect and assist victims of trafficking, and strengthen punishment of traffickers. In addition, the law establishes an interagency task force to monitor and combat trafficking and stipulates that antitrafficking measures be a key criterion in evaluating a state's human rights practices and qualification for U.S. foreign aid.[82] Given the United States' global status and power, this national legislation will have a significant impact on other states' actions. The Trafficking Victims Protection Reauthorization Act of 2003 not only provides funding for antitrafficking activities for 2004 and 2005 but also provides some amendments to the original Trafficking Victims Protection Act.[83] These include greater efforts to stem international sex tourism; expand benefits and allow more trafficking victims and their families to remain in the United States; prosecute sex-trafficking offenses under the Racketeering, Influenced, and Corrupt Organization Act; and establish watch lists of states that fail to comply with human trafficking guidelines.

Bilateral cooperation between select states such as Ukraine and Poland, which signed a cooperation agreement in 1998 to fight trafficking across their borders, is also important.[84] President Clinton cited joint efforts by Ukraine and the United States to combat trafficking of girls and women as a model for others.[85] The United States and the European Union are also providing some assistance to CEE states in sponsoring seminars to educate governmental officials, the media, and the public about this human rights problem.

While the passage of antitrafficking legislation and increased bilateral and multilateral cooperation implies increased funding, it may still be inadequate to contain the trafficking problem. Given the challenges of containing drug trafficking, gun smuggling, terrorism, and common crime, law enforcement budgets and personnel are stretched thin in the West. Europol, for example, has a budget of only $23 million.[86] High unemployment in the European Union states also limits the amount of revenues that CEE states can use to combat trafficking. However, those CEE states seeking to join the European Union or impress the United States have reason to increase enforcement, if not budgetary allocations, against trafficking.

The Optional Protocol to Prevent, Suppress, and Punish Trafficking in Persons, Especially Women and Children, supplementing the United Nations Convention against Transnational Organized Crime, was passed in November 2000.[87] This convention represents a historic milestone in the campaign against trafficking in girls and women. It provids a standard legal definition of trafficking and outlines various methods to prevent trafficking, penalize traffickers, and assist the victims. It serves as a model for national states to follow in their efforts to eradicate human trafficking and promotes more regional and international cooperation. As of December 2002, there were 117 states, including the European Union, that had signed the protocol on trafficking, including all twenty-two CEE states.[88] The protocol entered into legal force on 25 December 2003. The United Nations Convention against Transnational Organized Crime, also a landmark international measure to confront the challenge of transnational crime, had obtained 147 signatories by December 2002.[89] However, thirty-five of the states party to the Convention against Transnational Organized Crime have not signed the optional protocol against trafficking, possibly because appearing to be "tough on organized crime" is politically more salient than combating trafficking. So too, only 108 states have signed the optional protocol on the sale of children, child prostitution, and child pornography. Nevertheless, the antitrafficking protocol entered into legal force on 18 January 2002. The passage of antitrafficking legislation and programs at various levels—national, regional, and international—does represent a serious effort to address several supply-side factors, such as organized crime and corruption, through enhanced bilateral and multilateral cooperation in law enforcement and through the articulation of well-defined legal norms against trafficking.

## Phase Three: 2001–2003

The European Union's Council Framework Decision on Combating Trafficking in Human Beings represents a major effort to provide a comprehensive European approach to the problem of human trafficking for sexual and labor exploitation.[90] The framework decision was adopted in July 2002 and had a national compliance deadline of 1 August 2004. It seeks to ensure common legal definitions, effective and proportionate criminal penalties, and enhanced police and judicial cooperation. The framework decision stipulates a maximum penalty of no less than eight years' incarceration for a human-trafficking offense for sexual or labor exploitation. It also makes it legal to hold persons liable for trafficking offenses and formulates jurisdictional criteria in matters of prosecution. The European Union's council will assess member states' compliance with the framework decision based on adoption of appropriate national laws and will issue a report by 1 August 2005. The proposed enlargement of the European Union in 2004 by the addition of ten new members, mostly post-communist states from Central and Eastern Europe, was instrumental in the emergence of the framework decision. An expanding European Union needed a more coordinated regional approach to the human-trafficking problem—all the more so as several of the newest member states were among the countries of origin for sexual trafficking.

A major European Conference on Preventing and Combating Trafficking in Human Beings was held in Brussels in September 2002. The Brussels Declaration put forth diverse recommendations, standards, and best practices to prevent and combat human trafficking.[91] These included mechanisms for enhanced cooperation and coordination, such as the establishment of a European Experts Group on Trafficking in Human Beings, a European Forum on the Fight against Trafficking, improved intelligence gathering on the sex trade, and passport and visa changes for children—possibly requiring a passport for children six years of age or older. The experts group is a consultative body of twenty members that will forge an action plan to implement the Brussels Declaration and "help the Commission launch further concrete proposals at the EU level."[92]

The Council of Europe has also played an important role in combating human trafficking.[93] This Pan-European organization of forty-five member states is particularly focused on issues of human rights. It has established several special groups and issued reports on topics such as the impact of new technology on sexual trafficking (2003). The Council of Europe has also provided technical assistance and advice on legal reforms for Southeast Europe and a regional action plan for the Caucasus. Two major contributions by the council are in the areas of raising awareness and setting standards.[94] Most significant, the Council of Europe is drafting a European convention against trafficking in human beings, which should be completed by the end of 2004 or early 2005.[95] Given the more uniform regional context, a European convention against human trafficking can "contain more precise provisions and may go beyond minimum standards agreed upon in other international instruments."[96] Beyond anchoring human trafficking as a human rights problem, the convention can enhance victim protection, establish "a proper balance between respect for human rights and prosecution," and further develop antitrafficking standards.[97] Finally, the Organization for Security and Cooperation in Europe (OSCE), comprising fifty-five member states, also works with the Council of Europe and the European Union, as well as with international bodies, to combat human trafficking. In July 2003, the OSCE passed an "Action Plan to combat trafficking in human beings."[98]

## CONCLUSION

What are the future prospects of eliminating or significantly reducing the trafficking in children and women from Central and Eastern Europe? On the positive side, there is now more public awareness of the human rights problem of trafficking for prostitution. Public television stations in the CEE states show films shot on location from Turkey, for example, warning teenagers and others of the dangers of trafficking and forced prostitution abroad. Schools in Ukraine are covering antitrafficking and antiprostitution themes in high school classes. Media exposure of false scams that have lured girls and young women abroad has forced traffickers to shift away from open advertising in the big cities.[99] In the area of public education, noticeable progress has been made.

The passage of national, regional, and international legislation and the implementation programs against human trafficking also represent a mobilization of governmental and societal forces and resources. The optional protocol on trafficking as well as the optional protocol on the rights of the child[100] and the Convention on the Rights of the Child underscore the importance of protecting society's most precious resource: its children. These international conventions and protocols supplement a large body of international law and norms that identify the special needs and human rights of children. There now exists a set of international and national legal norms protecting children and others from trafficking and prostitution in Europe and elsewhere. The increase in bilateral and multilateral cooperation in Europe and beyond is both necessary and long overdue. Cooperation among police and judicial officials and governments and NGOs across borders is also welcome. More resources need to be devoted to the fight against human trafficking given the raised profile of the issue and the accompanying legislation. Significantly, social services and witness protection programs for girls and women who have been victims of trafficking are being established. The proposed European Convention against Trafficking in Human Beings should also help raise regional standards and facilitate more regional cooperation in the struggle against human trafficking. As a region, Europe has "one of the heaviest volumes of human trafficking and one of the most advanced responses to it. . . . However, recognition of the problem and regional and sub-regional cooperation in the fight against these practices is probably the highest of any area in the world."[101] Also, the heightened concern over border security and illegal immigration since September 11 could be helpful in cracking down on human trafficking in Europe and elsewhere.

On the negative side, although public education, legislative enactments, and an increase in allocated resources to fight trafficking may make some inroads in reducing supply-side factors, they may not be enough to eradicate the problem. Economic and social hardship in many CEE states will likely last another two decades or so, and organized crime and corruption will be difficult to extirpate. Traffickers may change routes and strategies to cope with successful law enforcement practices. Many desperate young people will still be vulnerable to traffickers and to their own dreams of better lives.

In the final analysis, attacking the problem of trafficking for prostitution will require not only more effective supply-side actions by governments and societies but will also require a serious effort to reduce demand for these girls and women in Western Europe and elsewhere. Global public education campaigns may educate men about the circumstances trafficked girls and women live under, and enhanced regulation (or removal) of Internet sites that exploit children and women may help to reduce demand. The fight for human rights for children and women is a long struggle but one that is a matter of social justice. As Kofi Annan states, "The fate of these most vulnerable people in our world is an affront to human dignity and a challenge to every State, every people, and every community."[102]

## NOTES

I would like to acknowledge the valuable research assistance provided by the following students: Kelly Harrington, James Quigley, and Todd Ziegler. Also, I would like to thank the anonymous reviewers for their constructive feedback.

1. Penelope Turnbull, "Memorandum for the Secretary of State, the Attorney General, the Administrator of the Agency for International Development, the Director of the U.S. Information Agency—11 March 1998," in *Illegal Immigration and Commercial Sex: The New Slave Trade*, ed. Phil Williams (London: Frank Cass, 1999), 215.

2. The U.S. government provides a more conservative estimate of the numbers of persons trafficked: eight hundred thousand to nine hundred thousand across international borders for purposes of sexual or labor exploitation. This figure excludes internal trafficking, within countries. See U.S. Department of State, Office to Monitor and Combat Trafficking in Persons, *Trafficking in Persons Report (2003)*, www.state.gov/g/tip/rls/tiprpt/2003/21262pf.htm. The higher estimate of four million is cited by Pino Arlacchi, the head of the UN Office for Drug Control and Crime Prevention. See Paul Goble, "World: Analysis from Washington—Globalization of Slavery," *RFE/RL Newsline*, www.rferl.org/nca/features/2000/12/05122000205456.asp.

3. "Trafficking in Women for the Purpose of Sexual Exploitation: Mapping the Situation and Existing Organizations Working in Belarus, Russia, the Baltic and Nordic States," *Foundation of Women's Forum*, August 1998, www.qweb.kvinnoforum.se/papers/traffickingreport.html.

4. The U.S. State Department, in the *Trafficking in Persons Report (2003)*, estimates that eighteen thousand to twenty thousand persons are trafficked annually into the United States, www.state.gov/g/tip/rls/tiprpt/2003/212262pf.htm. Amy O'Neill Richard, *International Trafficking in Women to the United States: A Contemporary Manifestation of Slavery and Organized Crime* (Washington, D.C.: Center for the Study of Intelligence, 2000), 3, cites a figure of forty-five thousand to fifty thousand.

5. Goble, *Globalization of Slavery*. Hamish McCulloch with Interpol provides the estimate of $9 billion.

6. See HR 3244, 106th Cong., for Trafficking Victims Protection Act of 2000, section 102.b.8 at http://thomas.loc.gov/cgi-bin/query/C?c106:.temp/~c1064cCsZE; and Robert McMahon, "UN: Exploitation of Children Gets Attention with Clinton Visit," *RFE/RL Newsline*, www.rferl.org/nca/features/2000/07/f.ru.000707151920.html.

7. Twenty-two states form Central Europe and Eastern Europe as defined in this chapter: Russia, Ukraine, Belarus, Moldova, Lithuania, Latvia, Estonia, Armenia, Azerbaijan, Georgia, Poland, Czech Republic, Hungary, Slovakia, Romania, Bulgaria, Albania, Yugoslavia, Croatia, Bosnia-Herzegovina, Slovenia, and Macedonia. It thus excludes the five Central Asian states of the former Soviet Union.

8. Press release SG/SM/7658 SOC/CP/233.

9. See Frank Laczko and David Thompson, eds., *Migrant Trafficking and Human Smuggling in Europe: A Review of the Evidence with Case Studies from Hungary,*

*Poland, and Ukraine* (Geneva, Switz.: International Organization for Migration, 2000), 18–24.

10. A/55/383.

11. A/55/383.

12. *Migrant Trafficking*, 18–24.

13. The Convention on the Rights of the Child can be found at www.unicef.org/crc/crc/htm.

14. Michael Specter, "Traffickers' New Cargo: Naïve Slavic Women," *New York Times,* 11 January 1998.

15. Richard, *International Trafficking*, 157.

16. *President of Ukraine Signs Law on Criminal Charges for Trafficking in Human Beings*, www.brama.com/issues/ukrainelaw.html.

17. U.S. State Department, *Human Rights Reports for 1999—Albania* (Washington, D.C.: Government Printing Office).

18. *Economist*, "In the Shadows," 24 August 2000.

19. E/CN/4/1999/71, 29 January 1999, 93.

20. Excerpts from United Nations General Assembly, Fifty-first Session, Agenda Item 106, 7 October 1996, in Williams, *Illegal Immigration*, 218–19.

21. *Child Protection: Sexual Abuse and Sexual Exploitation of Children,* www.unicef.org/programme/cprotection/traf.htm.

22. "Trafficking in Women for the Purpose of Sexual Exploitation: Mapping the Situation and Existing Organizations Working in Belarus, Russia, the Baltic and Nordic States," *Foundation of Women's Forum*, August 1998, www.qweb.kvinnoforum.se/papers/traffickingreport.html.

23. ECN.4/1999/71, 92.

24. David Montgomery, "Dreams of a Better Life End in a Nightmare of Sexual Slavery," *Chicago Tribune*, 3 January 2001.

25. ECN.4/1997/95/Add.1, 87.

26. A/RES/54/263 of 25 May 2000.

27. James Millar and Sharon Wolchik, *The Social Legacy of Communism* (New York and Cambridge: Woodrow Wilson Center and Cambridge University Press, 1994).

28. Kate Schecter, "The Social Sector: A Failure of the Transition," in *Nations in Transition 1999–2000* (New York: Freedom House, 2000), 33, http://freedomhouse.org/pdf_docs/research/nitransit/31–39.PDF.

29. Mark Field and Judyth Twigg, eds., *Russia's Torn Safety Nets* (New York: St. Martins Press, 2000).

30. Schecter, "Social Factor," 32.

31. *UNDP Report Exposes Transition's Dark Side*, www.worldbank.org/html/prddr/trans/julaug99/pgs19–21.htm.

32. *Children at Risk Report Summary*, euro/child/gla.ac.uk/Documents/monee/Monee%20Reports/report%204/care.htm.

33. UN Development Program, *UN Human Development Report 1999* (New York: Oxford University Press, 1999), 149.

34. UN Development Program, *UN Human Development*, 180–83.

35. Schecter, "Social Factor," 35.

36. Ben Hogan, "UN: Women Seen as Valuable, Wasted Resource," *RFE/RL Newsline*, www.rferl.org/nca/features/2000/06/f.ru.000606145751.htm.

37. UN Development Program, *UN Human Development*, 233.

38. *Gender in Transition—World Bank Conference in Bucharest*, www.worldbank .gor/html/prddr/trans/apr95/pgs15–16.htm.

39. U.S. State Department, *Annual Human Rights Reports for 1999* (Washington, D.C.: Government Printing Office).

40. UN Development Program, *UN Human Development*, 180–83.

41. *Children at Risk.*

42. UN Development Program, *UN Human Development*, 226–28.

43. UN Development Program, *UN Human Development*, 221–24.

44. John Kramer, "Drug Abuse in Post-Communist Russia," in Field and Twigg, *Russia's Torn,* 107.

45. Schecter, "Social Factor," 35.

46. *Children at Risk*, ix.

47. *The Monee Report*, TransMONEE 2000 Database, http://eurochild.gla.ac.uk/ Documents/monee/outputs/to7.asp?Region=All&variablesCRIMER&Periodfrom= 1998&Periodto=1998&Submit=Indice&Decimal=1.

48. *The Monee Report*, TransMONEE 2000 Database, http://eurochild.gla.ac.uk/ Doments/monee/outputs/to7.asp?Region=ALL&variable=JUVSENTT&Periodfrom =1990&Periodto=1998&Submit=Indices&Decimals=1.

49. UN Development Program, *UN Human Development*, 221–24.

50. *Children at Risk.*

51. *New York Times*, "Three Serbs Convicted in Wartime Rapes," 23 February 2001.

52. *Children at Risk*, 28–30.

53. Valerie Sperling, "The New Sexism," in Field and Twigg, *Russia's Torn*, 174.

54. *Children at Risk.*

55. *Children at Risk.*

56. E/CN.4/1997/95/Add.1, 17 February 1997.

57. Gerben Bruinsma and Guus Meershock, "Organized Crime and Trafficking in Women from Eastern Europe in the Netherlands," in Williams, *Illegal Immigration*, 111.

58. Gillian Caldwell et al., "Capitalizing on Transition Economies," in Williams, *Illegal Immigration*, 50–54.

59. Richard, *International Trafficking*, 57–61.

60. Caldwell et al., "Capitalizing on Transition Economies," 56.

61. Richard, *International Trafficking*, 57–61.

62. Caldwell et al., "Capitalizing on Transition Economies," 68.

63. Transparency International, *Annual Report 1999* (Berlin).

64. Caldwell et al., "Capitalizing on Transition Economies," 44.

65. Excerpts from General Assembly in Williams, *Illegal Immigration*, 219.

66. Williams, *Illegal Immigration*, 162–163.

67. Excerpts from General Assembly in Williams, *Illegal Immigration*, 219.

68. U.S. State Department, *Human Rights Report for 1999—Bulgaria* (Washington, D.C.: Government Printing Office).

69. Quoted in Williams, *Illegal Immigration*, 221.

70. Resolution submitted by the Coalition against Trafficking in Women, "Misuse of the Internet for the Purpose of Sexual Exploitation," *UN Working Group on Contemporary Forms of Slavery*, Geneva, Switzerland, May 1998, www.uri.edu.artsci/wms/hughes/catw/resolut.htm.

71. Gillian Caldwell et al., "Crime and Servitude: An Expose of the Traffic in Women for Prostitution from the Newly Independent States," *Global Survival Network*, www.globalsurvival.net/femaletrade/9711russia.html.

72. *Economist*, "Giving the Customer What He Wants," 12 February 1998.

73. Claire Snegaroff, "NATO Forces Spur Kosovo Prostitution Boom," *Central Europe Online*, 5 January 2000, www.centraleuropa.com/features.php3?id=122854.

74. See *Migrant Trafficking*, 112–18.

75. *Foreign Policy* interview, "Meet the World's Top Cop," *Foreign Policy*, January–February 2000, 33.

76. "Trafficking in Women for the Purpose of Sexual Exploitation: Mapping the Situation and Existing Organizations Working in Belarus, Russia, the Baltic and Nordic States," *Foundation of Women's Forum*, August 1998, www.qweb.kvinnoforum.se/papers/traffickingreport.html.

77. Karen A. Mingst and Margaret P. Karns, *The United Nations in the Post–Cold War Era*, 2nd ed. (Boulder, Colo.: Westview Press, 2000), 175–78, on the role of NGOs in the area of human rights.

78. E/CN.4/1999/71, 97.

79. E/CN.4/1999/71, 98.

80. Penelope Turnbull, "The Fusion of Immigration and Crime in the European Union," in Williams, *Illegal Immigration*, 208–9.

81. HR 3244, 106th Congress, Trafficking Victims Protection Act of 2000, http://thomas.loc.gov/cgi-bin/query/C?c106:.temp/~c1064cCsZE.

82. Most of the CEE states—fifteen of twenty-one (71.4 percent) evaluated in the U.S. State Department's *Trafficking in Persons Report (2003)*—were ranked as "tier two" in combating human trafficking. This signifies that they "do not as yet fully comply with the Act's minimum standards but are making significant efforts to bring themselves into compliance with those standards." Two were ranked in the lowest category, "tier three"—Bosnia and Georgia, along with the Western European states of Greece and Turkey—and thus were potentially subject to sanctions in 2004. Tier-three states "do not comply with the minimum standards and are not making significant efforts to bring themselves into compliance." However, a presidential determination and update indicated that "significant efforts" were being made in Bosnia, Georgia, Greece, and Turkey (in ten of fifteen tier-three countries), thus sparing them from sanctions. Note also that four CEE states ranked in "tier one" in 2003 (Czech Republic, Lithuania, Macedonia, and Poland). See *Trafficking in Persons Report (2003)*, www.state.gov/g/tip/rls/tiprpt/2003/21262pf.htm, and *Presidential Determination with Respect to Foreign Governments' Efforts Regarding Trafficking in Persons*, no. 2003–35, September 2003, www.state.gov/g/tip/rls/rpt25017.htm.

83. See the Trafficking Victims Protection Reauthorization Act of 2003, www
.state.gov/documents/organization/28225.pdf. Also see Office to Monitor and Combat
Trafficking, "Recent Developments in US Government Efforts to End Human Trafficking," fact sheet, 5 February 2004, www.state.gov/g/tip/rls/fs/28548.htm; and "US
Lauds OSCE Action Plan to Combat Trafficking," http://usinfo.state.gov/xarchives/
display.html?p=washfile-english&y=2003&m=July&x=20030730123638osnhojac0
.2282373&t=usinfo/wf-latest.html. Note also the passage of the Protect Act of 2003,
which allows for the prosecution of Americans who travel abroad to abuse minors,
raising the maximum penalty to thirty years imprisonment and having no statute of
limitations for sexual abuse of a minor.

84. "Poland and Ukraine to Fight Sex Slave Industry," *RFE/RL Newsline*, 17 July
1998, www.rferl.org/newline/1998/07/3–CEE/cee-170798.html.

85. Williams, *Illegal Immigration*, 217.

86. *Foreign Policy* interview, "Meet the World's Top Cop," 33.

87. A/55/383.

88. See www.unodc.org/unodc/crime_cicp_signatures.html.

89. See www.unodc.org/unodc/crime_cicp_signatures_convention.html and
A/55/383. Note that the Convention against Transnational Organized Crime entered
into legal force as of 29 September 2003, while the Protocol against Smuggling of Migrants by Land, Sea, and Air entered into legal force on 28 January 2004. Note that
thirty-five fewer states signed the Protocol against Smuggling of Migrants than those
who signed the Convention against Transnational Organized Crime.

90. See http://europa.eu.int.eur-lex/pri/en/oj/dat/2002/l_203/1_20320020801cn
00010004.pdf.

91. See www.belgium.iom.int/StopConference/Conference%20Papers/brude
claration.pdf.

92. See http://europa.eu.int/comm/justice_home/news/intro/printer/news_021003_
2_en.htm.

93. See http://www.coe.int/T/E/human%5Frights/Trafficking/1%%FOverview/
Introduction.asp.

94. "First Meeting of the Ad Hoc Committee on Action against Trafficking in Human Beings (CAHTEH)," 15 September 2003, address of Maud de Boer-Buquicchio,
deputy secretary-general of the Council of Europe, www.coe.int/T/E/humanrights/
Trafficking/2_Cahteh/speech.asp.

95. Address of Maud de Boer-Buquicchio.

96. Address of Maud de Boer-Buquicchio.

97. Address of Maud de Boer-Buquicchio.

98. Organization for Security and Cooperation in Europe Permanent Council,
"OSCE Action Plan to Combat Trafficking in Human Beings," PC.DEC/557, 24 July
2003, www.osce.org/press.rel/2003/pdf.documents/07-3447-pc1.pdf.

99. Specter, "Traffickers' New Cargo."

100. The optional protocols to the Convention on the Rights of the Child provide
"legal protection against the worst forms of exploitation" namely, the sale of children,
child prostitution, child pornography, and involvement in armed conflict. "An Optional
Protocol to a Treaty is an instrument that establishes additional rights and obligations

to a treaty. It is usually adopted the same day, but it is of independent character and subject to independent ratification. Such protocols enable certain parties of the treaty to establish among themselves a framework of obligations which reach further than the general treaty and to which not all parties of the general treaty consent, creating a 'two-tier system.'" See "Protocols" at http://untreaty.un.org/English/guide.asp.

101. U.S. Department of State, "Pathbreaking Strategies in the Global Fight against Sex Trafficking," *Conference Recommendations*, www.state.gov/g/tip/rls/rpt/20834.htm.

102. Press release SG/SM/7658 SOC/CP/233, 11 December 2000.

*Chapter Five*

# Three Prints in the Dirt: Child Soldiers and Human Rights

## Mary B. Geske with Mark Ensalaco

In September 1997, UN secretary-general Kofi Annan appointed Olara Otunnu, former foreign minister of Uganda, as his special representative for children and armed conflict. In part prompted by the 1996 report on children in war by Graça Machel, the secretary-general's appointment marked the beginning of active and public efforts by the United Nations to gather and disseminate information and advocate on behalf of children affected by war and armed conflict. This broad mandate covers an array of issues, from children displaced or orphaned by conflict to child victims of land mines and other forms of violence to sexual abuse and exploitation of children in warfare. One major issue that Otunnu's office addresses is the subject of this chapter: child soldiers.

Current estimates suggest that there are three hundred thousand child soldiers in the world. According to Machel, a "child soldier is any child—boy or girl—under the age of 18 who is compulsorily, forcibly, voluntarily recruited or otherwise used in hostilities by armed forces, paramilitaries, civil defense units or other armed groups. Child soldiers are used for sexual services, as combatants, as forced 'wives,' messengers, porters or cooks."[1] Reports of children as young as six being "recruited" as soldiers have come from countries throughout Africa, Asia, and Latin America. Perhaps most notorious and familiar to Westerners are the thirteen-year-old twins Luther and Johnny Htoo who, after leading the rebel Karen God's Army on the Burmese border, surrendered to Thai authorities. Most prominent and common, however, are children who serve as ordinary foot soldiers sent to front lines or into minefields ahead of adult troops. In various conflicts throughout the world, children are killing and are being killed, maimed, raped, and tortured.

International response to child soldiers followed the Machel report of 1996. Indeed, Otunnu referred to Machel's report as groundbreaking in providing "the first comprehensive assessment of the multiple ways in which children suffer in times of armed conflict."[2] In her report, Machel applied the principles and norms of the Convention on the Rights of the Child (CRC) to children in war. Following Machel's report and the creation of the office of the special representative, research and advocacy on child soldiers blossomed. Initially, children's rights groups, including Rädda Barnen of Sweden, did most of the research and advocacy on child soldiers. By the mid- to late 1990s myriad groups, including Amnesty International, Human Rights Watch, and the Center for Defense Information, began research. In 1998, various issue-specific nongovernmental organizations (NGOs) joined together to form the Coalition to Stop the Use of Child Soldiers.

From the start, the relationship between NGOs and intergovernmental organizations (IGOs) has been symbiotic and reciprocal. Both sets of actors have been influential in moving the international community toward adoption of specific measures to address the issue of child soldiers. These measures culminated in the May 2000 General Assembly adoption of the optional protocol to the CRC on the involvement of children in armed conflict. The optional protocol designates eighteen years as the minimum age at which children may directly participate in armed hostilities.[3] The optional protocol entered into force in February 2002. The collaboration between NGOs and IGOs over the issue of child soldiers suggests a new wave in global politics involving the growing influence of nonstate or suprastate actors in affecting the global agenda and state policy. While the substantive focus of this chapter is primarily on the evolving relationship between NGOs and IGOs regarding child soldiers, it also examines the U.S. position regarding the protocol, culminating in the United States' signing of the protocol in July 2000.

## THREE PRINTS IN THE DIRT:
## HUMAN RIGHTS DISCOURSE AND CHILD SOLDIERS

"Kids leave three prints behind: their two feet, and the rifle barrel dragging behind them."[4] The use of children in war is not particularly new. Indeed, "during the Middle Ages, thousands were sent off from Europe to martyr themselves in the Children's Crusade."[5] There are accounts of child soldiers involved in the U.S. civil war and, more recently, in the Falklands and Gulf War. Many argue, however, that the contemporary era is fundamentally different as children are deliberately targeted as both victims and combatants in war.

There are two sets of reasons for the increased use of child soldiers. The first and most frequently cited is the nature of modern warfare. Conflicts today are increasingly becoming intrastate based and frequently involve informal groupings fighting national armies within communities. The result is that the front line is everywhere and everyone is a combatant. Indeed, "in recent decades, the proportion of war victims who are civilians has leapt dramatically from 5 percent to over 90 percent."[6] Civilians, and especially children, are deliberately and indiscriminately targeted as victims and potential soldiers. Modern conflicts are also characterized by the use of light arms and small weapons. The lightweight feature of the M16 and AK-47, for example, makes them weapons even a child can use.[7] Second, domestic conditions within society make children more-ready targets for use as child soldiers. Specifically, poverty within society often leads children to "join" military and paramilitary forces.[8] Poverty and related economic and political problems have resulted in a rise of unaccompanied and often homeless children who are frequently conscripted into combatant roles. Finally, according to America's Defense Monitor, greater numbers of children and declining populations of adults also account for the growing numbers of child soldiers, a phenomenon that became apparent in 1986 when observers were shocked to see children as young as four years old marching into the Ugandan capital in the ranks of the National Resistance Army.[9]

Explanations of why children are targeted as combatants rely on three broad sets of factors.[10] First, there are societal reasons that explain child soldiers. Specifically, poverty within societies may drive children to become soldiers. Poverty may also drive children onto the streets unaccompanied by adults and vulnerable to exploitation. Another societal explanation centers on the prevalence of violence within societies. The result is that children come to see violence as both normal and permanent and are therefore willing to participate in violent acts themselves. Related, peer, and family pressure may also induce children into combat roles. The examples of Irish and Palestinian children are used in this context. Second, there are practical reasons why children are combatants. In many parts of the world shortages of adult soldiers make children obvious recruits. Children also might be used deliberately as instruments of war where they are pitted against their own people in civil conflicts. The Guatemala civil war is an example of this wherein Mayan children were deliberately recruited into anti-indigenous forces. Finally, children make desirable soldiers because they are obedient and malleable. Children do what they are told; they do not require much pay; they are easy to intimidate; and their size, agility, and fearlessness make them ideal soldiers for quite dangerous missions.

Children come to be combatants through "conscription, abduction or coercion."[11] Children also may "volunteer" for service—what at least one author has called "unforced recruitment."[12] Forced recruitment often entails abductions and what is called *press-ganging*, "wherein soldiers show up after school and literally line people up against the wall and pick and choose or load everyone on to a van."[13] Regardless of the means, upon becoming a part of armed forces, children are subject to brutal beatings, abuse, and sexual assault and are made to commit exceptionally violent acts against enemy soldiers, former neighbors, family members, and, occasionally, one another. The testimonies of children involved in armed conflict are horrific. Said a fourteen-year-old girl, abducted in January 1999 by the Revolutionary United Front in Sierra Leone,

> I've seen people get their hands cut off, a ten-year-old girl raped and then die, and so many men and women burned alive. . . . So many times I just cried inside my heart because I didn't dare cry out loud.[14]

An eleven-year-old girl recruited by Peru's Shining Path guerrillas recounted,

> They beat all the people there, old and young, they killed them all, nearly 10 people. . . . Like dogs they killed them. . . . I didn't kill anyone, but I saw them killing. . . . The children who were with them killed too . . . with weapons. . . . They made us drink the blood of people, we took blood from the dead into a bowl and they made us drink. . . . Then when they killed the people they made us eat their liver, their heart, which they took out and sliced and fried. . . . And they made us little ones eat.[15]

A thirteen-year-old former child soldier from Liberia said this:

> They gave me pills that made me crazy. When the craziness got in my head, I beat people on their heads and hurt them until they bled. When the craziness got out of my head I felt guilty. If I remembered the person I went to them and apologized. If they did not accept my apology, I felt bad.[16]

A fourteen-year-old boy recruited by the Guatemalan army remembered his experience this way:

> The army was a nightmare. We suffered greatly from the cruel treatment we received. We were constantly beaten, mostly for no reason at all, just to keep us in a state of terror. They forced me to learn how to fight the enemy, in a war that I didn't understand why was being fought.[17]

These testimonies speak not only to the horror child soldiers experience but also to the legacies child combatants leave behind. Many are quick to point out the range of physical and psychological effects that soldiering leaves on children. From permanent war-related injuries to drug abuse, STDs, and HIV/

AIDS, child soldiers experience a variety of physical disorders. Psychologically, the actions children have been forced to commit or witness leave them "permanently traumatized."[18] The use of child soldiers also increases societal insecurity and violence, breaking the bond between children and their families and between children and their communities. Wessells notes that "by damaging that social trust and breaking those social bonds, one is basically ripping out the fabric of civil society."[19]

NGO and IGO efforts to stop the use of child soldiers have focused on three broad strategies. First, both sets of groups have worked hard to get out information on child soldiers. Targets of these campaigns include, at various times, the UN and UN member states, state policymakers, and the public. Second, the groups have sought to get the issue of child soldiers on the international human rights agenda and into international agreements and protocols. Finally, both NGOs and IGOs have worked in tandem at the grassroots level to encourage the demobilization and reintegration of child soldiers, to aid in efforts toward the physical and psychological healing of child soldiers, and to foster agreements between governments and nonstate actors to cease using children as combatants.

IGOs and NGOs share a strong relationship over the issue of child soldiers. Over three thousand NGOs were invited to the preparatory meetings for the September 2001 General Assembly special session on children. This symbiotic relationship is not surprising given the nature of the issue of child soldiers; indeed, NGO fieldwork continues to be crucial in informing the UN of the issue. Moreover, the Security Council invited NGOs to report on the issue of child soldiers. This is significant because it is relatively rare for the Security Council to solicit the views of NGOs. Moreover, this move by the Security Council signals a willingness to open up international security discourse to include human rights issues like the use of child soldiers.[20]

## FROM ADVOCACY TO ACTION

Most concrete policy on child soldiers has occurred at the international level. As noted, the 1996 Machel report led to the incorporation of the issue of child soldiers onto the agenda of the United Nations. Using the 1989 Convention on the Rights of the Child, Machel advocated numerous policy initiatives, including the creation of the special representative of the secretary-general on children in armed conflict. Indeed, the Convention on the Rights of the Child speaks to the issue of child soldiers. Article 38 specifically calls on states not to recruit child soldiers or place children under the age of fifteen into hostile situations. Article 38 goes on to call for the protection of children in armed

conflict. Article 39 advocates the recovery and reintegration of children experiencing neglect, abuse, or inhumane treatment during conflict. Machel's
report, however, resulted in a number of additional specific actions intended
to address the use of child soldiers.

The major triumph in international efforts to address child soldiers was the
May 2000 adoption of the CRC optional protocol on the involvement of children in armed conflict.[21] The optional protocol entered into force in February
2002. Article 38 of the CRC in fact spurred the movement toward the optional
protocol. Many children's rights advocates believed the fifteen-year-old limit
for recruitment set by the CRC was too low. As a result, in 1994 negotiations
on the protocol began. The protocol establishes eighteen as the minimum age
for the conscription of children and for their direct participation in armed conflict. The protocol does not restrict the voluntary recruitment of children under eighteen, but it raises the minimum age to sixteen and establishes a variety of safeguards to ensure the voluntary consent of those individuals and
their parents or guardians. States are called on not only to enforce the protocol but also to see to it that any child soldiers are demobilized and accorded
"all appropriate assistance for their physical and psychological recovery and
their social reintegration."[22]

While not a momentous change, the optional protocol represents a symbolic shift toward addressing the concerns of many NGOs. Consequently, the
NGOs' response to the adoption of the protocol was supportive, though
guarded. According to the Coalition to Stop the Use of Child Soldiers, "the
adoption of this new protocol by the General Assembly signals that it is no
longer acceptable to use children in war."[23] The major criticism centered on
the failure of the protocol to establish eighteen as the minimum age for voluntary recruitment. A number of NGOs lamented Canada's being the first signatory of the treaty, hoping instead that a country adopting a uniform sub-
eighteen ban would be first. Importantly, a number of regional agreements
establish different guidelines for the use of child soldiers. For example, the
African Charter on the Rights and Welfare of the Child was the first agreement to establish a "straight 18" rule, banning all recruitment of children under eighteen along with their participation in conflict.[24] Finally, many NGOs
were critical of the protocol's differential treatment of state armies and other
armed groups within societies.

Adoption of the optional protocol must be seen as at least a partial success
given the strong opposition that countries, including the United States and
Britain, have for years expressed with regard to raising the minimum recruitment age from fifteen. Indeed, according to a Center for Defense Information
official, the United States was one of the key countries focused on in the negotiations. The protocol's "stand alone" status was primarily a concession to

the United States.[25] The protocol also must be seen as the product of years of effort and movement at the level of the United Nations, NGOs, and, in some cases, states. Finally, the protocol represents a small part of the ongoing efforts to effect change in the use of child soldiers. The office of the special representative of the secretary-general on children in armed conflict has been especially active in conducting studies, country visits, and negotiations to stop the use of child soldiers. According to Otunnu,

> the Special Representative strongly believes that the international community must now redirect its energies from the juridical task of developing standards to the political project of ensuring their application and respect on the ground. We must launch "an era of application"—the application of international and local norms for the protection of children in times of armed conflict.[26]

The office of the special representative has been working on a variety of activities addressing the three points noted here: collecting and disseminating information on child soldiers; getting the issue of child soldiers on the international human rights agenda; and working at a grassroots level to stop the use of child soldiers and to demobilize, reintegrate, and heal former child soldiers.[27] Along with their work for the optional protocol, the office of the special representative also has sought to achieve regional agreements on child soldiers.[28]

The agenda-setting work of the special representative has dutifully sought to get children on the agenda of the Security Council. While perhaps largely symbolic, Otunnu's success, as reflected in Security Council resolution 1261,[29] signals a shift in thinking on the part of the UN and the Security Council whereby the security consequences of war-affected children are recognized. In 2000, the Security Council went a step further in resolution 1314 "by putting in place more targeted, action-oriented building blocks to protect children during and after conflict."[30] In addition to urging all states to ratify the optional protocol to the CRC, resolution 1314 goes on to advocate the demobilization and reintegration of child soldiers, along with efforts to meet the special needs of former child soldiers. The resolution speaks to the work of grassroots organizations and other NGOs and calls on them to establish child protection units, including within-field units; to address cross-border activities affecting children (e.g., abductions and small-arms trade); to integrate considerations of gender into all projects and programs; and to encourage regional initiatives. Resolution 1314 also speaks to the UN in advocating various activities, from reunifying families separated during war to incorporating young people into the peace process.[31] The special representative's office, oftentimes with UNICEF, has successfully advocated for child soldiers at the global and regional levels. As is often the case in international agreements, state commitments to action and actual state policy frequently diverge. Thus, despite signing or ratifying the treaty establishing the International Criminal Court and/or the optional protocol, the use of child soldiers continues in many states.

At the grassroots level, the office of the special representative has sought to work along two fronts. First, it has positioned itself within the peace process of conflicts in an effort to advocate for children in negotiated settlements—for example, by working with parties to reach an agreement to end the use of child soldiers. In his 2000 report, Otunnu details these missions in a variety of countries, including Sierra Leone, Northern Ireland, East and West Timor, and Colombia. The emphasis in these negotiations is on advocacy and action. Advocacy for children takes the form of highlighting the particular issues affecting children in the given conflict. Linking these substantive issues to the broader economic, social, and political arenas is a part of the process. It is important to stress two aspects of the advocacy work surrounding child soldiers. First, since virtually all the conflicts are internal civil conflicts, child soldier advocates must work with both the leaders of the state and the state armed forces and the leaders of rebel groups. This work also can involve third-party states. For example, UNICEF, along with other intergovernmental organizations and NGOs, has been granted complete "access to a political military training camp [in Uganda] housing child soldiers from the Democratic Republic of Congo."[32] Uganda agreed to hand over to UNICEF all soldiers under the age of eighteen residing in the camp. Second, NGOs and grassroots organizations are deliberately and frequently consulted and/or incorporated into this process. Like many other parts of the UN, the office of the special representative works closely with international and grassroots organizations. Second, Otunnu's office has worked at the grassroots level to address the complex issues related to the demobilization of child soldiers. The special representative's efforts include reintegration efforts, care for psychological and physical injuries, education, and social programs. Like the peace process, these efforts incorporate local and global organizations.

Finally, Otunnu's office has worked subregionally to encourage work at the neighborhood level. These initiatives seek "to engage subregional actors in dialogue that would lead to specific agreements and concrete measures to protect children."[33] In these initiatives states both within and outside the region work to establish "neighborhood" solutions to problems that fuel conflict and its subsequent effects on children. Examples include efforts to curb cross-border flows in small arms and natural resources as well as cross-border abductions of children.

The issue of child soldiers has galvanized international efforts involving both intergovernmental actors and nongovernmental organizations. From gathering and disseminating information to advocating on behalf of child soldiers, these actors are increasingly affecting interstate relations and, importantly, state interests and practices. While it is instructive to examine the policies and practices of states that are often singled out as the major abusers of children in warfare, it is also useful to analyze U.S. policy. The United States has been reticent to support children's human rights generally and has had specific and pointed arguments against international efforts to curb the use of child soldiers. Thus, an analysis of U.S. policy offers an opportunity to assess the impact of NGO/IGO activities on state behavior.

## U.S. POLICY AND THE OPTIONAL PROTOCOL

Policy responses to international efforts to curb the use of child soldiers reflect a U.S. reluctance to ratify the major international human rights treaties generally. According to Michael Ignatieff, when it comes to international human rights, the United States is "a nation with a great rights tradition that leads the world in denouncing human rights violations but which behaves like a rogue state in relation to international legal conventions."[34] With respect to children's rights and specifically child soldiers, the U.S. record is consistent. In 1991 President Clinton signed the Convention on the Rights of the Child but never submitted it to the Senate for ratification.[35] Indeed, only the United States and Somalia have failed to ratify the CRC: Somalia, which has no central government, essentially cannot ratify a treaty. On July 5, 2000, President Clinton signed the optional protocol to the Convention on the Rights of the Child. In contrast to other treaties the administration supported, the protocol was submitted by Clinton to the Senate for ratification. The Senate ratified the optional protocol in December 2002. The politics surrounding the ratification debate are instructive. Beginning in 1999, a series of amendments were introduced that addressed the issue of child soldiers.[36] The earliest was Senator Paul Wellstone's successful amendment to the Foreign Relations Authorization Act for fiscal years 2000 and 2001. Wellstone's amendment does five things. First, it outlines the major issues surrounding the use of child soldiers. Second, the amendment calls on the Senate to condemn the use of child soldiers worldwide. Third, it urges the international community to move forward on the optional protocol. Fourth, the amendment calls for U.S. support of the protocol. Finally, it recommends that the State Department address the issue of child soldiers in its working group.[37] House members were similarly active in raising the issue of child soldiers and in calling on the United States to support the optional protocol. Wellstone and House member Tom Lantos supported concurrent resolutions condemning the use of child soldiers and urging U.S. support of the optional protocol. Throughout 1999 and 2000, members of Congress called on representatives from NGOs to testify on the problems surrounding the use of child soldiers.

Nongovernmental organizations were particularly active both in getting the issue of child soldiers on the U.S. policy agenda and in garnering support for the protocol. The potentially symbiotic relationship between members of Congress and NGOs is a product of the dual functions that NGOs perform: providing information and moral leverage. These roles were confirmed in interviews with individuals from the Senate Foreign Relations Committee and the NGOs themselves. While contention surrounds the motivations of various NGOs and although clear preferences exist for the views of some organizations over others, few doubt the influence of these organizations in raising issue awareness and using moral suasion to change lawmakers' views on U.S. policy regarding child soldiers.

There were a host of reasons why some senators felt initial reluctance to vote for ratification of the optional protocol. Three concerns were particularly salient. The first related to the possible legal ramifications of ratifying the protocol to a treaty that has not even been submitted to the Senate. According to a majority staff member, the specific concern was that ratification of the optional protocol would entangle the United States in legal obligations arising from the CRC.

A representative of the Center for Defense Information dismissed this concern in an interview, citing that the United States' success in gaining "stand alone" status for the protocol represents a negotiating victory for the United States. As for arguments surrounding the protocol's reference to the CRC, these are minimal, and, regardless, the United States currently takes part in other aspects of the CRC without having ratified the treaty.[38]

The second concern related to issues of U.S. military readiness, combat capabilities, and, therefore, U.S. national security. This concern was exaggerated. It is important to note the optional protocol would not prohibit the recruitment of children under the age of eighteen; it bans only their participation in combat. Moreover, the U.S. military's under-eighteen contingent is a small percentage of its troop total. Nevertheless, one majority staff member expressed concern over the effects of the ban on seventeen-year-old recruits who would not see combat until age eighteen. More specifically, he expressed concern about the possible impact of the protocol on the ability of the United States to conduct a full-scale mobilization of the U.S. population. He went so far as to suggest that the Joint Chiefs of Staff may not have examined the issue thoroughly. Essentially, he argued that they were so delighted that the ban did not extend to recruitment that their judgment was clouded on other issues.[39]

NGO representatives involved in the negotiations over the protocol countered these concerns as well. According to one State Department official, the protocol met with the approval of the Joint Chiefs of Staff and the Pentagon. In general, the official stressed that the recruitment policies of the United States were not the problem addressed by the protocol. Rather, the protocol was drafted to address the use by states and rebel armies of young children in combat.[40] The Center for Defense Information official concurs with this assessment stressing that the Joint Chiefs of Staff did not see insurmountable problems in the protocol and, in fact, saw it as a "battle that can be lost."[41]

The third concern related to the constitutional prerogatives of the Senate vis-à-vis the executive branch. The staff member interviewed suggested that President Clinton's handling of the child soldier issue, among others, demonstrated disrespect for the authority of the Senate. The Clinton administration gave the Senate only a few weeks' notice of the president's intention to sign the optional protocol. This apparent disregard of the Senate's authority may have motivated some lawmakers to oppose ratification of the optional protocol, not on its merits, but out of concern for the Senate's powers. Even so, many Senators on both sides of the aisle supported the protocol, a fact that eventually ensured its ratification. But ratification would have to wait until the end of the Bush administration's first year in office. A coalition of NGOs was critical to securing Senate ratification. These observations should diminish the fact that the United States has signed the optional protocol and, more important, that the protocol was submitted to the Senate. Moreover, opposition to the treaty is relatively limited. Significantly, the Pentagon and Joint Chiefs of Staff came to support the protocol. Also important was the virtual absence of significant vocal opposition to the treaty in the Senate. What delayed the ratification of the treaty was a reticence on the part of the majority of the Senate Foreign Relations Committee to move the protocol forward to the floor of the Senate for debate and ratification. Thus, a final push by NGOs was all that was needed to ensure ratification of the protocol.

On February 14, 2001, representatives of over forty NGOs—including Human Rights Watch, Amnesty International, the National Council of Churches, and Maryknoll Sisters of St. Dominic—called on President Bush to encourage the Senate to ratify the protocol. The support of the Pentagon and the Joint Chiefs of Staff for the optional protocol gave them additional leverage. Furthermore, U.S. negotiators were politically savvy in linking the optional protocol on the involvement of children in armed conflict to the optional protocol on the sale of children, child prostitution, and child pornography. This linkage effectively united senators across party lines and, just as important, won the support of senators from the religious right. The Senate ratified the optional protocol in December 2002.

## UNDERSTANDING THE POLITICS OF CHILD SOLDIERS

Scholars have taken note of the growing influence of transnational advocacy networks in international politics.[42] Critical in this regard is the role that norms, values, and beliefs play in shaping international interactions and state interests. Sikkink argues that Keck and Sikkink's concept of a transnational advocacy network is particularly relevant to human rights issues, especially efforts to stop the use of child soldiers.[43] Transnational advocacy networks are composed of "actors working internationally on an issue, who are bound together by shared values, a common discourse, and dense exchanges of information and services."[44] These networks are especially influential because of their "ability to mobilize information strategically to help create new issues and categories and to persuade, pressure, and gain leverage over much more powerful organizations and governments."[45] Indeed, the strategic mobilization of information and the application of pressure by a broad coalition of NGOs and IGOs forced the issue of child soldiers onto the agenda of the United Nations.

A number of NGOs and IGOs had been concerned with the problem of child soldiers for some time. As noted, in 1994 some NGOs began to argue the need for an optional protocol to the CRC. But publication of the 1996 Machel report and the secretary-general's decision to act quickly on the recommendations contained in it by creating the office of the special representative gave additional impetus to efforts to address the problem of children in combat. The adoption of Security Council resolutions 1251 and 1314 gave additional evidence of the influence of this emergent transnational advocacy network because those resolutions challenged the dominant thinking about international security. The strategic mobilization of information and application of pressure similarly contributed to the ratification of the optional protocol by the U.S. Senate. Critical in this regard was the NGOs' ability to educate sympathetic members of Congress, to pressure senators reluctant to vote for ratification, and, especially, to convince the Joint Chiefs of Staff that the battle over ratification of the optional protocol was one they could afford to lose. Essentially, this was a successful effort to change the norms and values of the Pentagon. Although the United States' concerns with respect to the under-eighteen ban and the stand-alone status of the optional protocol were met in the negotiation process, the protocol's critical norms are now ensconced in U.S. law. The campaign to stop the use of child soldiers demonstrates the efficacy of a transnational advocacy network. The future of international politics is likely to witness the growing influence of such networks over the global agenda and state behavior. This influence depends on effective collaboration among NGOs and between NGOs and IGOs, in addition to the strategic mobilization of information. But at the core of this growing influence is the moral force of human rights norms. Too many children continue to be exposed to the scourge of modern war in too many nations of the developing world. Ultimately, this threat to the survival and development of children will depend on efforts to reduce poverty and settle political conflicts fueled by poverty. But there has been progress toward a safer world for children at the level of values—the involvement of children in armed conflict is now unequivocally condemned.

## NOTES

1. Graça Machel, "The Impact of Armed Conflict on Children: A Critical Review of Progress Made and Obstacles Encountered in Increasing Protection for War-Affected Children, a Follow-Up on the 1996 Machel Report," *International Conference on War-Affected Children* (Winnipeg, Canada: 2000), 6.

2. Olara Otunnu, *Protection of Children Affected by Armed Conflict*, report of the special representative of the secretary-general for children and armed conflict, United Nations General Assembly, Fifty-fifth Session, agenda item 110, 3 October 2000, 3.

3. An overview of international efforts to protect children in armed conflict is at the end of the Machel report.

4. Tina Susman and Geoffrey Mohan, "Young Combatants, Easily Manipulated and Misled, Are Becoming a Source for Tools of Civil War," *Milwaukee Journal Sentinel*, 19 November 1999, 21A.

5. "Across the World, Children Are Molded into Ruthless Soldiers," *Milwaukee Journal Sentinel*, 19 November 1999, 21A–28A (special supplement based on *Newsday* articles).

6. America's Defense Monitor, *Child Soldiers: Invisible Combatants*, show transcript of documentary film, exec. prod., Gene LaRocque (June 29, 1997).

7. For a discussion of the links between contemporary conflicts and the increased use of child soldiers see America's Defense Monitor, *Child Soldiers*; Ilene Cohn and Guy S. Goodwin-Gill, *Child Soldiers: The Role of Children in Armed Conflict* (Oxford: Clarendon Press, 1994); *Economist*, "Kalashnikov Kids," July 10, 1999; Judith Miller and Paul Lewis, "Fighting to Save Children from Battle," *New York Times*, 8 August 1999; Mike Wessells, "Child Soldiers," *Bulletin of the Atomic Scientists* 53 (1997): 7. A number of NGO websites also discuss this link. See Save the Children, www.savethechildren.org.uk/scuk/jsp/index.jsp?flash=true; Human Rights Watch, www.hrw.org; and Amnesty International, www.amnesty.org. The Graça Machel report is on the UNICEF website, www.unicef.org/graca. In that report, Machel also makes this connection.

8. The idea of children volunteering to join military and paramilitary groups is contradicted by most experts. According to Mike Wessels, "I think one has to be very careful to recognize there is truly no voluntary joining, in the sense that the vast majority of children who join willing do so out of necessity or victimization, fear for security. Unaccompanied children who have no parents to protect them, people who are fearful that they will die of hunger or who have inadequate health care all may seek military activity." Some authors are quick to recognize the potentially culturally based arguments behind what might appear to be the arbitrary setting of eighteen as the age for adulthood in the Convention on the Rights of the Child. America's Defense Monitor, *Child Soldiers*; Wessells, "Child Soldiers."

9. America's Defense Monitor, *Child Soldiers*; *Economist*, "Kalashnikov Kids"; Graça Machel, *Impact of Armed Conflict on Children* (New York: UNICEF/UN, 1996). Uganda's rebel army had an estimated 3,000 child soldiers under the age of 16, including 500 girls.

10. Information regarding the use of child soldiers—that is, why children are used as combatants and how they come to be combatants—is in many of the sources already cited. Especially relevant is the America's Defense Monitor transcript *Child Soldiers* along with the Wessells article "Child Soldiers." Groups such as Save the Children and Amnesty International have issued reports detailing general and specific trends in the use of child soldiers. The 1996 Machel report and Machel's 2000 review offer similar details along with particular conditions in specific countries. The UN has issued similar reports, generally from the office of the special representative of the secretary-general for children and armed conflict (Otunnu, *Protection of Children*). The observations offered here come from these various sources.

11. Machel, "Critical Review," chap. 2.

12. Wessells, "Child Soldiers."

13. America's Defense Monitor, *Child Soldiers*.

14. Human Rights Watch website, www.hrw.org/campaigns/crp/index.htm.

15. Human Rights Watch website, www.hrw.org/campaigns/crp/voices.htm.

16. Human Rights Watch website, www.hrw.org/campaigns/crp/voices.htm.

17. Human Rights Watch website, www.hrw.org/campaigns/crp/voices.htm.

18. Otunnu, *Protection of Children*.

19. America's Defense Monitor, *Child Soldiers*.

20. Author interview with official from the Center for Defense Information, 8 February 2001.

21. United Nations General Assembly, *Optional Protocols to the Convention on the Rights of the Child on the Involvement of Children in Armed Conflict and on the Sale of Children, Child Prostitution and Child Pornography*, Fifty-fourth Session, agenda item 116 (16 May 2000).

22. United Nations General Assembly, *Optional Protocols to the Convention*.

23. International Coalition to Stop the Use of Child Soldiers. For information and press releases, among other information, see www.child-soldiers.org.

24. Otunnu, *Protection of Children*.

25. In this case, the stand-alone status of the protocol allows state ratification without prior ratification of the CRC.

26. Otunnu, *Protection of Children*.

27. It bears repeating that Otunnu's office deals with the broad topic of children and conflict. The issue of child soldiers is one of many substantive concerns of the special representative of the secretary-general for children and armed conflict. This discussion centers on its work with respect to child soldiers.

28. Otunnu, *Protection of Children*.

29. Security Council resolution 1261 was the first resolution to address the issue of children and war. The resolution not only recognizes the use of child soldiers as a violation of international law but goes further in both calling for an end to the myriad deleterious effects of war on children and recognizing the links between child soldiers and the international arms trade. United Nations Security Council resolution 1261, adopted by the Security Council at its 4,037th meeting, 25 August 1999.

30. Otunnu, *Protection of Children*.

31. United Nations Security Council resolution 1314, adopted by the Security Council at its 4,185th meeting, 11 August 2000.

32. UNICEF, "UNICEF Applauds Agreement with Uganda on Child Soldiers," press release, 9 February 2001.

33. Otunnu, *Protection of Children*.

34. Michael Ignatieff, "Human Rights: The Midlife Crisis," *New York Review of Books*, May 20, 1999, 58–62.

35. This was not unusual for the Clinton administration. Indeed, the administration signed many treaties that it never submitted to the Senate. Among them were the International Criminal Court, the Antiballistic Missle Treaty, and the Kyoto Protocol. This practice was not limited to the Clinton administration; the Reagan administration similarly signed a variety of treaties it never submitted to the Senate.

36. Before 1999 there were some congressional efforts to address the issue of child soldiers. Representative George Miller sponsored a 1989 resolution calling on the United States to support a ban on children in conflict, *Congressional Record*, November 7, 1989. Miller also advocated for the CRC, *Congressional Record*, November 2, 1989. In 1998 the topic of child soldiers was raised through a joint resolution condemning the situation in Uganda, *Congressional Record*, July 24, 1998.

37. "Amendments Submitted. Foreign Relations Authorization Act. Wellstone Amendment No. 697," *Congressional Record*, 18 June 1999.

38. Geske's interview with official from the Center for Defense Information, 8 February 2001.

39. Geske's interview with State Department official involved in the negotiation of the optional protocol, 2001.

40. Geske's interview with State Department official involved in the negotiation of the optional protocol, 2001.

41. Geske's interview with official from the Center for Defense Information, 8 February 2001.

42. Margaret E. Keck and Kathryn Sikkink, *Activists beyond Borders* (Ithaca, N.Y.: Cornell University Press, 1998); Martha Finnemore, *National Interests in International Society* (Ithaca, N.Y.: Cornell University Press, 1996).

43. Kathryn Sikkink, "Human Rights, Principled Issue-Networks, and Sovereignty in Latin America," *International Organization* 47, no. 3 (1993): 411–41.

44. Keck and Sikkink, *Activists beyond Borders*, 2.

45. Keck and Sikkink, *Activists beyond Borders*.

*Chapter Six*

# Children's Rights and the Tenuousness of Local Coalitions: A Case Study in Nicaragua

Richard Maclure and Melvin Sotelo

Since Nicaragua's endorsement of the UN Convention on the Rights of the Child and the legislative passage of its own Code of Childhood and Adolescence, improvements in the welfare of marginalized youth have depended largely on community-based actions that are sponsored by nongovernmental organizations (NGOs) and civic groups, many of which function in tangent with municipal government authorities and international aid agencies. In this chapter we review three community initiatives that have aimed at resolving problems associated with youth alienation and violence in a poor, heavily populated district of Managua.

## THE UN CONVENTION ON THE RIGHTS OF THE CHILD: PROBLEMS OF IMPLEMENTATION IN LATIN AMERICA

The UN Convention on the Rights of the Child (CRC), unanimously adopted by the General Assembly in 1989, was a landmark charter for the global human rights movement. Ratified by more than 170 countries and reinforced by the Declaration and Plan of Action that emanated from the 1990 World Summit for Children, the CRC signaled a major shift in official international perceptions concerning the status and welfare of children. No longer are children to be regarded as objects solely dependent on adult authority. Instead, because of their vulnerability, all children (deemed to be persons below eighteen years old) are entitled to special rights guaranteeing care and protection. Henceforth, the best interests of all children are to be a priority of governance. Accordingly, signatory states are to share with parents the responsibility for the upbringing and development of children (article 18).

"State parties" are enjoined to undertake legislation guaranteeing the protection of children's rights and to allocate maximum public resources for children's welfare (articles 3 and 4). For this endeavor to succeed, particularly in developing countries, international aid and cooperation are recognized as being significant (article 4).[1]

Throughout Latin America governments have had neither the financial resources nor the political capital necessary to implement the sweeping social reforms mandated by the CRC. Instead, in the wake of economic crises, burdensome national debts, and structural adjustment programs, central states have generally had to downsize social services and shift responsibility for addressing the plight of marginalized children and other vulnerable social groups to municipal levels of government.[2] Yet this in turn has placed onerous responsibilities on municipal authorities. Often without independent tax bases and rarely able to rely on substantive resource transfers from central ministries, cash-strapped politicians and bureaucrats working at local levels have been turning to NGOs and community associations to assist in providing social services and in dealing with pressing social problems.[3] This has been especially evident in heavily populated urban centers that are characterized by extensive poverty, high rates of unemployment, and a paucity of state-sponsored social assistance programs.

Nicaragua exemplifies many of the challenges confronting the discourse of children's rights and those who strive to transform the discourse into major improvements in the lives of disadvantaged children. Having ratified the CRC in 1990—one of the last acts of the revolutionary Sandinista (Frente Sandinista de Liberación Nacional) government before its defeat at the polls—the Nicaraguan state has undertaken several formal measures in line with its obligations as a signatory to the CRC. The most notable of these has been the formulation of the Code of Childhood and Adolescence (Código de la Niñez y la Adolescencia). At the time of its approval by Congress in early 1998, the code represented a triumph for children's rights advocates in Nicaragua, for it emulates many of the terms and objectives of the CRC. Yet more than half a decade later, the Nicaraguan state has demonstrated little capacity or will to implement the provisions of the code. Instead, NGOs and other local community groups that constitute civil society have continued to provide most of the impetus for improving the conditions of marginalized children and youth. However, although civil society clearly has a vital role to play in promoting and protecting children's rights in Nicaragua, there is little evidence that it has the cohesiveness and organizational capacity to make up for the social policy shortcomings of a fragile democratic state.

## CIVIL SOCIETY AS A FORCE FOR SOCIAL CHANGE IN NICARAGUA: ACCLAIM AND UNCERTAINTY

In Nicaragua many of the NGOs and local civic groups that constitute civil society have retained vestiges of the oppositional social movement and democratic culture that emerged during the revolutionary Sandinista period of the 1980s.[4] Although the elections of 1990 ended the leftist Sandinista government and ushered in a new era of centrist and right-wing national governments,[5] the Sandinista-inspired Communal Movement, a coalition of volunteer community associations, has attained prominence by juxtaposing political advocacy with the local mobilization of social services. Likewise, a growing number of autonomous NGOs have become increasingly involved in processes of national policy dialogue and social policy implementation.

Two interrelated factors have expanded the role of civil society as an arena of political activity and influence. First, as elsewhere in Latin America, the state in Nicaragua has been undermined by a host of problems that have weakened its ability to govern effectively. Prolonged economic stagnation and a debilitating international debt have forced government ministries to curtail their expenditures and downsize public services, especially those directed toward the social welfare of children and youth. Total state expenditures on education and health fell steadily throughout most of the 1990s, and inevitably this resulted in an increase in privately born costs for these services.[6] Further damage came in 1998 when Hurricane Mitch wrought severe devastation on the country's infrastructure and agricultural sector. Added to these difficulties has been the erosion of government credibility stemming from public service corruption and the protection of elite private interests, particularly during the Alemán regime of 1997–2001.[7] With the legitimacy of the state in question, many have looked to the diverse organs of civil society for social assistance and the promotion of social justice.

The second explanation for the strength of civil society in Nicaragua has been the influx of foreign aid that has been increasingly directed toward NGOs. Disenchanted with official development strategies that have often been seen as inefficient and skewed in favor of political elites, foreign donors now tend to regard NGOs as conduits of effective social service delivery and as vanguards of more participatory forms of governance.[8] Increased donor interest in the nongovernmental sector has consequently fostered a veritable boon in NGO activity in Nicaragua. By the year 2000 there were approximately eighteen hundred NGOs and community associations operating in Nicaragua, a tenfold increase from 1990.[9] Moreover, while official bilateral assistance to the Nicaraguan government fell from US$673 million in 1990 to $493 million in 1999, international aid to national NGOs in Nicaragua quadrupled, from US\$34.6 million to \$161 million during the same period.[10]

As many have argued, the heightened prominence of NGOs and civic groups in Nicaragua, and indeed throughout much of Latin America, represents a significant step in the transition to democratic governance.[11] From this perspective, besides supporting the provision of social services to marginalized and impoverished sectors of society, NGOs have helped to foster "secondary" citizenship among those excluded from participating in state-centered politics.[12] By encouraging dialogue, negotiation, and democratic resolution of conflict, NGOs have redirected social and political energy that has often been manifested as resistance to state institutions and policies of the state. Within the last decade, however, as treasuries have become depleted and the strength of state corporatism has diminished, NGOs and civic groups have gained political influence, forming social movements demanding legislation and policies oriented toward improving the conditions of marginalized social groups. In many respects this has facilitated processes of democratization and has helped to propel human rights issues into mainstream political discourse.[13] It has also fostered a new spirit of "pragmatism," which is reflected in a growing willingness among NGOs and local government authorities to cooperate.[14]

At the same time, however, although a vibrant nongovernmental sector has contributed to a reconfiguration of political processes in Latin America, there are those who nonetheless maintain reservations about the capacity of NGOs and community groups to ensure significant advancement of human rights and democratic institutions. For just as central states are constrained by transnational economic and political forces that are oblivious to conventional national boundaries, so too are civil societies vulnerable to economic oscillations and to the politics of foreign aid. As Macdonald has argued, throughout Latin America "the cards are stacked against the poor, and NGO activity can do little in the short term to reshuffle the deck."[15] From this perspective, expectations are likely to be misplaced that civil society can generate the structural changes necessary to reduce poverty and the marginalization of vulnerable social groups. While NGOs, civic and religious associations, and social movements can play a key role in improving the welfare of poor communities and in nurturing democratic rule, they generally rely heavily on voluntarist memberships and on resources that originate from outside local communities.[16] Similarly, although their diverse agendas may be strengthened through social networking, the different constituents of civil society are rarely able to establish institutionalized cohesion. As critics suggest, they may complement and indeed reinforce trends toward democratic rule, but they are no substitute for strong effective governments.[17]

A further criticism of the notion that civil society can be a catalyst of progressive change centers on the linkages that have increasingly bound NGOs and civic groups with national governments and international aid agencies. By embracing opportunities afforded by state accommodation and infusions of foreign assistance, many groups in civil society are becoming susceptible to hegemonic co-optation by governing elites.[18] Viewed in this way, many NGOs and community groups may be participating in a form of neoliberal subterfuge, through collaboration in the development and implementation of social policies and programs that are designed to offset the disintegrative tendencies of expanded global markets and reduced public services.[19] As they become more numerous and more formally structured, these organizations tend to preoccupy themselves with the technical and administrative dimensions of social assistance. Moreover, as critics have pointed out, since most NGOs and the growing number of community associations have come to rely heavily on foreign support, they tend to compete for funding and often become absorbed by external demands for fiscal accountability and project efficiency. In such circumstances, organizations of civil society may increasingly function as subcontractors for international donors and so be distracted from challenging the very structures of power that underlie situations of mass poverty and social injustice.[20]

Nowhere are these challenges more acute than in the realm of children's rights. While the nongovernmental sector in Nicaragua was instrumental in contributing to the formulation of the Code of Childhood and Adolescence, it is questionable whether civil society, even when aligned with municipal government authorities, has the capacity to generate fundamental changes to the status and conditions of the majority of marginalized Nicaraguan youth.

## CIVIL SOCIETY AND THE CODE OF CHILDHOOD AND ADOLESCENCE

By passing the Code of Childhood and Adolescence, the Nicaraguan government formally acknowledged the injustices of child poverty and reiterated its obligation to make children's rights a priority of public policy. All public policies and programs affecting the welfare of Nicaraguan children were to be guided by the articles of the code. Yet as outlined in the code, the onus for protecting children's rights does not reside solely with the state. Although the central government is expected to be the main guarantor of children's rights, the code stipulates that the welfare of children is a shared responsibility that necessitates the active participation of families, schools, and community organizations, as well as the participation of children and youth themselves (article

56).[21] Cooperation between state and civil society is thus deemed imperative for the promotion and protection of children's rights.

Within the last half decade, however, it has become clear that the state in Nicaragua has had neither the fiscal capacity nor the political and ideological will to satisfactorily enforce most of the code's provisions. Structural adjustment and debt servicing have led to the downsizing of public services that directly affect children and youth.[22] Despite admonitions by the UN Committee on the Rights of the Child that the national government of Nicaragua must "take all available measures . . . to guarantee the full implementation of the Code,"[23] it is generally accepted that much of the impetus for advancing children's rights continues to rest with NGOs, municipal authorities, and international aid agencies.

Yet it is far from certain whether locally based alliances, even when supported by external donor agencies, have the necessary organizational capacity, sustained leadership, and political strength to engender the structural reforms recommended by both the CRC and the Nicaraguan code. So far, little is known about the dynamics of specific municipal-level actions aimed at ameliorating the plight of indigent children and youth in Nicaragua nor on how these relate to the discourse of change as articulated in the Code of Childhood and Adolescence.[24] A challenge for researchers is to examine local initiatives aimed at improving the situations of marginalized young people and to assess the factors that are likely to enhance or confound the effectiveness of such initiatives. In the following sections of this chapter, we present a review of three community-level projects that were intended to address problems associated with youth violence and the conditions underlying youth marginalization in Managua's District VI. In all cases, while varied in terms of their success as small-scale local initiatives in their own right, there is no indication that they have helped to foster a structural transformation that might ensure long-lasting improvements in the welfare of Nicaraguan children.

## The Study

Research for this study was conducted as part of an overall inquiry into the effects of the Code of Childhood and Adolescence on social policies and programs affecting marginalized urban youth in Managua. From May 2000 to March 2002, one of the authors (Sotelo) was a research consultant working with the Centro de Información y Asesoría en Salud (CISAS). A national NGO founded in 1983, CISAS has worked for more than a decade in various neighborhoods of District VI, a large municipal zone in Managua. As part of his responsibilities, Sotelo served as CISAS's representative on the Intersectoral Commission for Integrated Care of Adolescents (CIS), one of the initiatives discussed here. During this period, he conducted extensive participant observations of community meetings and various social programs designed to improve the welfare of children and youth. He also conducted interviews with NGO representatives and public officials associated with the CIS. In addition, he reviewed two other civic activities in District VI—the Villa Libertad school program for at-risk youth and a community policing initiative. As both these latter activities had begun before Sotelo's research fieldwork, Sotelo obtained information through interviews with the Villa Libertad school director and with numerous public officials and community leaders. While documents obtained from different local government sources provided some background information on District VI, most of these were unedited and unpublished. Our knowledge of the district was therefore enhanced through participant observation and informal interviewing.

## District VI

District VI is the largest of Managua's municipal zones. It is governed locally by an elected municipal council that is responsible for taxation, security, and the coordination of state social services. It is also the site of a host of neighborhood civic groups, most of which are represented within Children's Rights and the Tenuousness of Local Coalitions 95, the districtwide nongovernmental Communal Movement. With a population of over three hundred thousand residents and a steady influx of immigrants arriving from the impoverished central and northern regions of Nicaragua, demographically the district is growing rapidly. Its social and economic problems are likewise multiplying.[25] Infrastructure such as potable water, electricity, and sewage are in short supply. Housing is seriously inadequate, with many instances of two or more families living under the same roof. Such is the cramped nature of family living arrangements that many teens simply abandon their natal homes to live in the streets. Approximately 30 percent of families are headed by single mothers. Poor health is endemic. While three health clinics offer free consultations in the district, many people are unable to afford the purchase of medicines required for treatment. Unemployment in the district is high—an estimated 60 percent of individuals who are eligible for work are without jobs. Another 20 percent are assumed to be working in the informal economic sector, mainly as street and market vendors.[26] This leaves approximately 20 percent of the district's working-age population employed in full-time jobs in either the public sector or as employees in private companies.[27]

Circumstances confronting the majority of youth in District VI are bleak. In 2001, out of an estimated fifty-eight thousand adolescents (aged thirteen to eighteen) who were eligible for formal schooling in the district, fewer than twenty thousand were officially enrolled in schools.[28] Two out of every three youth had thus either dropped out of school or had never enrolled at all. For these young people, the likelihood of obtaining any form of legitimate remunerative employment is sparse. In addition, since many are bereft of strong family and community support, large numbers of (mostly male) youth in District VI have been drawn toward neighborhood youth gangs. While serving as mutually reinforcing groups, gangs of young teens are also invariably engaged in illegal and often violent activities. Sometimes violence is inflicted on members of the general public, but for the most part assaults are perpetrated on other youth. According to district police, the most common forms of youth violence involve property damage, robbery with intimidation, assaults, and murder.[29]

Exacerbating the marginalization of youth in District VI, as indeed throughout Nicaragua and elsewhere in Latin America, is a commonly held view that children and adolescents are dependents who must be subjugated to the family, community, school, and the judiciary.[30] This perspective has been sustained by the powerful moral sway of the Catholic church and the dogmatic practices of a doctrinaire formal school system. As publicly stated by Humberto Belli, a minister of education in both the Chamorro and Alemán governments, the proper behavior of children in school is "to listen, to obey, and to be guided."[31] Traditional and still widely practiced methods of teaching emphasize discipline, conformity, and the transmission of a fixed body of curricular knowledge to passive child learners. This approach to teaching is reinforced by most parents in District VI, who hold to the belief that children must comply unquestioningly to all forms of adult authority.[32] Dominance and obedience are the foundations of relations between parents and children. In this cultural context, conventional approaches to youth delinquency generally involve punitive interventions designed to intimidate and control youth and, if necessary, to detain them indefinitely as a way to protect society.[33]

In light of these prevailing structural and normative conditions, not only are there serious concerns among children's rights groups about the overall well-being of the majority of youth in District VI, but there is also growing popular anxiety about the long-term social effects of youth marginalization on the general welfare of the district and on the city of Managua as a whole. Consequently, in the last decade, in order to respond to the plight of youth and allay popular fears of youth crime, a number of civic groups in District VI have initiated three separate and quite distinctive youth-related projects in the district. Each of these community projects has made inroads toward fostering changes in local perceptions of at-risk youth and in the way they are dealt with by institutional authorities. Yet, each of these youth-oriented initiatives has been limited in scope and has inevitably fostered doubts about the capacity of local coalitions to bring about the broad structural changes that are essential for the long-term advancement of children's rights.


## THE VILLA LIBERTAD SCHOOL INITIATIVE

In a social environment dominated by chronic poverty and disintegrating family bonds, many young males and (less visibly) young females have grouped themselves into neighborhood gangs. As peer enclaves that gravitated easily to violence and criminal activity, youth gangs inevitably generated disruption and fear among local inhabitants. This was particularly evident in and around the school of Villa Libertad, a neighborhood of District VI.

Established in the mid-1970s, the school in Villa Libertad is one of the largest public schools in Managua, offering both primary and secondary education to children in the district. By 1991, clashes between rival youth gangs frequently took place in the environs of the school. Students and teachers became victims of harassment and assault. As the school director, Doña Esmeralda Espinoza, recounted,

> There were nights that I would take youths who had been beaten up, shot or stabbed to the Carlos Marx Hospital. School desertion was tremendous, espe cially for the night shift, because that is when they attacked the most. Even teachers resigned because of the problem.

School appeals for police protection were met with insistence that the school pay the costs of police transportation and overtime expenses—veiled pretexts for avoiding night-time entry into what was considered a dangerous area for police officers.[34] Similar entreaties to the Ministry of Education, in writing and through face-to-face meetings, met with little more than a sympathetic hearing.

Faced with official nonresponsiveness to youth violence and to the subsequent endangerment of children's safety and loss of educational opportunities in Villa Libertad, Doña Esmeralda turned to the community's inhabitants. In due course, a group of parents and teachers decided to try to reduce the threat of continued gang harassment by forming what came to be known as the school Social Action Committee (SAC). Given their proximity to youth in the neighborhood and to the lack of action from local government authorities, the members of the SAC decided to approach the perpetrators of violence—the gangs themselves—directly. Among the first of its measures, the SAC invited gang members to several informal meetings at the Villa Libertad school so that all sides could express their mutual concerns.

Following these initial contacts, an agreement was established between the school and the neighborhood gang leaders. In return for gang acceptance of the school as a neutral safety zone, the SAC agreed to work with gang members and other out-of-school youth in organizing mainly recreational activities. Initially this involved the hosting of youth dances and bazaars. These events incorporated fund-raising components for purchases of sports equipment and books. By 1993, the threat of gang violence had been dramatically reduced at the Villa Libertad school. Yet rather than disband, the SAC decided to embark on a program of outreach for youth gangs and other out-of-school youth. Numerous adolescents were enticed to return to school, and several were able to complete their high school certificate examinations. As part of their educational outreach, Doña Esmeralda and SAC representatives undertook home visits to the families of at-risk youth. Doña Esmeralda also routinely visited gang members who had been incarcerated by the police or injured in fights and were confined in hospitals. More recently, a series of informal education projects focusing mainly on basic health issues has been established for youth and their parents at the school.

Over the past decade, largely because of the efforts of Doña Esmeralda and the SAC, over one hundred erstwhile gang members have completed their high school studies. Of these, an estimated seventy-eight youth have gone on to further studies, five have received university scholarships, and sixty-three have obtained paying jobs.[35] Among Villa Libertad inhabitants, a consensus exists that the efforts of the SAC, combined with the dynamic leadership of Doña Esmeralda, have had a positive impact among many at-risk youth in the district. This was acknowledged in 2001 when Doña Esmeralda was formally honored as the best school director of the year by the Ministry of Education. At the time of our inquiry, the school in Villa Libertad continued to maintain its reputation as a zone of safety.

Despite these positive outcomes, indications are that the Villa Libertad school initiative has encountered difficulties that have constrained its effectiveness. Notwithstanding conferral of the "best school director" accolade, the Ministry of Education has offered no exceptional support either to the school or to the SAC, nor has any other branch of government extended assistance. Similarly, the school received no support from NGOs or foreign donors. Even more troubling, apart from the rhetorical encouragement of the police and local Communal Movement leaders, the Villa Libertad school initiative has garnered limited interest from the population of District VI. Deeply fearful as they are of youth crime and accustomed to coercive forms of conflict resolution, many people question the value of assisting youth who are deemed to be hooligans. Steeped in traditional authoritarian values and a belief in rigorous coercion as the way to deter youth crime, vocal elements in the community continue to insist that only through higher rates of arrest, conviction, and punishment can the problems of organized youth crime and violence be resolved.

## THE COMMUNITY POLICING INITIATIVE

In 1998, responding to organized youth violence in District VI, representatives of the Communal Movement met with the district police chief to discuss ways in which local people and the police could cooperate more effectively in preventing youth crime. Mindful of the recently approved Code of Childhood and Adolescence and concerned about a lack of constructive community participation in local law enforcement, Communal Movement leaders proposed a form of collaboration that would combine conventional policing with efforts to resocialize youth gang members. The police chief was receptive to the proposal, and over the course of the following year several meetings were convened to develop a "community policing" initiative to foster cooperation between community representatives and the police. These initial meetings—which involved police officers, church officials, groups of parents, and members of the district Communal Movement—focused principally on methods of local surveillance and crime monitoring. Within two or three months, however, the meetings had expanded to include youth representatives. Dialogue consequently shifted to focus on ways of reducing gang activity and steering children away from association with gangs. On the basis of these discussions, police and community representatives formed several preventive "neighborhood watch" units. Informal workshops for police and youth were likewise arranged in order to foster awareness of the issues and concerns confronting each side. Several social events were also organized—notably, soccer football matches that included local gang members and police as players.

Although the idea of improved community–police collaboration was initially undertaken with some enthusiasm, by 2000 skepticism and resistance had begun to set in. There were mutterings among the police rank and file that collaboration with the local populace was an imposition above and beyond their law enforcement mandate, designed to diminish their authority to arrest and incarcerate young delinquents. As one police officer stated, albeit half in jest, "They wanted to change us into youth social workers." As a way of expressing their resentment, police officials began to demand remuneration or "overtime" expense, such as vehicle depreciation, fuel purchases, and additional hours of work. Gradually, too, it became apparent that some police were using information obtained through their ties with the Communal Movement to augment surveillance practices and apprehend youth suspected of

gang activity. Further disenchantment followed the misappropriation of locally raised funds that had been earmarked to attract a matching external
grant for community policing activities. By early 2001 the district police chief
was reassigned to another post. With the departure of this key figure, local
leaders lost interest in continuing formally organized community–police collaboration.

## THE INTERSECTORAL COMMISSION

In 1997 the German bilateral aid agency GTZ launched a study of the reproductive and sexual health of adolescents in District VI.[36] On completion of the
study, GTZ hosted a workshop to inform interested NGOs, community groups,
and local government authorities of the results of the study. In the ensuing dialogue, much attention was directed toward the socioeconomic dimensions of
adolescent sexuality and reproduction, as well as the lack of social services
available to teens in the district. Following recommendations of the GTZ study
and the resolutions of the workshop, further deliberations among NGOs and
local government authorities led to the formation in early 1998 of the District
VI Intersectoral Commission for Integrated Care of Adolescents—commonly
known as the Intersectoral Commission (Comisión Intersectorial; CIS). Composed of local public officials, representatives of various national NGOs and
local community associations,[37] and delegates from GTZ, which agreed to fi-
nance the initiative, the newly formed CIS proposed as its mandate the following principal objectives:

- to improve factors affecting adolescent health;
- to develop coordinated social programs for out-of-school and underemployed youth in District VI;
- to encourage active involvement of youth in the socioeconomic life of the
  district, thereby increasing opportunities for their personal, social, and occupational development;
- to foster the ideals of neighborhood solidarity, gender equity, and respect for
  children's rights as outlined in the Code of Childhood and Adolescence.[38]

Throughout its first year of existence, the CIS served as little more than a forum for encouraging its member organizations to develop or expand their
own program initiatives for youth in the district. Under the auspices of the
CIS, for example, GTZ financed the establishment of weekly adolescent-only
clinics at the three government health centers in the district. A key aim of
these clinics was to function not only as treatment centers for physical ail-

ments but to provide educational and informational services for youth, especially on issues related to reproductive health. These clinics have since been complemented by GTZ-sponsored health education outreach sessions conducted by government health officers for teens in the district.[39] Similarly, with assistance from UNICEF and the UN Drug Control Program, two district offices of the Ministry of the Family (both attached to the CIS) began to assist community associations in establishing counseling programs for out-of-school youngsters suffering from drug abuse and domestic violence. Several NGOs affiliated to the CIS likewise developed their own extension activities for youth. These included health education, diverse forms of vocational training, and individual counseling.

For a while, as these examples show, what appeared to be CIS activities actually consisted of the collected but separate youth-oriented initiatives of its members. Nevertheless, since 1999, drawing on an annual grant of approximately US$10,000 per year from GTZ, the CIS has emerged as a recognizably autonomous entity with its own youth program focusing on four areas of intervention. First, it has sponsored the creation of neighborhood youth clubs and a districtwide "adolescent commission" whose membership is drawn from the youth clubs. By supporting a regular schedule of adolescent commission meetings and by encouraging this assembly to articulate youth concerns and needs, the CIS has cultivated youth involvement in its own deliberations and decision-making processes. Several adolescents have become active participants at CIS meetings and in CIS-sponsored interventions.

A second program focus for the CIS is education and training, mainly through the youth clubs and the representative adolescent commission. Most prominent are educational forums on health and sexual relations, leadership and democratic governance, gender issues, youth violence, and the principles and objectives of the Code of Childhood and Adolescence. These forums have generally been conducted as seminars in which the youth participants are encouraged to discuss issues in small groups and in plenary sessions. In addition, the CIS has provided financial assistance for some youth to attend vocational training workshops and to complete formal schooling.

A third set of activities consists of sociocultural and recreational events that are organized for, and often by, adolescents. These include dances, theatre workshops, a festival of the arts, and an annual sports tournament. Most of these activities have attracted scores of youth and have helped to generate modest revenue for the adolescent commission. The fourth domain of CIS intervention consists of a series of discussion forums for parents and adolescents. With many families in District VI experiencing domestic violence and other types of abuse that often result in youth drifting away from their homes, the purpose of these meetings has been to foster stronger relationships between parents and youth.

In the last three years some three thousand adolescents and about a hundred parents have been directly involved in organizing and participating in this range of CIS-supported activities. The CIS has initiated dialogue and a degree of mutual empathy among seemingly directionless youth, on the one side, and parents and community leaders on the other. The establishment of the CIS as an intersectoral body composed of diverse state and nonstate member institutions has fostered a local discourse that reflects a broad perspective of disadvantaged youth. By connecting local government, NGOs, and neighborhood civic associations, it has provided these bodies with a legitimate forum to collaborate on specific district-level youth projects, to negotiate their differences, and to consider youth issues holistically and collegially. As one local official observed, before the CIS was created in District VI, "there was rivalry among the state institutions and the organizations of civil society: *we do this; you do that; we have this; you have that.* Now there is more cooperation."

Yet despite these encouraging developments, the CIS is not without its internal tensions. One frequent topic of debate has been the CIS preoccupation with community projects. As most of its NGO members have argued, the focus on project work tends to be technical and shortsighted. Some claim, therefore, that the CIS should move beyond discrete project interventions and take on a greater advocacy role by challenging government policies that reinforce the indigence of children and youth. For example, by openly denouncing compulsory school fees and the prohibition of sex education in the schools, the CIS would de facto assume a more critical and outspoken political stance. Not surprisingly, however, the prospect of openly denouncing the state does not sit well with local public bureaucrats. From the perspective of government representatives, collaboration between the state and organs of civil society requires consensus and the avoidance of politically charged declarations and actions. For this reason, to date the CIS has remained essentially apolitical and has confined its activities to information sharing and to project planning and administration. Yet these opposing views concerning the appropriate function of the CIS have sowed an element of discord among its state and nonstate members.

A further source of tension relates to the role of GTZ as the principal sponsor of the CIS. In 2001 the issue of financial dependency came to a head when a GTZ representative announced that German financial aid to the CIS was to be reduced in the following fiscal year. Abrupt withdrawal of the sole funding agency would probably have resulted in the demise of the CIS as a viable association in District VI. An agreement for a transition period was therefore worked out whereby GTZ would scale back its support gradually as new sources of financial input were established. However the issue of dependency on GTZ funding is resolved, it is clear that all interested parties anticipate the need for continued external donor assistance if the CIS is to continue to function.

## CONCLUSION

In District VI it is evident that collaboration among civic groups, NGOs, and local government authorities is essential if the conditions of children and youth are to be improved. In this brief descriptive review of three such collaborative initiatives, it is also clear that a shift in perspectives about youth and in the ways that they are engaged is critical to achieving any semblance of progressive change. Common to all of these initiatives was the democratic nature of their inceptions and the decision-making processes that were imperative for their continuances. In addition, all three initiatives attempted to depart from a conventional crime-control approach to youth delinquency and violence. Instead of focusing on intimidation and punishment, they all adopted strategies of prevention and dialogue that rested on relations of trust and interdependence. Attention was devoted not just to individual youth but also to immediate environmental risk factors that give rise to youth violence and crime. In this way, community activities were developed in an effort not only to alter individual attitudes and behavior but also to contribute to changing the social and physical environment of youth.

The conceptions that these interventions had of children and youth were parallel to those espoused by the CRC and the Nicaraguan code. Solutions to youth marginalization were sought as much through stakeholder discussion and participatory decision making as they were in the projects and activities that emerged from such processes. Youth were treated as "subjects" of special rights rather than as "objects" of authoritative interventions. Both the Villa Libertad school initiative and the more recent CIS were notable in establishing forums that enabled adolescents to voice their own concerns and participate in developing and managing youth-oriented activities. The CIS has likewise gone some way toward engaging youth as bona fide participants in planning and organizing CIS-sponsored activities and in promoting the Code of Childhood and Adolescence as an ideological framework for community action.

As we have observed, however, all three of these initiatives encountered difficulties that limited their scopes of action and influence. All were discrete endeavors conceived in response to pressing local concerns about youth crime and violence in District VI. They were neither affiliated with, nor did they arise from, a comprehensive nationwide or even citywide youth network. Instead, they were developed through strong local leadership whose focus of attention was the plight of youth in this one urban neighborhood. Invariably, therefore, questions of sustainability and long-term effectiveness have arisen. Despite dynamic leadership and shared local concerns about the problems associated with youth delinquency, discord among different stakeholders became evident in all three initiatives. Indeed, in the case of the community policing project, disagreements led to rank-and-file resistance and to disillusion among many inhabitants, a combination that hastened its demise.

While local leadership has been instrumental in addressing youth issues in District VI, there are also indications that reliance on the charisma and energy of prominent individuals in the community tends to hinder the expansion and institutional consolidation of otherwise innovative youth-assistance programs. The community policing initiative owed much to the combined stewardship of members of the District VI Communal Movement and the former district police chief. Unfortunately, the latter's reassignment to another post, coupled with the disinterest of his successor in continuing the initiative, spelled the end of participatory community policing. Likewise, while the Villa Libertad school program has been maintained largely due to the strength and commitment of Doña Esmeralda, the school director who has been recognized nationally for her efforts, it is open to question whether the program will continue after her eventual retirement or transfer. With no support from the Ministry of Education, and no indication that school-based outreach to youth gangs and other at-risk adolescents are being replicated in other schools in Managua, the prospects of sustaining—let alone expanding—the Villa Libertad school initiative are not promising. Strong local leadership, while essential for the advancement of children's welfare, cannot be guaranteed to last.

A further problem confronting all three of these initiatives has been that of external assistance. In the case of the Villa Libertad school, the inability to entice outside support from the Ministry of Education or from any other central government source has not only had the effect of limiting the scope of this community program but has greatly diminished the likelihood of its replication elsewhere in the school system. Likewise, those who promoted the community policing initiative did not connect with outside sources of expertise or funding, an oversight that left the project fragile until its demise. In contrast, the CIS emerged essentially as a result of donor agency support for collaborative youth projects in District VI. Ironically, however, an inherent weakness of the CIS lies in its dependence on one major funding source. To ensure its sustainability as a coordinated initiative, its members are now in the position of having to seek diverse sources of financial assistance.

Although our analysis of three youth-oriented programs in one district of Managua is clearly limited, it does raise a question about the capacity of community-based initiatives in Nicaragua to function as bases for long-term social change. In particular, while the Villa Libertad school and the CIS have assisted a small number of youth in District VI and have helped to heighten local consciousness of the structural and environmental antecedents of youth crime, they remain small "jewel boxes . . . beautifully crafted efforts,"[40] which nonetheless have had virtually no effect on either the magnitude or the systemic nature of youth marginalization in District VI and elsewhere in Managua.

Constrained by fiscal weaknesses and by deep-rooted corporatist traditions, Latin American governments have generally failed to consolidate their authority through genuine democratic processes. Yet it is far from clear whether civil societies possess the concentration of power that can generate a countervailing force for structural reforms and the enhancement of social justice. Consisting of loose coalitions that pursue diverse interests and tend to shift like nomads in place and time,[41] civil societies have for the most part been unable to compensate for weak democratic states. In Nicaragua, while a coalition of NGOs and civic groups, assisted by supportive international agencies, was able to unite in cajoling a rather chary government to pass landmark children's rights legislation, it remains to be seen whether this civic cohesion at the national level can be translated into a movement of interconnected and sustainable social actions at community levels. As the financial base of the Nicaraguan state is limited and as the privatization of social services and the reach of global markets have become more apparent, hopes for the resolution of severe social problems may simply reinforce situations in which resource-strapped municipal authorities and externally dependent NGOs struggle to initiate and sustain myriad short-term social assistance programs.[42] To the extent that this is true, it would seem to bolster the critique that NGO interventions and community-based social assistance programs help to strengthen the hegemony of a neoliberal agenda of vibrant markets and weak states. Certainly without a democratic central state that is fully engaged in protecting and promoting children's rights, it will be difficult to transform the pursuit of changes at household and community levels into nationwide structural reforms that fundamentally alter the prevailing conditions and treatment of marginalized youth.[43]

A key argument of contemporary social movement theorists is that the foundations of social transformation—which is the essential ideal of the Nicaraguan code and the UN Convention on the Rights of the Child—lie in diverse yet increasingly interconnected grassroots actions.[44] Parallel to Michel Foucault's notion of networks or webs of power, the struggle for change in attitudes and practices vis-à-vis millions of marginalized children and youth is one that is decentered, fragmented, and must derive from the agency of local people, including youth themselves. Yet it is also one that must penetrate the public sector, at national as well as municipal levels. Through daily interaction among many different community associations, public sector services, and growing numbers of youth groups, community-based alliances such as those that have been developed in District VI may help to augment a groundswell of critical awareness concerning the political and economic dimensions of children's rights. Thus, while the discourse of legislative reforms such as the Code of Childhood and Adolescence can serve the politically expedient ends of fragile states by placating forces of opposition, paradoxically in the long run it may contribute to an emerging solidarity among disparate forces working to improve the bleak livelihoods of many Nicaraguan children. For the time being, however, the consolidation of these forces into a broad social movement is still not apparent.

## NOTES

The full-length version of this chapter appears in the *Journal of Latin American Studies* 36, no. 1 (2004): 85–108. The authors are grateful to the International Development Research Centre, which provided a grant for this research project, and to the Centro de Información y Asesoría en Salud, which facilitated fieldwork in District VI between June 2000 and January 2002. We also wish to thank Hal Luft and Dan Dohan of the Institute of Health and Policy Studies, University of California (San Francisco), for their comments on an earlier version of this chapter. The authors are also grateful for the comments of two anonymous reviewers of the *Journal of Latin American Studies*.

1. United Nations, Convention on the Rights of the Child (Geneva, Switz.: United Nations, 1989).

2. Charles A. Reilly, "Public Policy and Citizenship," in *New Paths to Democratic Development in Latin America: The Rise of NGO–Municipal Collaboration*, ed. Reilly (Boulder, Colo.: Rienner, 1995), 1–27.

3. Although there is no definitive distinction between NGOs and community associations, for the purposes of this chapter we regard NGOs as those organizations that are quasi professional (i.e., with a formal organizational structure and usually some salaried staff) and are generally engaged in more than one locality. In contrast, community and civic associations are considered voluntary groups of citizens whose activities focus on their own neighborhood interests.

4. Florence E. Babb, "Negotiating Spaces: Gender, Economy and Cultural Politics in Post-Sandinista Nicaragua," *Identities* 4, no. 1 (1997): 45–69; Erika Ploako and Pierre LaRamee, "Grass-Roots Organizations," in *Nicaragua without Illusions: Regime Tran-*

*sition and Structural Adjustment in the 1990s,* ed. Thomas W. Walker (Wilmington, Del.: SR Books, 1997), 185–201.

5. The Unión Nacional Opositora government of Violeta Chamorro (1990–1996), the Alianza Liberal government of Arnoldo Alemán (1997–2001), and the current Partido Liberal Constitucionalista government of Enrique Bolaños (2002–present).

6. Alec Ian Gershberg, "Education 'Decentralization' Processes in Mexico and Nicaragua: Legislative versus Ministry-Led Reform Strategies," *Comparative Education* 35, no. 1 (1999): 63–80.34; Santamaria Sergio, *El costo de ajuste* (Managua, 1998), 17; Secretaria de Acción Social, *Evaluación del sector social* (Managua, 2001), 19.

7. Claudia Paguaga, "Enrique Bolaños Geyer: A Step towards Consolidating Democracy in Nicaragua" (policy paper, Canadian Foundation for the Americas, Ottawa, Ontario, 2002), 1–7.

8. Roger Charlton and Roy May, "NGOs, Politics, Projects and Probity: A Policy Implementation Perspective," *Third World Quarterly* 16, no. 2 (1995): 237–55; John Clark, "The State, Popular Participation, and the Voluntary Sector," *World Development* 23, no. 4 (1995): 593–601; Alan F. Fowler, "Authentic NGDO Partnerships in the New Policy Agenda for International Aid: Dead End or Light Ahead?" *Development and Change* 29 (1998): 137–39; Laura Macdonald, "A Mixed Blessing: The NGO Boom in Latin America," *NACLA Report on the Americas* 28, no. 5 (1995): 30–35.

9. Coordinadora Nicaragüense de la Niñez, *Segundo informe de la sociedad civil, sobre la situación de los derechos de la niñez y la adolescencia* (Managua, 1999), 1.

10. Foro de Cooperación, *El financiamiento externo de las ONGs nicaragüenses* (Managua, 2001).

11. Anthony Dewees and Steven J. Klees, "Social Movements and the Transformation of National Policy: Street and Working Children in Brazil," *Comparative Education Review* 39, no. 1 (1995): 76–100; Merilee S. Grindle, *Challenging the State: Crisis and Innovation in Latin America and Africa* (Cambridge: Cambridge University Press, 1996), 3; Francisco Panizza, "Beyond 'Delegative Democracy': 'Old Politics' and 'New Economics' in Latin America," *Journal of Latin American Studies* 32, no. 3 (2000): 737–63; Enrique Peruzzotti, "The Nature of the New Argentine Democracy: The Delegative Democracy Argument Revisited," *Journal of Latin American Studies* 33, no. 1 (2001): 133–55.

12. Reilly, "Public Policy and Citizenship," 2.

13. Dewees and Klees, "Social Movements"; Peruzzotti, "Nature of the New Argentine Democracy."

14. Reilly, "Topocrats, Technocrats, and NGOs," in Reilly, *New Paths*, 247–72.

15. Macdonald, "Mixed Blessing," 32.

16. Clark, "State, Popular Participation"; Alejandro Portes and Patricia Landolt, "Social Capital: Promise and Pitfalls of Its Role in Development," *Journal of Latin American Studies* 32, no. 1 (2000): 529–47.

17. Guillermo O'Donnell, "Reflections on Contemporary South American Democracies," *Journal of Latin American Studies* 33, no. 2 (2001): 599–609; R. S. Ratner, "Many Davids, One Goliath," in *Organizing Dissent: Contemporary Social Movements*

*in Theory and Practice; Studies in the Politics of Counter-Hegemony*, ed. William K. Carroll (Toronto: Garamond Press, 1997), 271–86.

18. Michael Edwards and David Hulme, "Too Close for Comfort? The Impact of Official Aid on Non-governmental Organizations," *World Development* 24, no. 6 (1996): 961–73; Fowler, "Authentic NGDO Partnerships."

19. Steven J. Klees, "NGOs: Progressive Force or Neoliberal Tool?" *Current Issues in Comparative Education* 1, no. 1 (1998), at www.tc.columbia.edu/~academic/ice/vol101nr1/v1n1; Ricardo Vergara, "NGOs: Help or Hindrance for Community Development in Latin America?" *Community Development Journal* 29, no. 4 (1994): 322–28.

20. Edwards and Hulme, "Too Close for Comfort?"; M. Powell and D. Seddon, "NGOs and the Development Industry," *Review of African Political Economy* 71, no. 3 (1997): 3–10; Anna C. Vakil, "Confronting the Classification Problem: Toward a Taxonomy of NGOs," *World Development* 25, no. 12 (1997): 2057–70.

21. Gobierno de Nicaragua, *Código de la Niñez y la Adolescencia* (Managua, 1998).

22. Richard Maclure and Melvin Sotelo, "Children's Rights as Residual Social Policy in Nicaragua: State Priorities and the Code of Childhood and Adolescence," *Third World Quarterly* 24, no. 4 (August 2003): 671–89.

23. UN Committee on the Rights of the Child, *Concluding Observations of the Committee on the Rights of the Child: Nicaragua*, 24/08/99 (Geneva, Switz.: United Nations, 1999), 3.

24. In part the reason was that the text of the code refers to "the state" and to "civil society" in general terms but does not elaborate on the specific role of municipal governments in implementing its provisions. Without such directives, municipal authorities have tended to view the code in rather abstract terms.

25. Manuel Fandiño, *Trabajo en red con adolescentes* (Managua, District VI: 2000), 15.

26. Centro de Salud de Villa Venezuela, *Clínica para adolescentes* (Managua: 1997).

27. Fandiño, *Trabajo en red con adolescentes*.

28. Figures procured from the education office of the district municipal council.

29. As we were unable to obtain statistics on the types and extent of youth crime, indications of youth crime were elicited from interviews with a former district police chief and with members of the government's district-level Youth Crime Prevention Commission.

30. Robert F. Arnove, "Education as Contested Terrain in Nicaragua," *Comparative Education Review* 39, no. 1 (1995): 28–53.

31. This sentiment was expressed in a speech delivered in May 1996 in which the minister also criticized the draft text of the Code of Childhood and Adolescence.

32. Emilio García-Méndez, *Child Rights in Latin America: From "Irregular Situation" to Full Protection* (Florence: 1998).

33. García-Méndez, *Child Rights in Latin America.*

34. Interview with Doña Esmeralda Espinoza.

35. Interview with Doña Esmeralda Espinoza.

36. The study focused specifically on teen sexual practices, on their knowledge and attitudes pertaining to sexual behavior, and on the available services providing

treatment and information on reproductive health. Deutsche Gesellschaft fuer Technische Zusammenarbeit, *Conocimientos, actitudes y práctica, sobre la sexualidad en adolescentes* (Managua: 1997). Melvin Sotelo was the principal researcher of this study.

37. Public services represented on the CIS include the Ministry of Health, the Ministry of Education, the Ministry of the Family, the Ministry of the Interior (police), and the municipal district council. The most prominent nongovernmental organizations represented on the CIS are CISAS, Quincho Barrilete, Dos Generaciones, Colectivo Ocho de Marzo, and the district Communal Movement.

38. Fandiño, *Trabajo en red con adolescentes*, 101.

39. Fandiño, *Trabajo en red con adolescentes*.

40. Dewees and Klees, "Social Movements," 93.

41. Alberto Melluci, *Nomads of the Present* (Philadelphia: Temple University Press, 1989).

42. Edwards and Hulme, "Too Close for Comfort?"; Sheelagh Stewart, "Happy Ever After in the Marketplace: Non-government Organizations and Uncivil Society," *Review of African Political Economy* 71 (1997): 11–34.

43. O'Donnell has argued that the enhancement of social rights in Latin America depends on the existence of genuinely democratic central states that are "more friendly" to social movements promoting human rights agendas; O'Donnell, "Reflections," 607.

44. Melluci, *Nomads of the Present*; R. S. Ratner, "Many Davids, One Goliath."

## Chapter Seven

# Protecting Children on the Margins: Social Justice and Community Building

### Laura M. Leming, FMI, and
### Bro. Raymond L. Fitz, SM

Marking the fifteenth anniversary of the 1989 United Nations Convention on the Rights of the Child is a challenge to intensify global investment in children's welfare. While global transformations are extremely complex, it is local contexts that circumscribe children's lives, and so attention to local communities becomes an urgent task. Children on the margins, both figuratively, in terms of their access to power and economic resources, and literally, by virtue of geographical locations, are a compelling subject for reflection on how the communities in which we live and work are meeting the challenge to protect children. The conviction underlying this chapter is that partnerships can best enhance our responsibility for children and their families marginalized by poverty, abuse, or other threats to their well-being. Our praxis as university educators is oriented to how the academy can best use its resources to partner with local, regional, and global entities on behalf of this precious, in many places endangered, resource, the world's children. Another key conviction, stemming from the philosophical tradition that guides our own institution, is that building communities that aim to do justice is a privileged practice for confronting urgent social problems. Children's rights are best protected in local communities where social justice is valued and practiced.

Children rivet attention to the human dimension of development issues against a background of very real obstacles to creating communities across national, ethnic, ideological, or economic divisions that can frustrate effective policymaking. This chapter argues that the critical needs of our most vulnerable citizens are best met by engaging in the process of building communities in purposeful ways, despite these divisions. This process informed with purpose entails three basic emphases: protecting children's rights means strengthening families' abilities to nurture and provide for them; strong families require a shared vision and effective collaboration on the part of various stakeholders within the community; and the institutional change demanded by the preceding statements is a work of social justice.

For well over a decade, the second author (Fitz) has been working on issues of children and families in Montgomery County, Ohio, and more broadly at the state level. As president of a large Catholic university, he accepted the task of chairing the Child Protection Task Force of Montgomery County in September 1993. Subsequently, the task force began fifteen months of reflection and deliberation on the status of the child protection system to examine the provisions for the safety of children in this urban setting. More recently, the first author (Leming) has been confronted with issues of child protection and children's rights while investigating the United States–Mexico border as a site for international experiences for students of sociology. One of the most compelling issues at the border is the tragedy of children whose lives bear the marks of the economic, health, and migratory struggles that characterize the "borderlands."[1] As in many developing world contexts, children who need to struggle for their own livelihoods come to be seen as a social problem rather than as a community responsibility. What follows is a collection of lessons gleaned in the efforts to link the academy and the community to provide the "special care and assistance" that the Convention on the Rights of the Child calls for, both on a local and a global scale. Systemic local efforts and working to protect children in the day-to-day are at the heart of the human rights project.

## TALES FROM TWO COMMUNITIES

The local efforts described and analyzed here are situated in two very different communities that are linked by some key characteristics—namely, significant changes in the employment structure and difficult challenges in responding to children and families in crisis. Attention to children's rights must include focus on how economic and social pressures on their families limit their life chances. It is telling that Dayton, Ohio, the largest city in Montgomery County, was featured in a 1996 *New York Times* report, "The Downsizing of America." The Dayton component of this report focused on shifts in employment opportunities dating from before the midcentury to the situation at the century's close. Whereas in the first period, an abundance of local factories attracted new populations to the city, by the early 1990s, tens of thousands of jobs had been lost as factories dispersed and opportunities were more likely to be found in the lower-paying service sector.

Dayton's loss of industrial jobs has exacerbated the plight of its families and children while the growth of industrial work in the *maquiladoras* (factories) of Nogales, Sonora, is having a similar effect. While it is not clear that the specific jobs lost to Dayton have moved to Nogales, surely the cities are linked by the economic shifts that have driven changes in both of them. Moreover, another bond is deep concern for children and the families raising them under difficult economic conditions. Both of these cities are exploring community-based solutions and partnerships among corporate, educational, and governmental institutions to meet the needs of those living on literal and figurative margins. While there is progress to report, families and children in both cities remain vulnerable.

Neighborhoods and *colonias* of concentrated poverty in Dayton and Nogales are isolated from the economic and social mainstream of the larger local and global communities, though for somewhat divergent reasons. Dayton suffers the impact of disinvestment in the city and the subsequent drain on population and resources. Nogales's rapid population and business expansions place high demands on the limited existing resources and create urgency around securing additional ones. Both of these cities illustrate the challenges to local urban and state governments that, though rarely considered as implicated in the Convention on the Rights of the Child, actually need to be understood as primary actors because of urbanization and government decentralization. Local ability to provide children and their families with avenues to economic and food security is a basic necessity of children's rights, but local capacity has not kept up with growing needs.[2]

Anzaldua describes a "borderland" as a place where two worlds merge to form a third, "a borderland . . . a vague and undetermined place . . . in a constant state of transition."[3] While Nogales sits literally on the border, where the United States has indeed built a steel wall, its transitional state in terms of population flow, employment structure, and as a place where First World and Third World cultures collide, makes it a borderland. Dayton's borderland identity stems from its history of racial segregation and the large segment of its population that lives near the edge in uncertain economic times.

Chaskin and colleagues note that "the needs and circumstances of individuals and families living in impoverished communities are interconnected."[4] The conditions in which families are working to survive are often tied to the specific needs of the family. A director of the juvenile detention facility in Nogales summed up the problem for investigator Miriam Davidson: "Without a house, without a stable job, without the possibility of social or economic advancement, the family falls apart. The kids end up on the street."[5]

Melton and Thompson argue that, in the face of social pressures on families and their increasing likelihood to be without necessary supports, it is imperative that child protection be "neighborhood-based and child-centered."[6]

More recently, Chaskin delineates the need to understand that the local community is both "the context for and the principle around which practice should be organized."[7] He reviews comprehensive community initiatives, which focus on strengthening the social fabric and social capital, and he stresses the need to articulate theories of change and ways to measure social support, such as network analysis and collective efficacy, as outlined by Duncan and Raudenbush.[8] This kind of analysis, when applied to pressing social needs, suggests a call for new partnerships that bring together the analytical expertise cultivated by the academy with the praxis orientation and experiential wisdom of service providers in the community, including the opportunity for cross-national research and information sharing.[9] This tale of children's rights issues in two communities—ones bound by employment shifts, the need for better child protection strategies and family supports, and the interest of an academic community—is a modest effort at exploring what can be learned about process and purpose in the view from the margins.

## Montgomery County, Ohio: The Child Protection Task Force

During the early 1990s, several indicators convinced Montgomery County officials of the need to better coordinate services on behalf of children in this community in southwestern Ohio. The young people in Montgomery County's largest school district, the Dayton Public Schools, were not faring well. Test scores were not good, attendance and graduation rates were poor, and teenage pregnancy was at a high level. Several collaboratives were trying to bring resources together in common cause for children and families, but their efforts tended to be more competitive than collegial. These included Montgomery County, with its myriad social service agencies; the city of Dayton, with its emphasis on neighborhoods; the Dayton Public Schools; and the Dayton business community, as future employers of the region's children. It was clear that there was need for a single forum that would focus the community on the needs of children while being a champion for change in the system.

Exacerbating this chronic state into a crisis was a number of child deaths in the fall of 1993 in Montgomery County. At least on the surface, these tragedies signaled that the child protection system in the county was not, in fact, ensuring children's right to survival. In response, county commissioner Donna Moon and university president Raymond Fitz cochaired a group that brought together most of the key stakeholders of the child protection system into one task force. Moon's role as a government official gave the task force political legitimacy and protected it from those who might want to derail its work in the short term. Fitz led the task force in deliberations to "review, study, and discuss the regulations and systems . . . in place and to make any recommendations deemed appropriate for the future of our children."[10] Together they designed a process that allowed the task force to understand the current child protection system, develop consensus on core community beliefs on children and families, design the desired future of the child protection system, and develop recommendations for the changes needed to move the different elements of the system from "where we were" to "where we wanted to be." The whole process took over fifteen months to complete and resulted in fifty-six recommendations made to the county commissioners.

The perspective of time shows real progress in Montgomery County. The county has implemented over 95 percent of the task force's recommendations. A County Family and Children Council brings together all of the stakeholders from the county, the city, the public schools, the business community, the universities, and a variety of other entities to work toward the vision of a community that supports families and protects children. The state of Ohio has adopted the Montgomery County model for the review of child deaths that was part of the task force report. A human service network enables individuals to share their case information with a variety of agencies rather than go through an intake interview each time they need to access services from a different agency in the community. Children's Hospital in Dayton opened Care House in early 1999, a comfortable setting where child abuse victims can be interviewed in an appropriate manner by an interdisciplinary team from children services, the police jurisdiction, the prosecutor's office, and the juvenile courts. Many other positive changes have been implemented.

### Developing a Process Model

The process of facilitating the Child Protection Task Force revealed several important elements that contribute to good community reflection and deliberation. Revising child protection was a monumental task. All of the stakeholders of the child protective system were involved, including the county commissioners, directors of major human service agencies, United Way agencies, child and domestic violence advocates, city police chiefs and sheriffs, representatives of the prosecutor's office, the juvenile court, foster parents, and court-appointed special advocates for children. Because there was very little common ground among the participants, finding the starting point was difficult. Despite the existence of plenty of manuals and pamphlets about different elements of the system, there was no agreed-on description of how the child protection system works or how people wanted it to work.

What emerged was a process of public reflection and deliberation that had four overlapping elements. We propose that these elements are a guide to working toward children's rights in other local contexts.

- *Telling stories*: Reviewing accounts of how the child protective system failed children and families, as well as stories about how it has worked well
- *Drafting community beliefs*: Formulating belief statements and commitments about how the community wanted to protect children and support families
- *Developing frameworks*: Developing an analytical framework that illustrates how child protection systems currently work and how they *should* work
- *Developing recommendations*: Drawing together what was learned into actionable recommendations that agencies could implement

*Storytelling.* The task force's work began with public and some private testimony in subcommittee. This storytelling allowed stakeholders of the child protective system to describe their experiences of failure in the system. Testimony was given by parents who believed they were harmed when their children were removed from their custody. Some foster parents believed that they were treated unfairly by the courts in the adoption process. The committee heard stories about the trauma experience of children, five and six years of age, who were having their abuse cases investigated by a multitude of strangers from different agencies. Particularly painful was the story of a drug-dependent mother who sought rehabilitation for the sake of her child but was not able to find an open slot in a drug treatment program because she was poor. There were also stories of success. The public testimony included accounts of how professionals and volunteers in the child protection system went to heroic lengths to help children and families.

*Drafting community beliefs.* One of the most important challenges facing the task force was to construct, debate, and refine a set of core community beliefs about children and families. Negotiating the agreement of the various stakeholders was equivalent to writing a community declaration on the rights of children and families for Dayton and articulating the obligation to protect those rights. In order to do this, the task force developed a set of beliefs about its children, about families, and about the best ways to support families while ensuring children's rights to protection. The goals for this part of the process were to lay a foundation that facilitated movement from a fragmented system oriented to crisis resolution to a comprehensive system oriented toward support and prevention. Overcoming fragmentation and polarization on the issues of the child protection system was critical. The task of constructing, debating, and refining the document was a breakthrough task. Through this conversation, task force members were able to create common ground on which to build frameworks and develop recommendations.

*Constructing analytical frameworks.* The third step, with the help of consultants, was to begin to build a number of frameworks to understand the stories and, most of all, what caused the rights violations they conveyed. Beyond understanding, the frameworks were needed to help move the core community beliefs into best practices for child protection.

The first framework was the pathways model of the child protection system. This model charts the major points of information gathering and decision making in the system. Previously, professionals had understood *their* piece of the system but not the other parts. In fact, the task force found that very few people in the community understood the whole system. Judgments were being made about child abuse and neglect across many police jurisdictions without clarity on the standards to be used. In complex cases, multiple interviews or interrogations of the alleged victim took place, by the police, by the public children services agency, and the prosecutor's office. Each of the units in the child protective system was working inefficiently, and collaboration between them was affected by poor systems of case management and a lack of trust of other agencies.

The second framework developed was the ecology of families and children. This framework explores the meaning of the African proverb "It takes a village to raise a child." Families are more capable of providing good environments for their children when they are part of vital neighborhoods and good communities that offer opportunities for self-sufficiency and growth as a family. When a community addresses the issues of support and protection of children, it must not only focus on parent and family functioning but also examine the larger social ecology of the family and ensure that neighborhoods and community institutions are working together to support families. The safety of the child must be primary when community intervention in a family situation is required to protect the child from injury, harm, and deprivation. However, interventions must be carried out in a way that respects parents' rights to raise their children safely and that offers parents neighborhood and community resources to allow them to demonstrate that they can be capable and successful parents.

A continuum of services was the third analytical frame used in the work of the Montgomery County task force. This framework built on the understanding of the social ecology frame and helped to distinguish among the roles of the extended family, neighborhood organizations and institutions, and the county government in protecting children. This framework stands on four premises:

1. Parents have the primary responsibility for raising their children, and most families fulfill this responsibility well and their children are safe.

All families need support in this endeavor, and most families receive this support from extended family members and members of their neighborhoods, ethnic, and religious communities.

2. Other families must receive this support from the larger community, represented by both voluntary organizations and government agencies. If this support is available, most families will use it and fulfill their parental responsibilities.

3. It is only when families do not use this available support and when children are not safe that a community must intervene through the public children services agency. If this intervention is supportive of the family, most families will safely care for their children.

4. It is only the small number of remaining families who cannot safely raise their children and with whom the public children service agency must intervene to find for the child or children of these families permanent, safe alternative homes.

A supportive community must find ways to deliver services to families and children in three overlapping areas designated as family support services, family intervention services, and child protection services.

Family support services include all activities by the community that are intended to strengthen family units, maintain the family as a self-sufficient social and economic unit, and prevent situations likely to deteriorate into family violence. Family intervention services are required in situations where families express a need for specialized help in personal functioning or family functioning or when a community agency such as children services or the juvenile court believes there are serious problems in family functioning. These services address family problems such as domestic violence and drug abuse, problems that have high correlations with occurrences of child abuse. These early intervention programs may use red flags such as excessive absences from school or reports of domestic violence as signals that the community should look into a family situation. Child protection services include those interventions triggered by suspected or substantiated child abuse and neglect and require action to protect the child from harm. This entails intervening in the family to restore a safe environment or, when necessary, removing the child or children from the parents. In these cases, children services personnel work with the prosecutor's office, juvenile court, local police jurisdictions, and a variety of community agencies to provide the necessary services for families and children in the child protection system.

*Developing recommendations.* Listening to the stories, drafting community beliefs, and forming analytical frameworks provided the basis for developing recommendations to restructure child protective services in Montgomery

County. This was a politically sensitive process, yet this final stage was where real potential for change was initiated. Consensus emerged on fifty-six recommendations only because of the time invested in the earlier steps of the process. Individual recommendations traced out the steps to accomplish three main goals: to create an integrated system of child protection, to create a comprehensive families and children services network, and to establish an ongoing issues forum on families and children. Using systems analysis combined with dedication to the support of individual families and children, the Montgomery County Child Protection Task Force challenged the disparate entities to dedicate their resources in new and collaborative ways and thus protect the rights of children in a far more effective way. Their work is testimony to the partnership of academy and community on behalf of children.

## Ambos Nogales, Sonora and Arizona

Taylor and Hickey's ethnography of Ambos Nogales, the twin cities straddling the United States–Mexican border sixty miles south of Tucson, describes them as a meeting of "the first and third worlds face to face, or back to back, across a fence."[11] Colloquially, Nogales, Sonora, Mexico, is known as *el trampolin* because it is a jumping-off point for both drugs and immigrants to enter the United States.[12] The population explosion at the border that gave rise to a serious problem of homeless children was largely created by the influx of global manufacturing at a time when poverty in Mexico was increasing. In the 1970s, a number of large companies came to Nogales that were drawn to the "shelter plant" model in which companies were provided support for buildings, workforce recruitment, and transportation. By the 1980s, twenty-three large companies were operating *maquiladoras* in Nogales, and traditional reliance on ranching, mining, and tourism had been weakened.[13] Sonoran statistics for the year 2000 put the number of *maquiladoras* in Nogales, Sonora, at ninety. This shift in the economic base, family employment patterns, and the sheer growth of the population created a strain on infrastructure and on families.

### Gathering the Stories

Rick Ufford-Chase is the director of a faith-based organization called Borderlinks, which had its roots in the sanctuary movement that grew up in Tucson when civil conflicts in Central America prompted many to attempt escape to *El Norte*. Ufford-Chase writes, "Whether you're a player in the emerging global economy or an out of work laborer discarded in your company's mad rush for ever-bigger profits, you need to know about Ambos Nogales. For Ambos Nogales is the reality behind the world's corporate glitter. It's the scar tissue underlying today's Wall Street 'miracles.'"[14] The Sonora side is a "city of desperation," where families may live only five feet from the other Nogales, on the Arizona side, but may not have running water, sewage systems, electricity, or weather-protected homes.[15]

One of the features connecting these two communities straddling the border is a set of parallel tunnels built in the 1930s, whose main purpose is to provide drainage during summer downpours. The tunnels became famous in the early 1990s when media attention was drawn to the band of adolescent children who used them as a gathering place and an underground economy site for drug dealing and exacting payment from those going back and forth across the border through the tunnels. Significantly, the media called the children "tunnel rats," which raised the ire of many, including a Nogales woman and civic leader that Leming interviewed. While speaking to a group of university students about her work with tunnel children, Cecilia Guzman asked pointedly, "How could they call children, rats?"

The conflict of interest between corporate profit and the rights of children struggling for survival became apparent when U.S. businesses near the border called for efforts to control the delinquency of the children from the tunnels. Capitalizing on media attention to the problem, local attorney Jan Florez Smith secured funding in 1994 from the Arizona Supreme Court juvenile crime reduction fund to create a center for homeless children on the Sonora side of Nogales. Called Mi Casa Nueva (My New Home), the center is a day shelter where homeless children can engage in activities as diverse as a chance to shower and wash their clothes, receive necessary medical and dental care, or work toward high school proficiency.

The negative media attention, coupled with the demands from the Arizona business community, created a situation screaming for innovative community response. In the Nogales case, collecting the stories that were integral to the public process of reflection in Dayton is now in the beginning stages. The growth of border studies programs in recent years, the specific interest in children and families living in the borderlands,[16] and cross-border linkages of various types are all contributing to developing frameworks of understanding leading to analyses and creative responses.[17]

## Community Beliefs and Frameworks for Action

The collaboration between the two cities named Nogales and their respective countries to craft a response to the critical needs at the border faces a number of challenges. One can be illustrated by the setback Mi Casa Nueva experienced when its second director—a Mexican American volunteer with the Border Volunteer Corps, a short-lived extension of the AmeriCorps Program—had to resign after just a few months because program rules clarified that volunteers were not allowed to work on the Mexico side of the border.[18] A number of United States foundations also place restrictions on funds so that Mexican agencies are not eligible. Mi Casa Nueva has applied for recognition by the Mexican government, which may facilitate eligibility for cross-national donations.

On the other hand, the situation of obvious critical need in Nogales, Sonora, has mobilized a number of faith-based organizations to create outreach programs that go beyond the immediate needs of the tunnel kids. A number of models exist to meet the needs of vulnerable children at "critical junctures."[19] The youth center model is illustrated by Casa Misericorde, founded in one of the poorest *colonias* of Nogales by a Catholic binational couple named Torres. A number of centers, established primarily by faith-based organizations, use elements of sports, music and drama, educational enhancement, vocational training, and nutrition to work at family and child support through prevention. Casa Misericorde's programs were able to access corporate sponsorship because Hope Torres, the female partner and a U.S. citizen, held a management position in a *maquiladora*. The premature death of her husband, José, who was raised in Nogales, Sonora, had the unexpected positive effect of institutionalizing the Casa Misericorde when Hope Torres was able to hand over the organization to Borderlinks, which was looking for a home base in Mexico to complement its center in Tucson. Borderlinks volunteers live at the center and work with child care workers, neighborhood parents, and local pastoral ministers to provide programs and services and to host immersion experiences for U.S. students and church groups.[20] Casa Misericorde is one example of binational cooperation initiated by a faith-based organization. Binational governmental efforts at collaboration are slower to develop.

Another challenge to meeting the needs of children on the margins in Nogales is eliciting and coordinating corporate participation. One effort, the Esperanza (Hope) Foundation, has aimed at addressing the housing needs of workers by soliciting corporate contributions. Business leaders' opposition to making general contributions has in some cases resulted in direct support for housing down payments to workers who qualify in length and consistency of employment. Thus, social pressure has increased corporate attention to workers' needs. The state of Chihuahua, Mexico, enacted legislation in 1994 that requires businesses with more than five employees to contribute to a fund for local development projects.[21]

Family ecology perspectives underline the broader environments that exert pressures and influence on children on the margins. At the border, preserving the natural environment and addressing sustainability issues in face of the large influx of factories and workers form another critical issue. One success of community effort was the incorporation of some environmental standards into the North American Free Trade Agreement, but access to water, air quality, and waste removal remain thorny issues in border towns.[22] The fragility of the natural environment, affordable and adequate housing, access to clean air and water, immigration practices, the impact on families of the local economy, and shifts both in employment opportunities and in the technological education needed to qualify for those opportunities constitute a long list of macroenvironmental issues that influence what happens in families. Cultural issues also condition families' abilities to care adequately for their children. In a binational study of drug use in Ambos Nogales, Quintero and Estrada argue that boys are more vulnerable to the negative excesses of drug use and violence associated with *machismo*, as a representation of masculinity idealized in Mexico, because of the structural limits they encounter and the fact that *machismo* provides social efficacy.[23] In a similar vein, Anderson's analysis of how inner-city teenage girls gain the respect afforded to women by becoming pregnant has applications to the stories of some of the tunnel girls profiled by Davidson.[24] Both cultural and structural influences need to be accounted for in any analysis of family support and intervention toward protection of children's rights.

In Nogales, preventive and rehabilitative programs for children and finding ways to engage families in positive patterns of community involvement directly involve children and their families. Indirect support for children comes from corporate sponsorship of programs that have short-term effects (housing, medical care) and long-term effects (creating positive peer and cross-generational interaction, education, and skill building) on their families in the workforce. Creatively navigating the obstacles that the border creates in terms of freely directing monetary and human resources where they are most urgently needed must be taken up by governmental entities, perhaps in partnership with business, educational, and religious leaders.

## PROTECTING THE RIGHTS OF CHILDREN: LESSONS LEARNED

Over the past decade, conditions have improved for many children in both Dayton and Nogales. But a significant number of children are being held back because they are part of fragile families or no families and are living on the margins of society. In both cities, neighborhoods are experiencing the interaction effects of concentrated poverty, low social cohesion, and family-level challenges that pose considerable risk for violations of children's rights to life and to develop their human capabilities.

In Dayton many neighborhoods have become disconnected from the mainstream through a gradual pattern of declining investments in the center city, resulting segregation, and the weakening or abandonment of established city institutions. Since World War II, the greater Dayton region, like most Midwestern industrial cities and regions, has been transformed into relatively affluent suburbs surrounding a core city with high concentrations of poverty and minority populations living in extremely distressed neighborhoods.

In the past thirty years, Nogales has been transformed from a sleepy border town reliant on agriculture to a city bursting at the seam that divides the First World from the developing world. New *colonias* continue to crop up as "invasion communities" occupying undeveloped land in the surrounding hills. Invasions consist of groups of workers who band together to take over a piece of undeveloped land. They then hire an agent to negotiate a form of retroactive land purchase after they have begun to build temporary shelters for their families and slowly develop the site into a neighborhood. Typically landowners agree since the land is more valuable if it is being developed, even if only informally, but it takes years for families to gain access to city services such as electricity, water, and sewage. Unlike Dayton, in Nogales the poverty is concentrated on the outskirts of the city, but the effect on families is the same. Social isolation and limited access to amenities that are taken for granted by other citizens create high levels of unemployment, a diminished sense of efficacy, and frustration that ultimately can jeopardize children.

In each of these cases major social dynamics, such as demographics (urban sprawl) and economic trends (globalization of manufacturing), have lead to the concentration of poverty in local communities. Poverty has isolated many families from the connections that are essential to provide the basic nurturing and support for children and their full human development.

## Protecting the Rights of Children by Community Building

How can we address the rights of children in the midst of these distressed communities? Research over the last decade indicates that children do better when their families do better, and families do better when they live in supportive communities.[25] Therefore, a family's ability to provide for their children depends both on its internal strength (e.g., providing love and support, setting expectations and boundaries, managing stress) and on the community's ability to support families in the task of providing for their children. Family strength is nurtured and enriched by a healthy community, and in turn, a family grows by making connections to its community. Recent research also indicates that positive outcomes for children are promoted by family involvement in community and social networks,[26] informal social control mechanisms,[27] and perceived levels of threat in the environment.[28] The community-building framework articulates a process of organization, community deliberation, and change directed toward a purpose of building the neighborhood so that it supports families and protects children.

A helpful way to view the connection between neighborhoods and their families and children is to see it as a social ecology, or webs of relationships between peoples, families, agencies, and organizations bound by a physical infrastructure and by a social fabric of norms, practices, and institutions. In distressed communities, the infrastructure—such as housing, local businesses, schools, and playgrounds—is often in poor repair and sometimes abandoned. Norms such as being vigilant about crime, expecting children to be in school, and taking care of one's own property are weakened in distressed neighborhoods and contribute to problems experienced by the community. Practices leading to organizing for positive change have atrophied. Institutions such as public schools and human services provided by government agencies often are not culturally appropriate for the people living in the community.

To support families in their task of nurturing their children, we must rebuild healthy neighborhoods and reconnect families to appropriate sources of support. These assertions are born of the emerging consensus in the work of major foundations and research groups: that families fare better when they have three kinds of broad support within their neighborhoods:

1. opportunities to work, earn a decent living, and build family assets;
2. access to a network of families, friends, neighbors, community institutions, faith-based organizations, and civic groups; and
3. support services from government and not-for-profit agencies that are accessible, responsive, and culturally appropriate.[29]

The purpose of community building in neighborhoods is to improve the lives of families and children; to create new and strengthened neighborhood assets, relationships, and institutions; and to set new standards and expectations for life within the neighborhood. To realize this purpose, residents and professionals must engage in a process that includes collective deliberation both on local problems and opportunities and on strategies for action, as well as the mobilization of people and resources needed for collective action. Community building requires an agenda for change and networks of relationships to implement change by renewing institutions. Neighborhood residents must focus or drive the agenda for change by addressing problems and opportunities to which they give high priority, such as violence in the neighborhood, absence of food and shelter, sanitary conditions, or the lack of educational and recreational opportunities for children. Working together, people build relationships of friendship and common interest, developing mutual trust and sharing information as well as the beliefs and convictions that provide a common ground for change.

The Dayton example illustrates a community-building process engaging many stakeholders in the community's child protection system, not only the professionals in the many agencies that make up the system, but also people who receive services from the system. The process undertaken by the Child Protection Task Force engaged these stakeholders in developing a constructive dialogue that gave them the space to tell stories, construct common beliefs and convictions about the child protection system, and redesign the system so that it did a much better job of supporting families and protecting children. This process developed not only an agenda of change but a new set of relationships between people and agencies in which there was less concern for agency turf and greater confidence that all were working for the good of children. Most task force recommendations were implemented because of the relationships of trust and collaboration that were built during the task force deliberations.

In Nogales, sites such as Mi Casa Nueva and Casa Misericorde came about because people joined together from various sectors to advocate for children's rights and develop an agenda for change. Seeking an agenda for change, these people maximized their ability to respond to children's needs by forming relationships with faith-based communities, employers, and government agencies. Community building in Nogales brought together attorneys, city and county officials, and private concerned groups on both sides of the border. Here, community building was a binational effort that also found success through building relationships of trust and collaboration focused on positive change.

## Community Building and Social Justice

Community building, in its fullest meaning, is a commitment to social justice. Social justice has many meanings in the literature. For some, social justice is a characteristic of societies that respect human dignity by treating all people as being of equal worth.[30] A related way of looking at social justice, based on Aristotle's concept of general or legal justice, is to view social justice as the act of organizing persons and groups to change the institutional structures of a community so that they advance the common good.[31]

As we saw in the previous sections, community building requires engaging a leadership group within the community to define the problems that it faces, to design action strategies that address these problems, and to implement the resulting plan of action. The Dayton example suggests that for deliberations on the problems facing the community, it is advantageous for the leadership group to reflect on principles and convictions and to focus on the desired future or a realization of the common good. Stakeholders at the table may hold different perspectives on the desired future for the community, but all are invited to articulate stories that illustrate frustrations as well as hopes. Out of these stories, beliefs and convictions are identified that can form common ground.

Designing action strategies necessitates coming to grips with the institutional dimension of protecting the rights of children and families. If children's rights in a community are to be protected, this occurs through the efforts of more than just one agency that provides service for children or one governmental body charged with protecting the rights of children. Rather, a complex institutional process of families and neighbors, educational communities, law enforcement agencies, children's services, the court system, providers of drug and alcohol services, and a variety of other agencies and organizations within the community must interact efficiently and effectively.

When change is required, it cannot adequately take place at the level of individual agencies and organizations. To appreciate why child protection systems fail, we need to examine not only the behavior of individual agencies, such as the children services agency or the juvenile court, but the patterns of interaction and communication that link these individual agencies as a system. Redesigning institutions requires a perspective and mode of reasoning and imagining that can see patterns and find leverage points for profound change. Moreover, these patterns of interaction must be examined at different levels. Interactions within agencies are important for effective operation, but what must also be analyzed is how agency representatives interact with their clients, with other organizations in the field, and with the community at large.

## CONCLUSION

Global transformations in economics and politics manifest themselves in the local realities of children and their families. We see a need to strengthen the bonds between the academy and the community at the local, regional, national, and international levels. First, we must orient our curriculum to help prepare a variety of thoughtful professionals who understand human rights and are able to be community builders at all levels, whether local or international. Urban educators, human service workers, criminal justice professionals, lawyers, health care workers, and a host of others must develop their capacity as community builders who understand the interactional processes that have created existing systems and who can work effectively to change them.

Second, we must find appropriate ways to link the many resources of the academy to the urgent needs of the communities we serve and to those of the international community as well. Making the expertise of analysis, evaluation, innovative thinking, and asset building that are integral to the university available to local, state, and even national and global entities has much potential to safeguard human rights and increase the life chances of the most vulnerable. This is a particular challenge in a time of economic uncertainty that creates pressure for us to be careful stewards of economic resources. Still, we challenge the academy to consider its links to the community as an equally important vision.

Third, we need to use existing relationships to invite creative partnerships with local government, businesses, school systems, public and private agencies, and faith-based groups to help leverage needed social change. Exploring linkages that spread the burden and protect the rights of children becomes imperative. Important to this process is recognizing and fostering the indomitable spirit of hope that cannot be quenched in our most vulnerable children and families as well as in those who work with and for them in both private and public arenas.

## NOTES

1. Gloria Anzaldua, *Borderlands–LaFrontera: The New Mestiza* (San Francisco: Spinsters/Aunt Lute, 1987); Lawrence Taylor and Maeve Hickey, *Tunnel Kids* (Tucson: University of Arizona Press, 2001): Miriam Davidson, *Lives on the Line: Dispatches from the US–Mexico Border* (Tucson: University of Arizona Press, 2000).

2. Sheridan Bartlett et al., *Cities for Children: Children's Rights, Poverty, and Urban Management* (London: Earthscan, 1999), 15.

3. Anzaldua, *Borderlands–LaFrontera*, 3.

4. Robert Chaskin, Mark Joseph, and Selma Chipinda-Dansokho, "Implementing Comprehensive Community Development: Possibilities and Limitations," *Social Work* 42 (1997): 435–44.

5. Davidson, *Lives on the Line*, 133.

6. Gary Melton and Ross Thompson, "The Conceptual Foundation: Why Child Protection Should Be Neighborhood-Based and Child-Centered," in *Toward a Child-Centered, Neighborhood-Based Child Protection System*, ed. Gary Melton, Ross Thompson, and Mark Small (Westport, Conn.: Praeger, 2002), 3–27.

7. Robert Chaskin, "The Evaluation of 'Community Building': Measuring the Social Effects of Community-Based Practice," in *Assessing Outcomes in Child and Family Services*, ed. Anthony Maluccio, Cinzia Canali, and Tiziano Vecchiato (New York: Aldine de Gruyter, 2002), 28.

8. G. J. Duncan and S. Raudenbush, "Assessing the Effects of Context in Studies of Child and Youth Development," *Educational Psychologist* 34 (1999): 29–41.

9. Anthony Maluccio, Cinzia Canali, and Tiziano Vecchiato, eds., *Assessing Outcomes in Child and Family Services* (New York: Aldine de Gruyter, 2002).

10. Child Protection Task Force, "A Community Which Supports Families and Protects Children: The Report of the Child Protection Task Force," Montgomery County Commission (Dayton, Ohio: February 15, 1995), vi.

11. Taylor and Hickey, *Tunnel Kids*, xi.

12. Gilbert Quintero and Antonio Estrada, "'Machismo,' Drugs and Street Survival in a U.S. Mexico Border Community," *Free Inquiry in Creative Sociology* 26 (1998): 3–10.

13. Davidson, *Lives on the Line*, 26.

14. Jerry Gill, *Borderlinks: The Road Is Made by Walking* (Tucson, Ariz.: Borderlinks, 1999), 125.

15. Ramon Ruiz, *On the Rim of Mexico: Encounters of the Rich and Poor* (Boulder, Colo.: Westview, 1998), 90.

16. Miriam Davidson, *Lives on the Line*; Taylor and Hickey, *Tunnel Kids*; Luis Alberto Urrea, *By the Lake of Sleeping Children: The Secret Life of the Mexican Border*, photography by John Lueders-Booth (New York: Anchor Books, 1996); Ruben Martinez, *Crossing Over: A Mexican Family on the Migrant Trail* (New York: Henry Holt, 2001).

17. Quintero and Estrada, "'Machismo'"; Gill, *Borderlinks*; Davidson, *Lives on the Line*.

18. Rachel Hays, "'Border Peace Corps' Experiment Killed," *Borderlines* 1, no. 9 (1995), web publication of the Inter-hemispheric Resource Center,www.us-mex.org/borderlines/1995/bl17/bl17bvc.html.

19. Richard Weissbourd, *The Vulnerable Child* (Reading, Mass.: Addison-Wesley, 1996).

20. Gill, *Borderlinks*.

21. Davidson, *Lives on the Line*, 184.

22. It shouldn't go unstated that cities such as Dayton also are beginning to awaken to similar issues. A *Dayton Daily News* exposé (January 26, 2003), around the time this chapter was first drafted, focuses on a hazardous-waste storage site left by one of the diminished corporations that adjoined one of Dayton's most desirable neighborhoods.

23. Quintero and Estrada, "'Machismo,'" 8.

24. Elijah Anderson, *Code of the Street: Decency, Violence, and the Moral Life of the Inner City* (New York: W. W. Norton, 1999); Davidson, *Lives on the Line*.

25. Robert Sampson, Jeffrey Morenoff, and Felton Earls, "Beyond Social Capital: Spatial Dynamics of Collective Efficacy for Children," *American Sociological Review* 64, no. 5 (1999): 633–60; Weissbourd, *Vulnerable Child*.

26. Frank Furstenberg, "How Families Manage Risk and Opportunity in Dangerous Neighborhoods," in *Sociology and the Public Agenda*, ed. William J. Wilson (Newbury Park, Calif.: Sage, 1993).

27. Robert Sampson, "A Neighborhood-Level Perspective on Social Change and the Social Control of Adolescent Delinquency," in *Negotiating Adolescence in Times*

*of Social Change*, ed. Lisa Crockett and Rainer Silbereisen (New York: Cambridge University Press, 2000).

28. Bartlett et al., *Cities for Children*.

29. See the Project on Human Development in Chicago Neighborhoods, conducted by the Harvard School of Public Health with funding from the John D. and Catherine T. MacArthur Foundation and others (Felton Earls, MD, principal investigator); also, report of the Annie E. Casey Foundation, Research Evaluation Conference, March 1999.

30. Martha C. Nussbaum, *Sex and Social Justice* (New York: Oxford University Press, 1999).

31. William J. Ferree, *Introduction to Social Justice* (Dayton, Ohio: Marianist, 1948; reprinted in 1997 with a new forward by the Center for Economic and Social Justice). A copy can be downloaded from www.cesj.org. Michael Novak, *Free Persons and the Common Good* (Lanham, Md.: Madison Books, 1989).

*Part III*

# CHILDREN'S RIGHTS IN THE UNITED STATES

The reduction of child labor has been one of the landmark human achievements of the labor movement. Today this victory threatens to be undermined by the impact of economic globalization on workers and the transfer of responsibility for children's life chances from government policies to market forces. Child labor represents a significant danger to children in the form of hazardous working and living conditions, economic exploitation, risks to health and survival, and impaired futures. The chapter "Child Farm Workers in United States Agriculture" examines recent reports of governmental agencies and NGOs on child employment in the multibillion-dollar agricultural industry in the United States. Children between the ages of fourteen and seventeen and younger children who are accompanying their migrant parents constitute one of the most disadvantaged segments of the domestic labor force. The presence of farm worker children who are minor teens and younger as laborers in crop agriculture is a reflection of families living in poverty. The consequences of beginning work life as an underage laborer in crop agriculture are serious. The work hours, seasonal intensity, and crop mobility disrupt education and limit children's futures. Children who are hired to do farm labor have a significant exposure to problems of health and safety, including fatalities. Social problems affecting farm workers in general create particular risks for minor teen and younger children. The authors argue that the fact that minor teens are a growing group of farm workers needs serious attention. Nearly half of these young laborers live without any family member or guardian accompanying them as they enter into the risky physical and social environment of migrant farm labor. As a group they are extremely poor and lack the income required to provide basic necessities.

Minor teen employment and labor by farm worker children must be understood in the context of a labor supply transition that is taking place in American agriculture. Today farm labor jobs come to be filled by more recent arrivals to farm work, more foreign-born workers, and more undocumented workers. The labor supply transition has been associated with a dramatic comeback of farm labor contractors (FLCs) as a type of labor recruitment and utilization in American agriculture. Migrant teens have been disproportionately connected to FLCs, especially those contractors who can help overcome language and cultural barriers and locate jobs for minor workers. The authors highlight conditions in California and Florida to explain some of the larger patterns and problems associated with FLC hiring of more new immigrants and unauthorized workers. Hiring through FLCs also has implications for recent patterns of immigration to the United States and issues of economic and social development in the sending countries.

The authors argue that public policies can counter the wage decline among the working poor that leads to conditions of child labor, especially in crop agriculture. The United States can enforce existing laws against child labor, such as the Fair Labor Standards Act, and extend the standards that regulate child labor in industry by applying them to agriculture. The United States can create a national strategy to enforce compliance with recognized international standards of child labor prohibitions, such as those of the CRC and ILO Convention 182, on the elimination of the worst forms of child labor.

The chapter "Human Rights and Juvenile Justice in the United States" addresses several issues in the human rights protections of juveniles and explores the challenges posed by the fact that the United States currently has the highest rate of juvenile incarceration in the world. The authors expose an array of existing conditions in several layers of the juvenile justice system that our constitutional protections were designed to prevent. While our nation has a longstanding system of juvenile protections that have been widely imitated internationally, our states' principles aimed at protecting the human dignity of children are compromised by the realities of the juvenile justice system today.

The authors outline some of the complex reasons for current conditions and highlight the role played by the porous boundary between juvenile and adult criminal justice systems and the increasing role of prosecutors in juvenile procedures. Conditions for juveniles are linked to declining public support for education and welfare and longstanding risks to life chances posed by high rates of joblessness and racial segregation. The authors question the escalation of juvenile punishments at a time of falling juvenile crime rates. They report on their own data collection and analysis concerning current conditions in the state of Michigan as well as on national studies to show the urgent need to address the underlying causes and find remedies. The authors emphasize the social cost of allowing present dangers to continue against the cost of making progress for children.

Some examples the authors examine are the problems of youth being transferred to adult criminal court at younger ages and for a wide array of offenses. Also, youth lack adequate due process protection in the processing stage and adequate defense counsel. At times, youth are placed in adult prisons without separation from adults. Minority youth are overrepresented in both transfer and placement decisions. Officials in juvenile programs have increased authority to use corporal punishment and segregation with little or no accountability. Conditions of confinement include severe overcrowding, abuse, and failure to meet basic health and safety standards. The authors particularly address the escalation of risks to children who are victims of abuse and neglect, since they can also be subjected to the same processing that applies to delinquent youth. The authors conclude with recommendations for actions that need to be taken in the United States in order to achieve compliance with standards present in such conventions as the CRC and the UN Standard Minimum Rules for the Administration of Justice.

The chapter titled "The Challenges of Human Rights Education and the Impact on Children's Rights" explores ways to forge new partnerships between children and adults through intergenerational dialogue and education for human rights. This highly usable chapter considers the challenges and potential for human rights education in the United States by exploring human rights linkages with related curricula currently available in many schools. The author suggests a variety of ways that human rights education can be connected with current curricula for democracy, peace, and multicultural education. She surveys pertinent programs, websites, and curriculum updates for incorporating human rights perspectives into teaching about tolerance, genocide, conflict resolution, current events, and practical law education.

This chapter regards human rights education as an essential experience to enhancing children's self-worth and cultivating their empathy. The goal is that dialogue between children and adults will motivate them to accept a sense of personal responsibility to advocate for and defend human rights. The author describes her direct observations and experiences as a human rights educator. She has created a valuable survey of human rights resources, including websites and free publications, for educators, students, professional organizations, and organizers of teacher training sessions and courses.

The existence of the Convention on the Rights of the Child and the landmark global consensus reflected in the extent of its support are a motivating force for child rights advocates in their efforts to promote human rights for all children. Even though political reinforcement of human rights norms is inconsistent, domestic laws and policies can be made congruent with the underlying principles of the CRC. If we regard the consensus around the convention as indicative of international customary law, human rights advocates can work in the United States for change in local legal culture, reform of statutes, and the development of legal precedent in alignment with its principles. There is a substantial educational role for advocates to play in persuading those charged with protecting and nurturing children in private lives and public roles to act upon the guiding values of the consensus on children's rights in the international community.

*Chapter Eight*

# Child Farm Workers in United States Agriculture

## Linda C. Majka and Theo J. Majka

The problem of child labor in the United States does not get public attention for very long. Even to those concerned with human rights, child labor does not seem as desperate as children being murdered, becoming homeless, engaging in prostitution, and falling victim to other tragic conditions. The problem of underage farm workers in the United States should, nevertheless, be a serious concern because the problems present in agriculture go far beyond simply the issue of children working.

Social scientists who reflected on the nineties called it a time of "selective prosperity." What they had in mind is the growth of worker incomes at the top of the scale even as the majority of worker incomes stagnated or fell behind. What is obscured by this generalized image is the extent to which conditions for the most vulnerable members of the American labor force, minor teen and child workers, reached an unacceptable level of risk and harm during a period of record-setting business prosperity. In particular, underage workers in our multibillion-dollar agricultural industry were exposed to hazardous working and living conditions that risked their health and survival and impaired their futures. Conditions that exist today in crop agriculture call into question America's commitment to its ideals of fair labor standards and legal protections for children.

The UN Convention on the Rights of the Child (CRC) affirms different types of rights that take into account the vulnerability of the child, who is defined as a person who is below the age of eighteen. Civil-political rights and economic, social, and cultural rights are interpreted as a means of protecting the child from exploitation and abuse. Article 32 of the CRC declares that "State Parties recognize the right of the child to be protected from economic exploitation and from performing any work that is likely to be hazardous or to interfere with the child's education, or be harmful to the child's health or physical, mental, spiritual, moral or social development."[1] Nations that ratify the convention are required to establish minimum ages for employment, regulate the hours and conditions of employment, and adopt penalties or sanctions to guarantee effective enforcement of the article.

The CRC obliges states that have ratified it to ensure that the requirements to implement the convention are met. States file reports and are answerable if conditions in the nation fall short of the obligations within the CRC. The responsibilities of the convention are implemented through a combination of measures, including legislation, administrative regulations and enforcement, and information. While the United States has not ratified the CRC, in 1999 it ratified the international treaty on child labor known as convention 182 of the International Labour Organization (ILO). Accordingly, the United States is obliged to undertake a national program of action to comply with convention 182, the Convention Concerning the Prohibition and Immediate Action for the Elimination of the Worst Forms of Child Labor. Like the CRC, the convention applies the term *child* to every person under the age of eighteen. It defines "the worst forms of child labor" as "work which, by its nature or the circumstances in which it is carried out, is likely to harm the health, safety or morals of children."[2] The types of work comprised by this article of the convention are expected to be determined by national laws and specified by a process of consultation by authorities with employers and workers. ILO convention 182 recognizes that child labor is a fundamental reflection of poverty and cannot be eliminated without addressing the needs of families. It asserts that poverty alleviation and universal education are important forms of action that will lead to a long-term solution.

Beginning in the late 1980s, several national agencies began to more systematically collect, analyze, and report data concerning the use of child labor in various sectors of the economy and document the impact for children and the society. This chapter focuses in particular on recent reports of the Department of Labor, the General Accounting Office, the National Institute for Occupational Health and Safety, and the National Advisory Commission on Migrant Health, which have all issued studies of the nature, extent, and consequences of child labor in agriculture.

## RESEARCH ON YOUTH EMPLOYMENT IN AGRICULTURE

Beginning in 1988, the Department of Labor has carried out a periodic nationwide survey called the National Agricultural Workers' Survey (NAWS) that interviews field workers in crop agriculture to monitor basic demographics and seasonal agricultural wages and working conditions. A random sample of farm workers are contacted at their place of employment and, at a later time and location, administered a detailed questionnaire. NAWS selects workers using a multistage procedure that takes into account seasonal and regional fluctuations in forty-seven crop reporting districts, chosen for the variety of crops and the number of farm labor employees. NAWS data are available for youths between fourteen and seventeen years old, who constitute their sample of farm workers in this age category. NAWS does not directly interview children under the age of fourteen, but the survey does ask farm worker parents about their children with respect to demographics, schooling, work, and migration.[3]

Research based on the NAWS survey shows two distinct categories of minors doing hired farm work. The first group of minors identified by NAWS are teenagers, who are interviewed as members of the general farm worker population. The summary portrait of teen farm workers is a group who is very poor. Nearly half (48 percent) live without any family member accompanying them.[4] They constitute a new and growing group of farm workers, according to the Labor Department.[5] The second group of minors identified by NAWS is farm worker children working alongside their parents in the fields. The majority of teens doing wage labor in agriculture was from this group, one composed of poor, often migrant households with incomes under $25,000.[6]

It is important to distinguish the circumstances of this majority from a third category, which is a radically different group of hired teens: A minute proportion of employed minors in crop agriculture is formed by rural young people whose parents are local residents and not farm workers. Many from this third group are local teens from middle-class families who do farm work for pay when school is not in session. For example, they perform such tasks as detasseling corn on Midwest farms.[7] While teens in this category do fit a common mental image of American rural youth, they are not the majority and are not disadvantaged to the same degree as migrant teens and farm worker children. This chapter is not about local resident youth or children working on their parents' farms.

NAWS surveys during the 1993–1998 period found that 6 percent to 7 percent of all crop farm workers in the United States were minor teens between the ages of fourteen and seventeen, with another 9 percent at eighteen and nineteen years. Less than 1 percent were under fourteen years old. Similarly, the Commission on Agricultural Workers estimated that 7 percent, or approximately 126,000 out of 1.8 million farm workers, employed annually were minors between fourteen and seventeen years old. Over half were born in the United States and were citizens.[8]

In general, farm labor remains one of the poorest-paid occupations in the United States. Teen farm workers (thirteen to nineteen years old), representing about 15 percent of total farm workers, earned even less than adults, with at least 30 percent earning minimum wage or less. Teens were most common in the lowest-paid jobs. The average number of weeks that teens worked was fourteen. This means that a significant proportion (estimated at 40 percent) worked for at least part of the school year. Their median annual earnings were far below those of adults: 59 percent received less than $1,000 a year for doing agricultural work. Teens typically needed an intermediary person to find jobs for them: only 11 percent of teens found their farm job on their own. Most significant, many teens were de facto emancipated minors, living without any kind of family supervision. Among migrant teens, four of five constituted unaccompanied minors, and 91 percent were foreign-born, usually recent arrivals, and their percentage rose over the last decade.[9]

A second category of child farm worker is composed of children who labor alongside their farm worker parents. Children with a migrant parent were more likely to do farm labor than children whose parents settled out of the migrant stream. In this category, three-quarters of underage farm workers are born in the United States, even though three-quarters of farm worker parents are foreign-born. According to the NAWS surveys, 31 percent of underage farm workers in the age group of sixteen and seventeen were working in the fields, as were 18 percent of farm worker children aged fourteen and fifteen. Two out of five child farm workers in this category were female.[10]

Most farm worker children are not employed in agriculture, but, through random surveys with their parents, NAWS found that one in four children who are working in the fields with their parents was under the age of fourteen. Another 28 percent were fourteen- and fifteen-year-olds, and 45 percent were sixteen- and seventeen-year-olds. Also, approximately 7 percent of teenagers between thirteen and seventeen were given the responsibility of taking care of younger siblings while their parents did farm work. Most children of farm workers are very young, with 83 percent under the age of fourteen and 40 percent under six. The parents themselves are a young population, according to NAWS data, with two-thirds of all farm workers less than thirty-four years old, a reflection of the fact that they are mostly young immigrants.[11]

The presence of farm worker children who were minor teens and preteens as laborers in crop agriculture is a reflection of the survival needs of families whose incomes are far below the amount required to provide necessities. Almost two-thirds of farm worker families with children living with them fell below federal poverty levels. Families who have children working alongside the parents are more likely to be poor than other families. Farm worker families with children are overwhelmingly located at low income levels: 87 percent have incomes less than $25,000 a year, and 60 percent have family incomes under $15,000. In spite of the fact that so many families lived below the federal poverty level, very few receive any form of public assistance based on need. Many children of farm worker families endure serious difficulties whether they work or not. Only 10 percent of farm worker children had a parent who was eligible for employer-provided health insurance.[12]

## CONSEQUENCES OF CHILD LABOR

A serious consequence of beginning work life as a minor teen or preteen hired in crop agriculture is that the long hours, seasonal intensity, and crop mobility demanded by the occupation disrupt a young person's education. Data show that minor teen farm workers are at a high risk of not completing a high school education. Fewer than half (47 percent) were attending school at the grade levels that corresponded to their ages. A high proportion (37 percent) of workers had not attended school within the last year and were considered dropouts who did not obtain a high school diploma. The second major category, farm worker children who worked alongside their parents, was more likely to be behind in school than farm worker children who were not employed. Only 62 percent of child workers were learning at their appropriate grade levels; 22 percent were behind at least one grade; and 16 percent had dropped out of school.[13]

Agricultural employment poses particular risks of injury and death for all workers, so children who are hired to do farm labor have a significant exposure to problems of health and safety.[14] Minor teen farm workers aged fifteen to seventeen had a risk of fatality per hour worked that is 4.4 times higher than the average worker of the same age. Job deaths in farm work are more likely to happen among the youngest workers. More than half of youth fatalities in farm labor happen to young workers under the age of fifteen. A common cause of death is associated with farm machinery, such as harvesting equipment. Nationally, during the past decade, more than 40 percent of children who were killed because of injuries on the job were working in agriculture, especially crop production.[15]

The general risks in the occupation extend well beyond the possibility of fatal accidents. The National Advisory Commission on Migrant Health cited the results of hearings, congressional testimony, and research studies in a report that shows why agricultural work is sometimes categorized as the second-most hazardous occupation in the United States. The characteristics of work and environmental health risks have particular dangers for children, but the conditions of risk extend to all farm workers. Some of these negative conditions are disruption of education due to the timing of seasonal labor and long work days; social problems, such as child abuse and domestic violence in overcrowded labor camps; accidents associated with farm equipment; constant stoop labor; lack of clean water and toilets at the work site; illness and disease caused by substandard, crowded, and pest-filled housing; exposure to weather elements and exposure to chemicals used in crop agriculture; inability to qualify for basic health benefits; and an array of illnesses, including severe ones that are commonly associated with agricultural work.[16]

Comprehensive information on the acute and chronic health effects on children due to pesticide exposure are not available, but the General Accounting Office reported significant recent concerns about the health of children exposed to pesticides, such as by doing farm work, being caught in the drift when pesticides are applied to fields, and direct contact with treated plants and soil. Apart from the evidence that children are working in agriculture, NAWS surveys indicated that farm worker parents sometimes took children five years of age or younger with them to the fields because of a lack of child care.[17] Children's developing systems absorb chemicals more readily and excrete some chemicals less effectively than do those of adults. Exposure to toxins can permanently change the human body at critical periods of growth and development. Children may have greater contact with poisons because they are less likely than adults to wear protective clothing. Children also have greater oral transfer rates of pesticides from objects, dust, or soil, and they breathe more per unit of body weight than do adults.[18]

The Fair Labor Standards Act remains one of the most important basic protections regulating child labor in the United States, but the act offers fewer protections for underage workers in agriculture than it does in other industries.[19] It is legal for children to do farm labor under conditions that would be illegal in other work sectors.[20] Farm workers who are minors are legally allowed to work at younger ages, in more hazardous jobs, and for longer hours than young workers in other sectors of the economy.[21] As minor teen workers, they are especially at risk for unsafe work assignments, harassment, and intimidation. Many are working in agriculture for the first time and do not comprehend the long-term consequences of disease, injury, and disability.[22]

## PROTECTING THE RIGHTS OF CHILD FARM WORKERS

A human rights emphasis on patterns such as child and underage labor has the potential for offering universal standards for assessing existing patterns. While not replacing struggles among different interest groups and advocates, human rights norms can provide a context for social and political actions. Although violations of human rights have been asserted in areas such as massacres and genocides related to wars and ethnic animosities, it has been more difficult to establish human rights norms related to labor standards, including child labor. One obvious reason is that to do so would challenge powerful economic organizations that profit from existing arrangements, such as large agricultural corporations.

In their discussion of the nature of human rights, Sjoberg, Gill, and Williams place special emphasis on "organized power relationships," the fact that power is wielded through organizations. It is not sufficient simply to hold individuals responsible for human rights violations.[23] Rather, because most contemporary human rights abuses occur through institutional structures, it is necessary to examine and hold accountable the powerful organizations that create and shape patterns leading to human rights violations. In our increasingly interconnected world, this has come to mean not only nation-states and their policies but also the activities of corporate and transnational organizations.[24]

More specifically, underage labor in United States agriculture fits the perspective of understanding violations of international human rights norms as a result of the actions and policies of large-scale, powerful, and influential organizations. The perspective offered by the CRC can be used to evaluate the patterns of labor employment by United States agricultural firms as well as policies in immigrant-sending countries, particularly Mexico, that contribute to the prevalence of underage immigrant farm workers.

A number of serious operational difficulties present themselves in securing United States compliance with the CRC. The Health, Education, and Human Services Division undertook a study for the House of Representatives to assess the numbers of children working in agriculture and the characteristics and legality of their work. The division reported in 1998 that the number of minor teens between the ages of fifteen and seventeen who were hired in crop agriculture could be estimated at 155,000 on average, with the number reaching 300,000 at some point during the year.[25] The report also cited limitations in available information and methodological problems that likely produced an undercounting of the total number of children working.[26] The report acknowledged that similar difficulties apply to the information about children's working conditions and their illnesses and injuries associated with working in the fields.

Experience with enforcement of key provisions of the Fair Labor Standards Act shows that relatively low resources are devoted to agriculture by the Labor Department's Wage and Hours Division and by the Occupational Health and Safety Administration. There are simply not enough labor investigators to conduct the necessary inspections. Also, the nature of agriculture and its type of workforce make it more difficult to enforce child labor laws and other health and safety regulations.[27] Much of the workforce is mobile and willing to have children work because families need the additional income. Even if workers are willing to report employer violations, the employees can be deterred by a normal fear of employer retaliation. Workers may also distrust enforcement agencies. Labor officials reported that when they found agricultural crews with children, adults told them to stop working until the investigator left; therefore, it was impossible to witness child labor violations.

Employer records make it difficult to detect underage labor because children working with a parent often work under the parent's payroll numbers. This makes it hard to establish that there is an employment relationship with the child. The practice also results in minimum-wage violations because wages paid to the parent were for work actually done by the parent and the child.[28] Finding acceptable documentation of the child's age is made more difficult when the child is a migrant or not attending school or when the parent and child are willing to lie so that the child may continue to work.

Further obstacles to enforcement reflect the citizenship status of the labor force. The proportion of farm workers who were citizens has declined throughout the eight-year period of 1989 to 1996. The share of citizens has fallen by half, to 21 percent in 1996.[29] The proportion of unauthorized or undocumented workers increased to 52 percent by 1998.[30] The past decade has seen increases in both the percentage of children who entered the United States illegally to work in agriculture and the percentage of those who did not have their parents or other family members accompanying them.[31]

Data from California, the state with the largest number of crop workers, show that a full two-thirds of all minors in wage labor on crop farms reported that they were unauthorized, compared with one-quarter of adult farm workers. Only one out of seven underage farm workers had Immigration and Naturalization Service authorization. More than one-third of minors working on crop farms in California were hired by farm labor contractors.[32]

A distressingly large share of children working as hired crop farm workers are living and working on their own without a family member accompanying them and without supervision by a parent or guardian. Nationally 37 percent of child farm workers are living and working unaccompanied. Occupational health specialists regard the circumstances of these child workers with particular concern because these children have less chance of receiving adult advice and training in an occupation having many hazardous working and living conditions. Some minor teens may react to the absence of adult restrictions by involving themselves in high-risk behavior when they are away from the job.[33] Further perils are entailed in the border crossing itself, which has become far more hazardous since a nationwide border-control strategy began during the mid-1990s to deter illegal crossings by causing migrants who attempt entry to use remote and hostile terrain with extreme weather conditions.[34] News reports of migrant deaths that have averaged over three hundred annually from fiscal years 1998 through 2003 suggest that perhaps 20 to 25 percent of the deaths involve underage migrants.[35]

## RECENT IMMIGRATION AND UNDERAGE WORKERS

The evidence on child labor in crop agriculture must be understood in the larger context of shifting trends in agricultural production over the past quarter century. Our argument is that the extent of underage, and especially unaccompanied, teen crop workers needs to be placed in the context of two patterns that are intertwined and that support one another. The first is a significant increase in immigration from Mexico, much of it unauthorized. The second is the growing importance of a pattern of agricultural employment: the farm labor contractor system.

Mexican immigration during the past two decades represents the acceleration of a century-old pattern. However, some believe that the precursor to recent immigration was the Bracero Program from 1942 to 1964. As an alternative to unauthorized immigration, the Bracero Program brought almost five million Mexican farm workers into the United States legally for the duration of the harvest season, after which they returned to Mexico. The termination of the Bracero Program did not end the social networks that had been built between sending villages in Mexico and jobs and communities in the United States. Consequently, many workers continued to come but now illegally. Work in this country had simply become part of the survival strategy of many Mexican families and their villages. As migration networks became stabilized over time, the cost of migration was reduced. Once begun, immigration continued as a self-sustaining process, nurtured by a culture of migration and numerous relatives and other personal contacts in the United States.[36] In fact, as more people became involved in migration networks over time, the economic motivations behind migration, such as economic incentives and individual cost-benefit calculations,[37] became less-important factors in individuals' and, in effect, communities' decisions to migrate.[38]

An internal migration within Mexico has been fostered by the growth of Mexican agro-export enterprises, and this development appears to facilitate migration to the United States. Agricultural production primarily for export has been expanding in the Culiacan Valley in Sinaloa and the San Quintin Valley in Baja during the past several decades. Many of the companies in these agricultural regions are enterprises under joint venture by Mexican growers and U.S. distributors. The proximity to the border (for example, the San Quintin Valley is only a five-hour bus trip to Tijuana) makes both locations suitable recruiting spots for "coyotes" (smugglers) with connections with employers.[39] It must be kept in mind, however, that the demand aspect of labor entry to the United States has remained critical. Some analysts believe that the demand for manual labor now predominates over other factors in accounting for Mexican immigration.[40]

The transition in the agricultural workforce made possible by recent immigration has been documented by NAWS and other studies that show that the farm labor supply has come to be filled by an increasing proportion of recent unauthorized immigrants. These studies show that changes in the labor force have been associated with increased turnover in farm labor jobs, increasing poverty of farm worker families, minor teen employment and labor by farm worker children, and stagnating incomes of farm workers compared with those of other workers and earlier data within this occupation. An important shift in migration patterns from Mexico is the context for a major transformation in the labor supply in crop agriculture. In this respect, the increase in underage farm workers is partly a culmination of this migration trend.

According to the latest published NAWS data, 81 percent of all crop farm workers were foreign-born, with 95 percent of these (or 77 percent of the total) being from Mexico. Of those foreign-born in crop agriculture, 32 percent had entered the United States within two years of the survey. The proportion of unauthorized workers has been steadily rising, as many of the previously unauthorized who were legalized under the Special Agricultural Workers program of the 1986 Immigration Reform and Control Act (IRCA) left the fields for better prospects. Unauthorized workers composed 52 percent of the crop agricultural workers by 1998, up from 40 percent in 1995 and 17 percent in 1990. Legal permanent residents ("green carders") made up 24 percent and United States citizens 22 percent. The median age of farm workers, twenty-nine years in 1998, has also been gradually declining: 6 percent are fourteen to seventeen years old. Farm workers below the age of twenty-five, including underage ones, were at least twice as likely to be unauthorized than they were to be authorized or United States citizens.

Corresponding to the labor force transition has been a decline in real wages for crop workers, from $6.89 per hour in 1989 to $5.98 per hour in 1997 (in constant 1997 dollars). The ratio of hourly wages of crop workers to private non–farm worker wages declined from .543 to .480 during this same period.[41]

## FARM LABOR CONTRACTORS AND UNDERAGE WORKERS

The labor supply transition has been associated with a dramatic comeback by farm labor contractors (FLCs), particularly in California, where farm labor unionization under the United Farm Workers (UFW) reduced their presence from 1970 to the mid-1980s. FLCs are intermediaries who match workers with jobs. They typically command the work crew, provide their transportation to fields, and sometimes coordinate their housing and board as well as other services, such as loans for emergencies. New immigrants, particularly unauthorized ones, are those most in need of contractors' services.[42] Not unexpectedly, migrant teens have been disproportionately connected to FLCs, especially those contractors who can help overcome language and cultural barriers and find jobs for minor workers. Even though FLCs were prohibited under union contracts with the UFW in California, FLCs never disappeared, and after the decline of unionization, FLCs rapidly reappeared in agricultural operations where they had been absent. For example, FLCs now dominate the supply of peak-season labor for fruits and vegetables in California's San Joaquin Valley.[43]

Many growers prefer contractors since this arrangement allows growers to avoid the paperwork, and sometimes the legal liability, of complying with immigration laws and labor regulations, such as adhering to child labor laws, paying the minimum wage, abiding by pesticide exposure and other safety rules, and in California, complying with the state's Agricultural Labor Relations Act. Using FLCs also shifts the threat of IRCA-mandated employer sanctions from individual growers to contractors. When an oversupply of workers is available, FLCs compete among themselves and thereby reduce growers' production costs and transfer the costs of labor force instability to workers.[44] FLCs are essentially private agents supplying abundant numbers of new immigrants to the farm labor market, both in the United States in general and California in particular.[45]

The share of agricultural workers employed by FLCs in California increased by more than one-quarter from 1984 to 1988.[46] One study concluded that FLCs supply more than one-third of the nine hundred thousand workers who have farm jobs at some time during the year and over half of the six hundred thousand with seasonal farm jobs.[47] NAWS reports place the figure at 31 percent for the years 1990–1991 and 30 percent for 1997–1998.[48] The California share is considerably greater than the nationwide average of 19 percent seasonal agricultural workers who are employed by FLCs, although this increased from 11 percent in 1989.[49]

The expanded usage of FLCs is important for several reasons. First, FLCs play a significant role in recruiting and employing minor teen migrants, who are more prevalent in the lowest-paying jobs.[50] Nationally, among minor teens working for FLCs, two-fifths were unauthorized, and only one of seven was a United States citizen. The reverse is the case for minor teens working directly for a farm operator: 70 percent were United States citizens, and only one out of five was unauthorized. California data show, in contrast, that an absolute majority of minor teens working for either FLCs or farm operators reported that they were unauthorized.[51]

Also, labor costs for growers are reduced considerably from those under union contracts that did not permit child labor. Unlike other immigrants, unauthorized Mexicans showed little wage returns for longer experience in the United States as long as they stayed in agriculture. By contrast, those who initially took agricultural jobs but moved to other occupations showed a 15 percent wage advantage to that of their counterparts who stayed in agriculture.[52]

The increasing importance of farm labor contractors in particular has been associated with an imbalance between a large supply of workers and existing jobs. Research findings indicate that FLCs are not employment stabilizers; rather, employees of contractors have higher turnover rates and less job tenure than non-FLC employees. In fact, many contractors do not maintain stable crews; instead, the number hired changes frequently due to daily needs and terms of labor contracts. For example, Miriam Wells, in her study of strawberry production in the Salinas area, described FLCs who hire daily from one of several "shape-up points" where job security is virtually nonexistent.[53]

Of those channeled into the fields by FLCs, a greater proportion are newcomers, particularly unauthorized ones, when compared to that of workers hired directly by individual growers. The results are predictable. Studies by agricultural economists indicate that compared with direct grower hires, workers employed by FLCs not only have lower earnings but also have less experience with the same grower, less consecutive employment with the same grower, fewer hours and shorter days at work when employed, and more time without work than other farm workers in California.[54] Their annual earnings are therefore lower. They are less likely to receive unemployment insurance. Extra charges further reduce take-home pay as they must often pay for equipment, rides to the job, food, and housing. Job conditions are also less sanitary. FLC hiring has contributed to the large wage gap that exists between native-born and immigrant workers, including children, by increasing the immigrants' uncertainty of employment and by expanding the farm labor oversupply.

Another reason to focus on labor contractors is that they are associated with the more sensational cases of abuses among farm workers. A series of articles in the *Palm Beach Post* in December 2003 and an article in the *New Yorker* in April 2003 described recent cases in Florida's agriculture that approximate modern-day slavery.[55] The articles described actions such as labor contractors who locked up workers, including underage ones, when not in the fields and controlled every aspect of their lives, such as shelters, meals, transportation, and even phone calls. Five slavery cases prosecuted by the United States government in recent years with roots in Florida appear to be the leading edge of a more widespread pattern of child and labor abuse.

Further violations of children's rights are connected to farm labor contractors. For example, the *Palm Beach Post* series described two fifteen-year-old Mexican girls who escaped confinement and told authorities that they had been smuggled into this country believing they would work in health care but instead were forced to become prostitutes in south and central Florida and offer services to migrant workers who were mostly under the supervision of contractors. Other cases involve female workers raped by supervisors.

It is no coincidence that labor contractors dominate Florida's agricultural employment. One of the *Palm Beach Post* articles cites a federal study that showed that contractors serve as the employers of roughly half (50.4 percent) of Florida farm workers as opposed to their direct employment by growers and as compared to 20.6 percent hired by contractors elsewhere.

In summary, more new immigrants and unauthorized workers are hired by FLCs than by the growers themselves. By sustaining an oversupply of workers and low-wage employment conditions, FLCs create downward pressure on wage rates, force a lowering of union benefits in comparable jobs covered by union contracts, and charge more than growers do for work and housing requirements. FLCs contribute to high turnover rates in farm labor jobs, less job tenure for workers, falling hourly wages, falling numbers of hours of employment, and declining annual incomes.

Nevertheless, labor contractors need to be seen as only one part of the institutional arrangements of agricultural production that lead to human rights violations. Although contractors may be the most visible element, they are part of a system of employment that includes agricultural companies and individual growers. And the international migratory patterns associated with underage farm workers are facilitated by conditions and changes in sending countries whose families depend on the wages of their underage members as part of their economic survival strategies.

The importance of a focus on interrelated patterns and organizations is epitomized by the comments of a federal judge, K. Michael Moore, who presided over a modern-day case of slavery in Fort Pierce, Florida, in November 2002. When a defense attorney for three individuals charged with involuntary servitude asked that the charges be dismissed because the prosecution of his clients was selective and arbitrary, he asked, "Do you not think for one moment . . . that the growers don't know what's going on? . . . Everyone knows that somebody has to buffer them." Judge Moore replied, "That's the way the whole system works." The judge suggested at the sentencing that prosecutors redirect their resources away from the middlemen labor contractors on trial and toward others in the system, and he observed that "others at a higher level of the fruit picking industry seem complicit in one way or another with how these activities occur."[56] When commenting on the contractor system, the director of the Migrant Farmworker Justice Project, a legal advocacy group in Florida, noted, "The richest, most powerful people in the state are benefiting from this."[57]

## CONCLUSION

Conditions of wage labor prevalent in crop agriculture that are described in this chapter create particular difficulties for implementing the CRC in the United States. Nevertheless, the perspective of the convention encompasses a long-term dimension. The CRC provides a unique form of leverage for gradually upgrading conditions for children in all societies; rather than through an abrupt and sometimes dislocating set of changes, progress is effected through an ongoing process of changing attitudes and amending laws, rules, and standard practices.

It must be acknowledged that child labor has been a perennial problem in the United States for at least two centuries.[58] Nevertheless, the nature of child labor hired in crop agriculture has changed in recent decades. Currently, there is a national oversupply of farm workers, and many are seriously underemployed. Today's farm labor force is increasingly composed of young single males who are newly arrived to the United States. A small but growing proportion is composed of minor teen newcomers who are unauthorized, underage, and unaccompanied. Their presence reflects one dimension of a fundamental transformation in the agricultural labor supply. Recent appeals for action against child labor in the fields fail to recognize the connection between underage workers and the underlying basic transformation of the farm labor market in this country.

The following discussion on policies and practices that would reduce the number and proportion of underage workers in crop agriculture has a particular emphasis on unaccompanied underage minors. Since 10 percent of rural Mexican households report receiving remittances from the income generated by work in the United States by some of their members, drastic measures, such as "sweeping the fields," to detain and deport unauthorized underage workers would likely be counterproductive. Even if feasible, measures like these would likely lead to undesirable, unintended consequences, such as a sharp increase in unauthorized immigration as individual households scramble to adjust to changing realities.

Instead, changes should be made in patterns of Mexican immigration and employment in crop agriculture in ways that would, over time, alter the underlying conditions that produce unaccompanied underage Mexican teen immigrants to the United States and their employment as crop farm workers.

For its part, the Mexican government needs to develop better postprimary education opportunities (grades 7–12) for its young people, especially in those states and regions that send the largest numbers to the United States. Underage employment in this country should not be justified by the fact that the average education level of recent male immigrants to the United States from Mexico is only 8.5 years (and 8.3 years for females), which is about a half year above the Mexican average, and that most of those employed in crop agriculture had already completed their schooling. Various UN and other public documents have emphasized the necessity of secondary education for achieving a reduction in poverty. In his 2000 presidential campaign, current Mexican president Vicente Fox said he would give priority to increasing educational attainment for young people and to reducing the vast disparities of access and quality within the educational system, where the federal government provides 80 percent of all funds. But so far, improvements have been difficult to achieve.

Nevertheless, increased educational opportunities in Mexico are a crucial part of any strategies to reduce underage migration to the United States. While actions taken in this country have been unable to alter the network-driven nature of much Mexican immigration, at least Mexico can attempt to reduce its underage–unaccompanied component.

In the United States, strategies should focus on reducing the "incentives" or "advantages" for utilizing underage teens in crop agriculture. If we are serious about this, the patterns described in this chapter need to be reversed — that is, the growing proportion of unauthorized among crop farm workers, the decline in real wages for farm workers, the "revolving door" of farm labor employment, and the virtual disappearance of employment benefits such as health care. What is necessary is a multifaceted approach, since action in a single area is unlikely to bring about the desired changes.

One way to reverse the proportion of unauthorized farm workers is simply to legalize the presence of a large number. This has been done several times in the past, from the "drying out" of Mexican farm workers during the 1950s to the legalization programs under IRCA that expired in 1989. However, what has proven difficult is to translate legalization into a stable, authorized farm labor force. As previously pointed out, many of those legalized under IRCA left the fields and were replaced by recent unauthorized immigrants. Any legalization must be sensitive to farm labor markets and must be accompanied by improvements in the conditions of work in crop agriculture if reform is expected to have any impact on the "revolving door" nature of agricultural employment—that is, the steady outflow of workers from agriculture that makes necessary the continual influx of new workers, including many underage ones.

Currently, competing proposals from the Democratic and Republican parties have put legalization on the public agenda. However, both proposals, as they now exist, fail to address the distinct characteristics of farm labor markets and would most likely be unable to counter unauthorized underage crop farm workers in the longer term. One alternative or complement to either proposal is the Agricultural Job Opportunity, Benefits, and Security Act (AgJOBS), introduced in both houses of Congress in September 2003. Although narrower in concern than either the Democratic or the Republican proposal, it has the potential to reverse some of the patterns that facilitate underage employment in agriculture.

Because of compromises that resulted in its current version, AgJOBS is supported by both employer and worker organizations, including the UFW, the Farm Labor Organizing Committee (FLOC), and several farm worker advocacy organizations. AgJOBS would attempt to legalize unauthorized farm workers and give them eighteen months after the bill became law to apply for a six-year temporary resident status (TRS). To qualify, applicants would need to document that they did the lesser of at least 575 hours or 100 days of farm work in a consecutive twelve-month period ending August 31, 2003. To qualify for permanent resident status, or a green card, those with a TRS through AgJOBS would have a multiyear farm labor requirement, needing to work at least 2,060 hours or 360 days of farm work during the next six years. Spouses and minor children of TRS workers would not be deportable but would not be allowed to work legally. If TRS workers obtain permanent resident status, then this status would be applied to spouses and minor children as well.

To assist agricultural employers, AgJOBS would make it easier to obtain seasonal nonimmigrant "guest workers" under the existing H-2A temporary foreign agricultural worker program of the United States Department of Labor. AgJOBS would streamline the process by reducing employer's paperwork and time frames for H-2A applications being authorized by the Labor Department. The current requirements for government certification have resulted in few growers in the western United States utilizing H-2A workers. The H-2A program requires employers to pay H-2A workers the higher of federal or state minimum wage, the prevailing wage in the occupation and area of intended employment, or the adverse effect wage rate (AEWR) that is calculated for each state to prevent wage stagnation or decline due to the use of immigrant workers. As of 2004, the AEWR is $8.50 in California, $8.73 in

Washington, $8.18 in Florida, and $8.06 in North Carolina, where many H-2A workers are hired.[59]

If AgJOBS is approved, its impact will depend on its implementation. It does have the potential to reverse the recent trends of an increasing unauthorized workforce and the "revolving door." And if unaccompanied underage farm workers are ineligible to apply for temporary residency, then their numbers may begin to decline.

Besides immigration laws, there is a potentially large area of public policy initiatives that also can help counter the wage stagnation or wage decline among the working poor that leads to conditions such as underage labor. Enforcing minimum wage laws and, more important, increasing the mandated minimum wage are two examples of mechanisms that have been historically effective in assisting working families by allowing adults to support their families on low-wage jobs. Individual states do not need to wait for the federal government to act. A California ballot initiative passed in the November 1996 election increased the state's minimum wage to $5.75 an hour as of March 1998. California's minimum wage further increased to $6.25 in 2001 and $6.75 in 2002 while the federal one remained at $5.15. Another initiative is to increase the earned income tax credit (EITC), whose increase early in the Clinton administration was perhaps the most effective antipoverty measure taken by that administration. Further examples include enforcing current laws against child labor and extending the laws that protect children in industrial occupations into agriculture.[60]

Internationally, there is a strong association between labor rights and human rights, and this is true in the United States as well. Unionization, of course, has been associated with improvements in low-paid employment, and the hope of many AgJOBS supporters is that the law will encourage unionization. During the 1970s, union contracts negotiated by the UFW for crop farm workers in California succeeded in improving wages and working conditions and created job benefits such as health care. Even nonunionized workers benefited with better wages and some benefits, as growers sought to counter the attractiveness of unionization.[61] However, the number of California farm workers covered by UFW contracts plummeted during the 1980s, and many former union members were replaced by recent immigrants supplied by FLCs. In contrast, in northwest Ohio, southeast Michigan, and northeast Indiana, ongoing three-way contracts initially signed in 1986 between the FLOC of Toledo, Ohio, processing companies such as Campbell and Heinz (Vlasic Pickles) and grower associations have raised wages, ended an exploitative "share-cropping" or "share-farming" arrangement, and brought more stability to individual farming operations.[62] FLOC's contracts with both the Mt. Olive Pickle Company and the North Carolina Growers Association, signed in September 2004, promise to raise wages several dollars above the current AEWR for eighty-five hundred (mostly Mexican) H-2A workers imported legally to harvest North Carolina's cucumber crop.[63]

Finally, the United States should comply with recognized international standards, such as the child labor prohibitions of ILO convention 182 and the UN Convention on the Rights of the Child. Issues regarding the poverty of children and families need to come back into the national agenda. Conditions that have increased underage farm workers in the United States are part of a larger complex of forces that have lowered the wages and working conditions for workers in crop agriculture.[64] The decline in wages and working conditions of farm labor in most of California's agricultural areas has stimulated an upsurge of scholarly and journalistic publications detailing the deplorable conditions in the fields,[65] the increasing poverty among farm workers,[66] and that of their communities.[67] Descriptions of child labor today are reminiscent of national conditions described by Ronald B. Taylor in his exposé of child labor exploitation, first published in 1973, in which he argued that children were being used to depress wages in the agricultural labor market.[68]

Today, the labor market in agriculture is one of intense competition that reflects experiences with a massive influx of new and recent immigrants to a particular occupation and industry. The deterioration in living and working conditions of farm workers in the last two decades can be seen as a labor subsidy to the industry that has become steadily more prosperous. At the same time, the financial and human costs of this market transformation are borne by the workers themselves and their families, the displaced workers who can no longer work at the customary wage, and ultimately society as a whole, in the form of diminished life chances for the workers and their children.

It is also important that the focus of national attention be shifted from immigrants themselves, regardless of their immigration statuses, toward an examination of the conditions of work and employment to which many new immigrants and lesser-skilled domestics typically have access. We need to recognize the importance of upgrading low-wage, low-skill employment in areas including, but not limited to, agriculture.[69] Increased pay and improved employment circumstances have the potential to reduce the "revolving door" characteristic of farm labor employment. In fact, for almost a century, farm labor advocates have held the goal of stabilizing the agricultural labor force.

Changes such as legalization, unionization, increased minimum wages, and "tax rebates" such as the EITC divert some of the costs of labor force instability from low-paid workers back to employers and perhaps consumers. As opposed to policies penalizing immigrants, raising the rewards and desirability of traditionally poorly regarded occupations offers a more substantial promise for countering the considerable economic and social costs of labor force transitions.

We need to reassert the balance between the market and the needs of children and families. Ultimately, progress is needed toward compliance with important international standards, such as the CRC and ILO convention 182, in order to respect the human rights of disadvantaged children and demonstrate ethical leadership in a prosperous industry in the world's wealthiest society.

## NOTES

1. United Nations, "Document 60: Convention on the Rights of the Child," in *United Nations Blue Books Series*, vol. 7 (New York: UN Department of Public Information, 1995), 340.

2. International Labour Organization, *Convention 182: Convention Concerning the Prohibition and Immediate Action for the Elimination of the Worst Forms of Child Labour* (Geneva, Switz.: International Labour Organization, 1999).

3. References in this section indicate parts of chapter 5, "Youth Employment in Agriculture," for the U.S. Department of Labor's *Report on the Youth Labor Force* (Washington, D.C.: U.S. Department of Labor, Bureau of Labor Statistics, June 2000, revised November 2000). Information for this chapter of the report was obtained by NAWS interviews with 13,380 workers during fiscal years 1993 through 1998.

4. Ruth Samardick, Susan M. Gabbard, and Melissa A. Lewis, "Youth Employment in Agriculture," in *Report on the Youth Labor Force* (Washington, D.C.: U.S. Department of Labor, Bureau of Labor Statistics, 2000), 53.

5. U.S. General Accounting Office, *Child Labor: Labor Can Strengthen Its Efforts to Protect Children Who Work*, GAO-02-880 (Washington, D.C.: U.S. General Accounting Office, 2002), 13.

6. Samardick, Gabbard, and Lewis, "Youth Employment," 56.

7. Samardick, Gabbard, and Lewis, "Youth Employment," 56.

8. Samardick, Gabbard, and Lewis, "Youth Employment," 53.

9. Samardick, Gabbard, and Lewis, "Youth Employment," 54; U.S. General Accounting Office, *Child Labor*, 13.

10. Samardick, Gabbard, and Lewis, "Youth Employment," 54–55.

11. Samardick, Gabbard, and Lewis, "Youth Employment," 54–55.

12. Samardick, Gabbard, and Lewis, "Youth Employment," 55–56; Don Villarejo, *The Health of Children Hired to Work on U.S. Farms*, final performance report to the National Institute for Occupational Safety and Health and the Centers for Disease Control (Davis: California Institute for Rural Studies, 2002), 7.

13. Samardick, Gabbard, and Lewis, "Youth Employment, 54–56.

14. A. L. Mardis and S. G. Pratt, *Preventing Deaths, Injuries, and Illnesses of Young Workers: NIOSH Alert*, DHHS (NIOSH) publication no. 2003-128 (Washington, D.C.: National Institute for Occupational Safety and Health, July 2003); J. R.

Myers and K. J. Hendricks, *Injuries among Youth on Farms in the United States, 1998*, publication no. 2001154 (Washington, D.C.: National Institute of Occupational Safety and Health, 2001).

15. Samardick, Gabbard, and Lewis, "Youth Employment," 58–60; U.S. General Accounting Office, *Child Labor*, 22.

16. National Advisory Council on Migrant Health, *Losing Ground: The Condition of Farmworkers in America* (Bethesda, Md.: Department of Health and Human Services, 1995), 27.

17. U.S. General Accounting Office, *Child Labor*, 6.

18. U.S. General Accounting Office, *Child Labor*, 17.

19. U.S. Department of Labor, *Child Labor Requirements in Agriculture under the Fair Labor Standards Act* (Washington, D.C.: U.S. Government Printing Office, 1989).

20. U.S. Department of Labor, *Report on the Youth Labor Force*; National Research Council, *Protecting Youth at Work*, report of the Committee on the Health and Safety Implications of Child Labor (Washington, D.C.: National Academy Press, 1998).

21. U.S. General Accounting Office, *Child Labor in Agriculture: Characteristics and Legality of Work*, GAO/HEHS-98-112R (Washington, D.C.: U.S. General Accounting Office, 1998); U.S. General Accounting Office, *Child Labor in Agriculture: Changes Needed to Better Protect Health and Educational Opportunities*, GAO/HEHS-98-193 (Washington, D.C.: U.S. General Accounting Office, 1998); U.S. Department of Labor, *State Child Labor Laws Applicable to Agricultural Employment– January 1, 2000* (Washington, D.C.: U.S. Department of Labor, 2000), 1–10.

22. M. Vela Acosta and B. Lee, eds., *Migrant and Seasonal Hired Adolescent Farmworkers: A Plan to Improve Working Conditions* (Marshfield, Wis.: Marshfield Clinic, 2001).

23. Gideon S. Sjoberg, Elizabeth A. Gill, and Norma Williams, "A Sociology of Human Rights," *Social Problems* 48, no. 1 (February 2001): 11–47.

24. Richard A. Falk, *Human Rights Horizons: The Pursuit of Justice in a Globalizing World* (New York: Routledge, 2000).

25. U.S. General Accounting Office, *Child Labor in Agriculture: Characteristics*, 2–5.

26. The GAO Reports primarily reflect data from the Current Population Survey (CPS). The CPS is a monthly survey conducted by the Bureau of the Census for the Bureau of Labor Statistics. The GAO Reports recognize several major sources of data on children working in agriculture, but note that the surveys measure different populations and include different age categories.

27. U.S. General Accounting Office, *Child Labor in Agriculture: Characteristics*; *Child Labor in Agriculture: Changes Needed*.

28. U.S. General Accounting Office, *Child Labor in Agriculture: Characteristics*, 17.

29. Villarejo, *Health of Children*, 5.

30. Kala Mehta et al., *Findings from the National Agricultural Workers Survey (NAWS), 1997–1998: A Demographic and Employment Profile of United States Farm-*

*workers*, research report no. 8 (Washington, D.C.: U.S. Department of Labor, Office of Program Economics, March 2000), viii.

31. U.S. General Accounting Office, *Child Labor: Characteristics*, 13.

32. Villarejo, *Health of Children*, 5–6.

33. Villarejo, *Health of Children*, 9.

34. *Los Angeles Times*, "INS Chief Targets Risky Rural Crossings," 7 September 2000.

35. *Los Angeles Times*, "They Keep Dying," 25 February 2001.

36. Miriam Wells, *Strawberry Fields: Politics, Class, and Work in California Agriculture* (Ithaca, N.Y.: Cornell University Press, 1996), 155; Douglas Massey et al., *Return to Aztlan: The Social Process of International Migration from Western Mexico* (Berkeley: University of California Press, 1987); Susan Gabbard, Richard Mines, and Beatiz Boccalandro, *Migrant Farmworkers: Pursuing Security in an Unstable Labor Market*, research report no. 5 (Washington, D.C.: U.S. Department of Labor, Office of Program Economics, May 1994), 22–26; Douglas S. Massey, Jorge Durand, and Nolan J. Malone, *Beyond Smoke and Mirrors: Mexican Immigration in an Era of Economic Integration* (New York: Russell Sage Foundation, 2003).

37. George J. Borjas, *Friends or Strangers: The Impact of Immigrants on the U.S. Economy* (New York: Basic Books, 1990); George J. Borjas, "Economic Theory and International Migration," *International Migration Review* 23, no. 3 (1989): 457–85.

38. Massey et al., *Return to Aztlan*; Monica Boyd, "Family and Personal Networks in Recent International Migration: Recent Developments and New Agendas," *International Migration Review* 23, no. 3 (1989): 638–70; Pierrette Hondagneu-Sotelo, *Gendered Transitions: Mexican Experiences of Immigration* (Berkeley: University of California Press, 1994).

39. Carol Zabin and Sallie Hughes, "Economic Integration and Labor Flows: Stage Migration in Farm Labor Markets in Mexico and the United States," *International Migration Review* 29, no. 2 (1995): 397–422.

40. Jorge A. Bustamante, "The Mexicans Are Coming: From Ideology to Labor Relations," *International Migration Review* 17, no. 2 (1983): 323–41.

41. Mehta et al., *Findings*, 43–44.

42. Philip L. Martin, *Promises Unfulfilled: Unions, Immigration, and the Farm Workers* (Ithaca, N.Y.: Cornell University Press, 2003), 28; Gabbard, Mines, and Boccalandro, *Migrant Farmworkers,* 37.

43. Don Villarejo and Dave Runsten, *California's Agricultural Dilemma: Higher Production and Lower Wages* (Davis: California Institute for Rural Studies, 1993); Don Villarejo, *Privatizing the Costs of the California Farm Work Force* (Davis: California Institute for Rural Studies, 1995).

44. Gabbard, Mines, and Boccalandro, *Migrant Farmworkers*, 37.

45. J. Edward Taylor, Philip L. Martin, and Michael Fix, *Poverty amid Prosperity: Immigration and the Changing face of Rural California* (Washington, D.C.: Urban Institute Press, 1997); Philip L. Martin and J. Edward Taylor, *Merchants of Labor: Farm Labor Contractors and Immigration Reform* (Washington, D.C.: Urban Institute,

1995); Commission on Agricultural Workers, *Report of the Commission on Agricultural Workers* (Washington, D.C.: U.S. Government Printing Office, 1993).

46. J. Edward Taylor and Dawn Thilmany, "Worker Turnover, Farm Labor Contractors, and IRCA's Impact on the California Farm Labor Market," *American Journal of Agricultural Economics* 75, no. 2 (1993): 350–60.

47. Philip L. Martin and J. Edward Taylor, "Immigration Reform and Farm Labor Contracting in California Agriculture," in *The Paper Curtain*, ed. Michael Fix (Washington, D.C.: Urban Institute, 1991), 239–61.

48. Howard R. Rosenberg et al., *Who Works on California Farms: Demographic and Employment Findings from the National Agricultural Workers Survey (NAWS)*, NAWS report no. 7 (Washington, D.C.: U.S. Department of Labor, Office of Program Economics, 1998).

49. Mehta et al., *Findings*; Richard Mines, Susan Gabbard, and Jimmy Torres, *Findings from the National Agricultural Workers Survey (NAWS), 1989: A Demographic and Employment Profile of Perishable Crop Farm Workers*, research report no. 2 (Washington, D.C.: U.S. Department of Labor, Office of Program Economics, November 1991), 60.

50. Samardick, Gabbard, and Lewis, "Youth Employment."

51. Villarejo, *Health of Children*, 6.

52. Marta Tienda and Audrey Singer, "Wage Mobility of Undocumented Workers in the United States," *International Migration Review* 29, no. 1 (1995): 112–38.

53. Wells, *Strawberry Fields*, 197.

54. Philip L. Martin, "The Missing Bridge: How Immigrant Networks Keep Americans Out of Dirty Jobs," *Population and Environment* 14, no. 6 (1993): 539–64; Philip L. Martin, "Collective Bargaining in Agriculture," in *Contemporary Collective Bargaining in the Private Sector*, ed. Paula B. Voos (Madison: Industrial Relations Research Association, University of Wisconsin, 1994), 491–528; J. Edward Taylor, "Earnings and Mobility of Legal and Illegal Immigrant Workers in Agriculture," *American Journal of Agricultural Economics* 74, no. 4 (1992): 889–96; Taylor and Thilmany, "Worker Turnover."

55. Christine Evans et al., "Modern-Day Slavery: A Cox News System Special Report," *Palm Beach Post*, 7 December 2003; John Bowe, "Nobodies: Does Slavery Exist in America?" *New Yorker*, 21 and 28 April 2003.

56. John Bowe, "Nobodies."

57. Evans et al., "Modern-Day Slavery."

58. U.S. Department of Labor, *Report on the Youth Labor Force*.

59. Philip L. Martin, "AgJOBS: New Solutions or New Problems?" http://migration.ucdavis.edu/cf/; *Migration News* 11, no. 3 (July 2004), http://migration.ucdavis.edu/mn.

60. Human Rights Watch, *Fingers to the Bone: United States Failure to Protect Child Farmworkers* (New York: Human Rights Watch, June 2000); National Consumers League, *Child Labor in the United States* (Washington, D.C.: National Consumers League, 2000); Child Labor Coalition, *First Annual Report by Non-governmental Organizations on the International Labour Organization's Convention 182* (Washington, D.C.: Child Labor Coalition, December 2000); Association of Farmworker Opportunity

Programs, *Children in the Fields Campaign* (Arlington, Va.: Association of Farmworker Opportunity Programs, 2000).

61. Linda C. Majka and Theo J. Majka, *Farm Workers, Agribusiness, and the State* (Philadelphia, Pa.: Temple University Press, 1982); Patrick H. Mooney and Theo J. Majka, *Farmers' and Farm Workers' Movements: Social Protest in American Agriculture* (New York: Twayne Publishers, 1995); Philip L. Martin, Daniel Egan, and Stephanie Luce, *The Wages and Fringe Benefits of Unionized California Farmworkers: 1976–1987* (Davis: Department of Agricultural Economics, University of California, 1988).

62. Mooney and Majka, *Farmers' and Farm Workers' Movements*, 199–215.

63. Steven Greenhouse, "Growers' Group Signs the First Union Contract for Guest Workers," *New York Times*, 17 September 2004; Kati Hodges, "FLOC Pact in North Carolina 'Historic': Agreement with Growers Calls for Better Wages, Conditions," *Toledo Blade*, 17 September 2004; John Chavez, "Local Union, North Carolina Pickler to Sign Contract: Pact to Affect 8,000 Migrant Workers," *Toledo Blade*, 16 September 2004.

64. International Labour Organization, *A Future without Child Labour* (Geneva, Switz.: International Labour Organization, June 2002), 24–26.

65. Daniel Rothenberg, *With These Hands: The Hidden World of Migrant Farmworkers Today* (New York: Harcourt Brace, 1998); David Griffith and Ed Kissam, *Working Poor: Farm Workers in the United States* (Philadelphia, Pa.: Temple University Press, 1995); Eric Schlosser, "In the Strawberry Fields," *Atlantic Monthly* 276, no. 5 (November 1995): 80–108; Steven Greenhouse, "As Economy Booms, Migrant Workers' Housing Worsens," *New York Times*, 31 May 1998.

66. Richard Mines, Susan Gabbard, and Anne Steirman, *A Profile of U.S. Farm Workers: Demographics, Household Composition, Income, and Use of Services*, based on data from the National Agricultural Workers Survey (NAWS), research report no. 6 (Washington, D.C.: U.S. Department of Labor, Office of Program Economics, April 1997).

67. Elaine M. Allensworth and Refugio I. Rochin, "Ethnic Transformation in Rural California: Looking Beyond the Immigrant Farmworker," *Rural Sociology* 63, no. 1 (1998): 26–50; Taylor, Martin, and Fix, *Poverty amid Prosperity*.

68. Ronald B. Taylor, *Sweatshops in the Sun: Child Labor on the Farm*, foreword by Carey McWilliams (Boston: Beacon, 1975).

69. Abraham T. Mosisa, "The Working Poor in 2001," *Monthly Labor Review* (November/December 2003): 13–19.

*Chapter Nine*

# Human Rights and Juvenile Justice in the United States

Rosemary C. Sarri and Jeffrey J. Shook

The United States was founded on the principles of individual freedom, equality, and due process in a democratic society, but in the area of the justice system, these principles have often been challenged or neglected. The United States strongly advocates for the extension of human rights enforcement throughout the world, but when it relates directly to the United States, there is resistance not only to adoption but also to the enforcement of those rights by United Nations agencies. Nowhere are the principles of human rights and democratic society more at risk today than in the United States' juvenile justice system.

This chapter uses principles outlined in international human rights conventions and standards to analyze U.S. adherence to international conventions that have particular relevance for juveniles. We address some of the dramatic changes that have occurred in the laws governing juvenile justice in the United States, specifically the legal representation of juveniles in the courts, the processing of children as adults, the treatment of juveniles in the courts and facilities of the system, the overrepresentation of youth of color, and the application of the death penalty and life-without-parole sentences against children. We focus primarily on those behaviors of juveniles that result in charges of delinquency rather than on protective services related to neglect and abuse.

The five international conventions we use include

1. The Convention on the Rights of the Child (1989)
2. International Convention on the Elimination of All Forms of Racial Discrimination (1969)
3. International Covenant on Civil and Political Rights (1976)

4. Convention against Torture and Other Cruel, Inhuman, or Degrading Treatment or Punishment (1987)
5. American Convention on Human Rights (1978)[1]

Further, we focus on human rights requirements found in UN standards and rules that have not been adopted as treaties but that have been negotiated by governments and adopted by the international community to guide practice in specific areas. Two of these standards—United Nations Rules for the Protection of Juveniles Deprived of Their Liberty (1990) and United Nations Standard Minimum Rules for the Administration of Juvenile Justice (1985)—apply directly to juveniles. The other two—Standard Minimum Rules for the Treatment of Prisoners (1957) and United Nations Standard Minimum Rules for Noncustodial Measures (Tokyo Rules)—apply more broadly to justice administration. In addition to discussing the aforementioned conventions and standards, we explore how the United States recently objected to provisions establishing the International Criminal Court. While that court does not pertain directly to the juvenile justice system, one of the United States' objections to the court was the potential for its investigation of the U.S. criminal justice system as well as the concern about actions that might be taken against U.S. military personnel.

## THE JUVENILE JUSTICE SYSTEM

The establishment of the juvenile court in 1899 in Cook County, Illinois, created a separate system of justice for children. The principles underlying this court were that children were developmentally immature and required protection; they were malleable and could be rehabilitated; the court should aid children suffering from a broad range of problems, including dependency, neglect, abuse, and status offenses, as well as crime. Because the defendants were children, it was further assumed that hearings should be informal and that judges should have broad discretion in the handling of their cases so that the proceedings themselves would not have a negative impact upon youth. The primary focus of the court was on rehabilitation or habilitation.[2] Soon after its implementation in Cook County, the juvenile court spread throughout the rest of the country, and it has been modeled in many Western countries.[3]

Before the establishment of the juvenile court, children who were charged with delinquent acts were primarily tried in the criminal justice system, but age did play a role in presumptions of criminal responsibility. Individuals under the age of fourteen were presumed not to possess the sufficient criminal responsibility to commit a crime, though the presumption was refutable between the ages of seven and fourteen.[4] Individuals fourteen and older were presumed criminally responsible. The creation of the juvenile court altered this presumption in part, providing almost exclusive jurisdiction over individuals under the age of eighteen in most states.

The juvenile court differed from the adult criminal court in many ways, namely through its philosophy and practice. First, its terminology did not speak about guilt, innocence, trials, or sentences but created a framework similar to civil transactions by speaking of adjudications and dispositions.[5] Second, the focus of the court was less on the immediate offense behavior of the child and more on the needs or "best interests" of the child. Rehabilitation and treatment were considered the primary goals of the system, rather than punishment.[6] Third, the court structure featured an informal procedural system that allowed broad judicial discretion. Fourth, privacy was an important function of the juvenile court system, and proceedings and records were closed to the public. Finally, the juvenile court maintained jurisdiction over youth for both criminal and noncriminal behavior. These tenets constituted a separate system of justice that recognized differences between children and adults.

In the late 1960s critics addressed the operation of the juvenile court, charging that despite its rehabilitative rhetoric, it often treated children punitively, largely on the basis of race, class, and gender. Because of the volume of cases that were processed in many urban courts, implementation of rehabilitation was nearly impossible. Moreover, some criticized the court for having a conflict of interest in its legal processing of children because of its serving as the services provider, as in the control of detention and probation. This conflict was particularly apparent in the handling of youth in detention before and after adjudication. During the 1960s and 1970s, the decades often referred to as the human and civil rights era, there were national commission reports, legislation, and Supreme Court decisions that led to many new federal juvenile-justice initiatives.[7]

These initiatives had positive effects in several areas of the juvenile justice system. Policies of decriminalization, deinstitutionalization, community-based programs, and the extension of education were implemented and extended in many states.[8] This progress was associated with the extension of social justice and human rights to persons of color, women, children, the disabled, and the mentally ill. With regard to the juvenile court, Supreme Court decisions provided children with several due process protections but stopped short of equating juvenile proceedings with adult trials. Children were still acknowledged to be less competent because of their immaturity and limited experience. By the mid-1970s, the progress made in the 1960s resulted in substantial reductions in institutional placement, the development of community-based services, and procedural checks on the court.[9]

The progress of the 1960s and 1970s was dramatically reversed in the 1980s and 1990s with the passage of federal and state legislation that emphasized incarceration and punishment, along with withdrawal of the distinction between juveniles and adults as far as certain criminal behavior was concerned. As one hundred years of juvenile justice was celebrated in 2000, the laws and philosophy had returned to many of the practices in place before the invention of the juvenile court. Thousands of juveniles were held in adult jails and prisons, often under extremely punitive conditions.[10] Zimring posits that legislative changes have not reduced the power of the court but instead have reoriented its mission toward punitive ideals.[11] Feld argues that judicial, administrative, and legislative decisions have transformed the court into a second-class criminal court that does not serve the interests of children.[12] In many courts, the increased authority of prosecutors and the reduced authority of judges have produced pronounced differences in both the processing and the outcomes for juveniles. This shift ceases to recognize differences in development, maturity, capacity, and culpability between children and adults. It primarily seeks punishment or "accountability" instead of rehabilitation, the hallmark of the original juvenile justice system and the focus of many human rights standards and rules.

Much of the transformation was "justified" because there was an increase in violent crime by juveniles between 1985 and 1994. Juveniles involved in violent crime were not viewed as children able to benefit from rehabilitation, and the vocal public sought to provide appropriate "adult" sanctions to these individuals. Legislatures focused on violent juveniles and responded with an emphasis on law enforcement and punishment, which affected the entire juvenile justice system. This occurred despite the fact that the actual numbers of juveniles involved in violent crime never equaled 10 percent of all of the juveniles arrested for delinquency.[13] Thus, the entire system shifted toward punishment and accountability although the crime data did not support such a shift. Furthermore, punitive lawmaking continues into the twenty-first century despite the fact that juvenile crime, including violent crime, has declined dramatically to levels similar to those of the early 1980s.[14]

## PERSPECTIVES ON CHILDREN'S RIGHTS IN THE UNITED STATES

The importance of rights and standards for the treatment of children is heavily contested terrain in the United States, as is evidenced by the United States' unwillingness to ratify the Convention on the Rights of the Child. A number of perspectives exist regarding whether rights should be afforded to children.

*Children are viewed as vessels needing care and guidance to develop into productive citizens, not as citizens who could or should possess and exercise rights.* In the United States, families are viewed as the primary institution to care and protect youth, but the state retains power to intervene in the "best interests of the child." Children do not possess many substantive or procedural rights.[15] They were afforded some procedural rights by the Supreme Court regarding court processing, free speech, search and seizure, reproduction, and control over their sexuality. However, these rights were limited in scope and effect, have been limited by subsequent legal decisions and legislation, and are often not exercised given social realities concerning children.

*Children must have substantive and procedural rights in their own persons when families and the state do not appropriately care for children.* The human rights conventions and standards underlie this view. The discretion of various actors is limited, and there are specific safeguards to ensure protection and treatment, along with monitoring to ensure that interventions are effective, fair, and humane. The research, policy, and popular literature is filled with reports of the abrogation of children's rights today.[16]

*Children, depending on their ages, are in various stages of development and maturation.* The right to be acknowledged as a child in the process of development and maturation is being more actively discussed in the United States as concerns have increased about the use of life-without-parole sentences and the thousands of children who are tried and incarcerated as adults every year despite dramatic declines in crime by children. In addition, several states have now implemented legislation to protect children who are abused and/or neglected in foster care and residential facilities. Because many of these cases over time drift into the justice system, some have suggested that these rights apply to juvenile delinquents as well.[17] Research by Steinberg, Grisso, and Scott raises questions about the criminal culpability of juveniles.[18] They and their colleagues surveyed fourteen hundred juveniles in four states to assess their competence to be tried in an adult court. The authors argue that juveniles should not be held to the same standards of criminal responsibility as adults because children's decision-making capacity is not fully developed: they are less able to resist coercive influence; their assessment of risk is limited; and their personal identity is less well-formed.

## HUMAN RIGHTS CONVENTIONS

The 1989 Convention on the Rights of the Child (CRC) includes a preamble and forty-one substantive articles that note that the inherent dignity and equal and inalienable rights of all members of the human family "are the foundation of freedom, justice and peace in the world."[19]

After nearly universal ratification, the UN called on all states in 1998 to implement the provisions without any discrimination, to ensure the education of children, to ensure that all children charged with any penal violation be treated with dignity and with awareness of the developmental maturity of the juvenile. Among the reasons given for the United States' failure to ratify the CRC are that its enforcement would interfere with family rights and individual state's rights, that rights acknowledged under the UN are not acknowledged as rights in the United States, and that U.S. laws conflict with the principles of the CRC. Specifically, U.S. law permitted the use of capital punishment of children, which is forbidden by article 37 of the CRC and by several of the other conventions that have been adopted, including the regional American Convention on Human Rights, which the United States signed in 1977 but did not ratify.

Despite the resistance of the United States in ratifying the CRC, human rights conventions and standards serve as a valuable framework for guiding the treatment of children in the juvenile and criminal justice systems because they establish minimum rules and standards addressing the care and control of children in these systems. As discussed, five separate conventions and four separate standards are used to analyze the treatment of children in these systems. The CRC provides the comprehensive framework for establishing the positive need–based rights and the negative rights of children. It sets eighteen years as the age of majority and specifies a number of personal rights, including safety, education, culture, housing, food, and protection from harm by the family or by the state. The CRC includes articles pertaining to criminal processing. Article 40 provides children with due process rights, the right against criminal processing before gaining sufficient capacity, the right to be processed outside of judicial proceedings whenever applicable, and the right to dispositions to match the child's circumstances. Article 37 refers to the rights of children who have been deprived of their liberties and sets out specific protections governing their treatment and the prohibition of capital punishment.

The International Covenant on Civil and Political Rights was adopted by the UN in 1976 and ratified by the United States Senate in 1992 with the reservation that it would not implement certain articles. Specifically, the United States specified a reservation about the prohibition of the death penalty for juveniles under the age of eighteen (article 6.5). It provides that juveniles have the right not to be subject to cruel, inhuman, or degrading treatment or punishment (article 7). Juveniles are to have speedy and fair trials (article 14); juveniles have the right to be kept separate from adults when they are incarcerated. The Convention against Torture and Other Cruel, Degrading, and Inhuman Treatment and Punishment, ratified by the United States in 1994, is also relevant to juvenile justice in the United States because of some of the conditions in which juveniles are held in both juvenile and adult facilities. The United States' past use of the death penalty against persons who committed their crimes as juveniles was probably the most egregious violation. The International Convention on the Elimination of All Forms of Racial Discrimination, ratified in 1994, has particular relevance for the United States because there is such a serious problem of a disproportional presence of youth of color in all aspects of the criminal justice system. Moreover, there is federal law that requires that states receiving grants under the Juvenile Justice and Delinquency Prevention Act must attempt to achieve proportional representation of youth of color.

There are further provisions that provide standards and rules that govern the processing and institutionalization of children in the justice systems. The UN Standard Minimum Rules for the Administration of Juvenile Justice (1985) focuses specifically on systems developed to adjudicate the offenses of children. It provides a framework to guide the development of juvenile justice systems, the processing of cases through those systems, the range and function of dispositions, and the treatment of children in institutions. The UN Rules for the Protection of Juveniles Deprived of their Liberty (1990) focuses on the rights and needs of children detained, imprisoned, or otherwise held in public or private custody and establishes a framework to guide their treatment in facilities and community-based programs.

The Standard Minimum Rules for the Treatment of Prisoners set standards that primarily refer to adult correctional facilities but pertain to juveniles in those facilities and can be viewed as basic guidelines to govern juvenile facilities as well. The UN Standard Minimum Rules for Noncustodial Measures (Tokyo Rules) are important because of their focus on human rights issues with regard to the inclusion of noncustodial measures in the justice systems. These rules advocate reductions in imprisonment and the development of community-based programs. Interestingly, many of the provisions contained in these conventions and standards we use are quite similar to policies governing the juvenile justice system that have been adopted by the American Bar Association during the past several years.[20]

## LEGAL REPRESENTATION OF CHILDREN IN THE JUVENILE AND CRIMINAL JUSTICE SYSTEMS

Only in 1967 did the Supreme Court acknowledge a juvenile's right to counsel, in *In re Gault*.[21] In a famous line in that decision, Justice Fortas declares that "under our Constitution, the condition of being a boy does not justify a kangaroo court."[22] Essentially, *Gault* held that despite the rehabilitative rhetoric of the juvenile court, children faced and often received punitive consequences. Therefore, the Court determined that children required safeguards in the juvenile court, including access to counsel.[23] Several other cases regarding the juvenile court were decided before and after *Gault.* These decisions provided youth with a hearing before being transferred to the adult criminal court[24] and required that evidence of a crime be proven beyond a reasonable doubt,[25] but they did not provide children with the right to trial by jury.[26] In conjunction with *Gault*, these cases were viewed as an opportunity to impose minimum standards and due process rights for children in the juvenile court, starting with access to counsel. As Snyder says, through *Gault* the "Court teaches that even the most well-intentioned court cannot replace the child's attorney when it comes to protecting and promoting the child's legal interests."[27] Not only has the absence of substantive standards resulted in the lack of individual treatment, but it has also failed to produce fair and effective procedures.

Human rights provisions are clear in their agreement with *Gault* about the right to counsel for children alleged to have committed criminal offenses and children who face the deprivation of their liberty. Article 37.d of the Convention on the Rights of the Child states that "every child deprived of his or her liberty shall have the right to prompt access to legal and other appropriate assistance." Article 40.2.b.ii states that every child alleged to have committed a crime shall "have legal or other appropriate assistance in the preparation and presentation of his or her defense." Rule 15.1 of the UN Standard Minimum Rules for the Administration of Juvenile Justice states that "throughout the proceedings the juvenile shall have the right to be represented by a legal adviser or to apply for free legal aid where there is provision for such aid in the country." Similarly, a number of U.S. standards call for the appointment of counsel for children in the juvenile court at the earliest stages of proceedings.[28] However, the available evidence indicates that this often does not happen.

## Importance of Counsel

Recent juvenile code changes signify an increasingly important role for attorneys in all stages of juvenile proceedings. These code changes have reoriented the mission of the juvenile court toward more punitive goals.[29] Between 1992 and 1997 alone, every state and the District of Columbia enacted legislation easing the process of transferring children to the adult criminal court; providing for mandatory minimum, determinate, or blended sentences; making correctional programming more punitive; and/or increasing access to juvenile records and proceedings.[30] In a study of code changes in four states, Shook found that legislative changes in each of these areas interact to increase the costs associated with juvenile crime.[31] Additionally, he found that states vary greatly in their strategies for dealing with juvenile crime at various points in the system, including transfer, sentencing, and correctional programming.

The processing of juveniles in the juvenile court has steadily increased over the last several decades, despite drastic fluctuations in the crime rate and a significant decline since 1995.[32] Increasing numbers of cases in the system raise the likelihood that more youth will be sanctioned. This is evidenced by the increase in the rate of children incarcerated in public or private facilities at the same time that juvenile crime rates continue to drop. Thus, it is apparent that both legislative provisions and court practice have increased the costs of crime. The increasing role of prosecutors in the juvenile court further adds to the costs associated with juvenile crime. Even in the juvenile court, prosecutors primarily maintain a public safety perspective with regard to case decisions, influencing their processing of cases away from serving the best interests of the child.[33]

Defense attorneys can serve to protect youth against these increased costs. They can appear early in cases to reduce the likelihood of pretrial detention, transfer, or the filing of a formal petition. Attorneys can prepare strong cases, negotiate pleas, and advocate for beneficial disposition alternatives. Furthermore, they can remain with their cases after disposition, advocating for lower placements and filing appeals when necessary. Because defense attorneys are often the party that speaks for the juvenile, their ability to speak for the needs and interests of the juvenile is essential to providing juveniles with a voice in the proceedings. Finally, a strong and organized defense bar can also move beyond individual cases and advocate for policy change at the local, state, and national levels. Consequently, it is increasingly important that juveniles receive access to adequate representation at all stages of proceedings.

## Access to and Effectiveness of Counsel

Juveniles are either represented by public defenders, contract attorneys, or retained counsel. Retained counsel is rare in the juvenile court due to the high correlation between class and court processing. Contract attorneys (or appointed attorneys) are assigned cases and paid by the court and are typically sole practitioners. The existence of public defender or legal aid offices varies by jurisdiction. Public defender offices typically provide centralized structure and support to juvenile attorneys but suffer from a variety of other limitations.

Although the appearance of counsel in the juvenile court has increased dramatically since *Gault*, counsel still does not appear in a significant number of cases, and when it does appear, many factors—structural, legal, and cultural—limit its effectiveness. Before *Gault*, counsel appeared in the juvenile court in 5 percent of all cases.[34] In their national study of juvenile courts following *Gault*, Sarri and Hasenfeld report that counsel was only employed full-time in 17 percent of the courts and part-time in 11 percent of the courts.[35] Nationwide data on the access to counsel are currently not available. However, available data indicate that counsel does not appear in many instances.[36]

There are numerous explanations for the lack of access to counsel for children in the juvenile court. Some of these explanations are related to the lack of available public and contract attorneys in a court or to the lack of court resources to supply defense counsel to each youth, but often the deficiency may simply be the result of the court not providing adequate information about how a juvenile can formally request an attorney.[37] Other explanations are related to issues involving the administration of justice in juvenile courts. For example, in courts that are informal and have a culture reflecting this informality, court actors may advise juveniles not to use counsel. Parental wishes and the inability of children to fully comprehend the importance of counsel also may explain why juveniles do not access defense counsel in juvenile proceedings. Finally, children who are poor or whose family do not strongly advocate for them are often the least likely to have a counsel. Many of these children will be held for extended detention both pre- and postadjudication while awaiting placement.

The ineffectiveness of counsel in juvenile courts is a second issue that requires examination.[38] Feld and the ABA found effective counsel to be lacking in the juvenile court, and both identify a number of reasons that explain the ineffectiveness of counsel.[39] In public defender offices, experienced juvenile attorneys are rare as tenure in juvenile courts is typically less than two years. Juvenile caseloads among public defenders are extremely high, and training is limited. When contract attorneys represent a large number of cases, they may become beholden to the court for continued assignment of new cases, thus negating their ability to function independently for their clients. Attorneys are appointed at various points in the proceedings, limiting their opportunities to affect cases early in the process. This is crucial for cases where preadjudication detention may be unnecessary. Postdispositional representation is lacking, as most attorneys do not participate in postdispositional proceedings and many contract attorneys end representation after the disposition. Juvenile attorneys typically do not appeal cases, and many attorneys are not even authorized to take appeals. The lack of appellate cases reduces the ability to develop further legal precedent governing the juvenile court. Currently, children are not uniformly provided with counsel in accord with human rights or United States legal standards. Defense counsel can assist children in all stages of the proceedings as well as monitor postdisposition conditions. Attention must be paid to structural factors limiting the provision of counsel and the quality and effectiveness of counsel—attention through both research and a commitment to provide resources, training, and involvement of defense counsel in the juvenile court.

## TRANSFERRING CHILDREN TO THE ADULT CRIMINAL COURT

The transfer of children to the adult criminal court represents another area where human rights standards are relevant to juvenile justice. Specifically, according to article 40.3 of the Convention on the Rights of the Child, "states shall seek to promote the establishment of laws, procedures, authorities and institutions specifically applicable to children alleged as, accused of, or recognized as having infringed the penal law." Articles 40.3.a–b and 40.4 further state that this system should establish a minimum age for children to maintain the capacity to infringe on the penal law, that measures should seek to process children outside of formal proceedings wherever possible, and that a range of dispositional alternatives should be created to ensure that children are being treated appropriately based upon their circumstances. Rule 2.3 of the UN Standard Minimum Rules for the Administration of Juvenile Justice similarly requires that states create a separate system of justice to adjudicate the criminal offenses of children and that this system be designed to meet their basic needs. These provisions have been read to require a distinct system of justice for *all* children.[40]

The United States does not adhere to the requirement to maintain a separate system of justice for all children. The borders between the juvenile system and the adult criminal justice system have increasingly become porous, as children are transferred to the adult criminal court system by a variety of actors; under a variety of criteria (or sometimes no criteria); often with no minimum age specified by the transfer provision; and for a range of person, property, and drug offenses.[41]

*Kent v. United States* addressed the issue of standards and criteria for transferring youth to the adult criminal court, and the Court held that transfer required a hearing comporting to minimum standards of due process.[42] Known as *judicial waiver*, this mechanism provides increased protections to children considered for transfer because it requires a judicial hearing and set of criteria that must be considered in the hearing based on the evidence presented.

Many states, however, have increasingly enacted or expanded alternative transfer mechanisms over the last several decades. *Statutory exclusion* involves the state's setting of age and offense criteria in the juvenile code that excludes youth meeting those criteria from the jurisdiction of the juvenile court. This mechanism relies merely on the age and offense as indicators of adult responsibility, not a hearing where evidence can be presented about the circumstances of the youth. *Prosecutorial discretion* provisions allow prosecutors to determine the choice of forum in which to file a case. Under these provisions, prosecutors can make the decision without the necessity of a hearing, providing prosecutors with ever-increasing power in the juvenile court. These two mechanisms serve to decrease the power of judges to make decisions regarding transfer; they both focus primarily on offense-related criteria in the transfer decision; and they both take away the due process protections provided to juveniles in the transfer process.

Transfer legislation has been a site of major change in the rules governing the juvenile court over the last several decades. Between 1992 and 1997, forty-four states and the District of Columbia enacted at least one provision easing the process of transferring children to the adult criminal court for trial. The lowering of minimum-age requirements, or otherwise expanding the population of juveniles eligible to be treated as adults, has been a primary focus of the transfer legislation. Currently, twenty-three states do not specify a minimum age for transfer for one or more of the offense classifications in their transfer statutes.[43] The minimum age in the remaining states ranges from ten to fifteen years and varies by offense and transfer mechanism. The number of states without a minimum-age limit does not even include a state such as Michigan, which sets a minimum age of fourteen years for a juvenile to be tried as an adult in the criminal court but allows for juveniles to be tried as adults in the juvenile court at any age. An example of the risks of this provision can be found in several recent Michigan cases. Michigan maintains a prosecutorial discretion statute that allows prosecutors to determine whether to try a juvenile as a juvenile in the juvenile court, as an adult in the juvenile court, or as an adult in the criminal court. Under this statute, Nathaniel Abraham was tried as an adult in the juvenile court for an offense he committed at the age of eleven, despite the fact that he was evaluated and found to be functioning at the level of a six-year-old.[44] According to the statute, the judge held the discretion to impose an adult sentence, a juvenile sentence, or a blended adult–juvenile sentence and chose the juvenile sentence. Although Nathaniel did not receive the adult or blended sentence, he is now locked up in a maximum-security institution until the age of twenty-one.[45] In another Michigan case, a thirteen-year-old boy was tried as an adult in the juvenile court, convicted of second-degree murder, and received a life sentence.[46]

The recent trend has been to focus on more offense- and neglect-based characteristics of the youth, particularly with statutory exclusion and prosecutorial discretion provisions. In addition, the trend has been to shift power from judges to prosecutors in the transfer decision, as many states use statutory exclusion and prosecutorial discretion for more serious offenses and use judicial discretion as a blanket provision for juveniles charged with an act that would be a felony offense if committed by an adult.[47] This shift has led to numerous questions regarding the fairness and focus of the decision-making process.

Once convicted in the adult criminal court, juveniles are often subject to adult sanctions. In an in-depth study of four Midwestern states, Shook found that transferred children were subject to straight adult sentences in three states and subject to juvenile sentences only under particular circumstances in the fourth.[48] Increasingly, more states are allowing blended sentencing, permitting judges either at the juvenile or criminal court level to decide whether to impose a juvenile or adult sentence. Some states even add a third option where a juvenile can be sentenced as both a juvenile and an adult, with the adult sentence stayed, pending the successful completion of the juvenile sentence.[49]

## Processing Children in Adult Courts

It is estimated that approximately 210,000 to 260,000 children under the age of eighteen were processed in the adult court in the mid- to late 1990s.[50] This includes between 30,000 and 40,000 transferred juveniles and between 180,000 and 220,000 juveniles tried in states that end juvenile court jurisdiction before the age of eighteen. These estimates reflect an increase from a previous estimate in which approximately 200,000 children were processed in the adult criminal court in 1991. The number of transfers alone reflects a substantial increase from 1978, when there were approximately 12,600 transfers.[51] Data are currently available on children transferred through judicial waiver but not for statutory exclusions and prosecutorial transfers. The lack of data is a substantial limitation to understanding the treatment of children in the adult criminal court. From what we know about judicial waiver on a national scale, between 1988 and 1994 the total number of children waived through the judicial waiver mechanism increased from 6,700 to 11,700. From 1994 to 1997, this number dropped to 8,400, corresponding to decreases in the juvenile crime rate.[52]

Data available on the outcomes for children convicted in the adult court indicate that juveniles are often treated equally or more punitively for many offenses than are adults. Among defendants convicted of aggravated assaults in 1994, children were more likely to receive a prison sentence than adults, 74 percent to 49 percent. For other offense categories, there was relatively little difference in the likelihood of receiving a prison sentence. Children sentenced to prison for property crimes received a similar length of sentence as did adults, but for weapons, drug, and violent offenses they received longer sentences. For many offenses, children sentenced to jail or probation received longer sentences than adults did.[53] This may in part be a function of transferred youths' having committed more serious offenses, but it is also an indication that these youths are not receiving a youth discount in the criminal court.

The human rights implications of transfer are dramatic. Human rights standards clearly indicate that a separate system of justice should be established for all children. Additionally, standards state that children should be treated in the least restrictive ways possible. Despite such a system for children in the United States, the boundaries between it and the adult criminal court are increasingly porous. Children may now be tried in the adult criminal court at very young ages and for a variety of offenses. Significant numbers are processed in the criminal court for property, drug, and public order offenses. Children are often treated more harshly in the criminal court, receiving prison sentences more often than adults and receiving sentences longer than those of adults. Whereas *Kent* sought to standardize transfer decisions through judicial hearings, current practice allows the prosecutor to make transfer decisions in many situations. Within a "get tough on crime" climate, these decisions often reflect law and order, not the best interests of the child. It is a situation where children are treated as adults, without clear standards or rationale, clearly in violation of human rights provisions that seek to treat children differently and in the least restrictive way possible.

## OVERREPRESENTATION OF YOUTH OF COLOR

One of the most critical issues facing the entire justice system in the United State is the disproportionate representation of persons of color in all phases of the system. The Convention on the Elimination of all Forms of Racial Discrimination is particularly applicable in the United States because youth of color are increasingly overrepresented in the juvenile justice system relative to their proportion in the total youth population. The federal Juvenile Justice and Delinquency Prevention Act of 1974, as amended in 1988, mandates that states who participate in programs under the act make "every effort" to achieve proportional representation of youth of color in the juvenile justice system in order to continue to receive funding. As of 2001 youth of color compose 36 percent of the total juvenile population but 62 percent in detention facilities and 67 percent confined in juvenile institutions.[54] Disproportionality is greater in the juvenile system than in adult criminal justice. In several states (California, Connecticut, Louisiana, New Jersey, New Mexico, and New York), the proportion of youth of color confined in training schools exceeds 80 percent, so unless some substantial action is undertaken, it could well reach 100 percent nationally as the proportion of youth of color in the total population becomes the majority.[55]

## Factors Explaining Overrepresentation of Youth of Color

Serious personal and property felonies remain a small proportion of juvenile crime, so the severe response to delinquency is punitive and particularly so for youth of color. Examining the rate of juvenile confinement during the past century reveals findings that deserve further attention. There was a steep increase in the rate of confinement between 1950 and 1970 in the period in which the adolescent population grew rapidly and the juvenile crime rate also increased substantially. Then in 1970, following the passage of the Juvenile Justice and Delinquency Prevention Act, there was a sharp decline in confinement until 1990. However the "deinstitutionalization effect" of the 1970s and 1980s occurred for white youth while the rate of confinement for youth of color continued to increase. In actuality, there was a nearly 80 percent reduction in Anglo-American institutionalization and a 90 percent increase in confinement of youth of color.

Bonczar and Beck estimate that 5.1 percent of all persons born in the United States in the mid-1990s can expect to be incarcerated in a prison, but 28.1 percent of all black males can expect to be incarcerated.[56] For African American males, that number is six times the rate of whites and eight times the rate for white women. In fact, by age twenty-five, 15.9 percent of black males, 6.3 percent of Hispanic males, and 1.7 percent of white males can expect to have served time in a state or federal prison. Miller estimates that 75 percent of all eighteen-year-old African American males in Washington, D.C., can look forward to being arrested and jailed at least once before they reach age thirty-five.[57] The reality of these predictions is supported by the fact that in 1994, 11.7 percent of African American males aged twenty to twenty-nine were incarcerated.[58]

While numerous study findings support the argument that youth of color are punished for crimes at disproportional rates, different explanations are provided about the causes of disproportionality:

1. Youth of color are said to have higher rates of offending, especially for more serious and violent crimes.[59]

2. Crime levels are higher in neighborhoods where poor people and people of color live and where police are likely to do more surveillance.[60] Bynum, Wordes, and Corley show that the degree of concentration of people of color in an area is correlated with increases in apprehension, even when controlling for crime rates.[61]

3. Factors used in decision making to confine reflect the lack of opportunity for minority youth in education and employment, the quality of life in inner-city ghettos, the pervasiveness of the drug culture, and housing segregation.[62]

4. Juvenile justice agencies treat minority youth more severely than nonminority youth, particularly in the early stages of processing.[63]

5. The application of structured decision making may inadvertently result in the disproportionate confinement of minority youth. There may be discriminatory attributions about the behavior of minority youth or about the characteristics of their families (e.g., single-female-headed families).[64] Bridges and Steen in 1998 found that the attitudes probation officers held toward juveniles were significantly influenced by the race of the offender.[65] Nunn argues that the oppression of African American youth (especially males) appears normal because we have been socialized to undervalue the lives and realities of African Americans.[66]

6. Diversion and similar community-based programs are more frequently available in suburban communities that have lower proportions of youth of color. The lack of such programs in inner-city areas results in more local youth being processed in the formal justice system and thus institutionalized.[67]

Not only does the disproportionate presence of youth of color occur at the time of apprehension or detention, but it often increases at later stages of juvenile justice processing: adjudication, commitment, placement in public/private facilities, and reintegration services.[68] Even when controlling for class, family structure, and offense, there was a residual effect associated with race. The differential processing of persons of color by both the juvenile and the adult criminal justice system is a matter of increasing national concern. Despite the provisions and policy priorities of the Juvenile Justice and Delinquency Prevention Act, little concrete action has been taken to reverse this pattern of minority overrepresentation in the justice system, in arrests, jail, or detention; court convictions; commitments to secure facilities; and probation or parole.[69] In fact, in 1999 a serious effort was initiated to eliminate the policy priority of reducing minority overrepresentation in the juvenile justice system through Senate bill 254, but it did not pass.

## Human Rights Implications—Overrepresentation of Youth of Color

Youth of color are overrepresented in the juvenile justice system from the initial stages of arrest through to confinement in juvenile institutions and ultimately to commitment to adult prisons. Moreover, they remain longer than whites and tend to receive fewer services when they return to their communities following confinement. Discrimination in violation of the International Convention on the Elimination of Racial Discrimination is clearly evident and increasing on a rather dramatic rate from year to year. By midcentury, more than 50 percent of youth in the United States will be children of color, but it is possible that their proportion in the justice system will be far higher. Attention to organizational, policy, and community variables will be necessary to change these practices, not just individual-level action, because the former are critical in justice system processing.

The international convention is specific about racial discrimination. Article 2 states that governments are to amend, rescind, or nullify any laws and regulations that have the effect of creating or perpetuating racial discrimination. Thus far, few policies or practices have been implemented to reverse racial discrimination in the justice system, nor is there even serious acknowledgment of the problem. The CRC positive rights provisions are also implicated because youth of color require the same guarantees as those of white youth for youth well-being. The convention also specifies a number of civil rights for all people, such as the right to education, equal participation, and access to any public place.

## CONDITIONS OF CONFINEMENT

In the mid-1990s, Lerman reported that there were 230,700 youth confined in twenty-four-hour institutions on any given day, with approximately 75 percent of that population in correctional or detention facilities.[70] This number results in a rate of 336 per 100,000 youth, probably the highest rate of juvenile incarceration in the world. It is also important to consider the total number of youth who are incarcerated in a year since that is much higher than a single-day count. For example, it can be estimated that 85,000 juveniles spend some time in an adult jail or prison in one year, although many remain for only a few weeks in jails.[71] Nonetheless, the impact of those few days can be grave, as we had reported in an earlier study.[72]

The several international conventions provide excellent guidelines against which we can assess conditions in United States' facilities, both juvenile and adult. Recent reports of Amnesty International,[73] Human Rights Watch,[74] and the Youth Law Center[75] document the intolerable conditions for juveniles in many U.S. juvenile correctional facilities, from detention through to confinement in training schools and other correctional institutions. However, these reports do not represent new phenomena. A national study of juvenile courts and correctional institutions in the 1970s reported widespread human rights violations, increased suicide attempts, and lack of treatment and educational programming.[76] In addition, facilities were often located far from the juveniles' homes so that parents and relatives could not maintain frequent contact.[77] Although the United States has been negligent about signing and ratifying many of the conventions, several state courts have charged juvenile and adult correctional programs with violations of the Eighth Amendment against cruel and inhumane punishment. Recently, Judge Mark Doherty ordered that a private facility for juveniles in Louisiana be closed because of the severe abuse of juvenile inmates.[78] Similar conditions were reported for facilities in Mississippi and Georgia, but the facilities remain open.[79]

Some of the most egregious violations at present occur in facilities that operate under private ownership with little surveillance by state administrative agencies or by committing courts. Juveniles may be placed in solitary confinement for extended periods with no opportunity for physical exercise or participation in programming. Investigations by reporters about two adult facilities in Michigan within the past year clearly indicated daily and continuing human rights violations of nearly every type that is prohibited by all of the conventions and rules that we have referred to.[80] Cruel and inhuman punishment in violation of the Eighth Amendment of the U.S. Constitution continues without any attempt to stop or punish those responsible.

The lack of interest in juveniles by civil rights attorneys and the punitive laws that prohibit suits against the state or the facility inhibit exposure of much abuse. The Prison Litigation Reform Act of 1995 has stymied actions on behalf of juvenile and adult offenders. A report by Amnesty International in 1998 documents the many violations of human rights in the justice system, affecting juveniles in all parts of the United States. There are almost weekly reports in the media in the majority of states about punitive issues of confinement for juveniles, both delinquents and child welfare youth. Among the most common types of abuses found by Amnesty International (1998)[81] and others in both juvenile and adult correctional facilities are the following, all of which violate provisions of the CRC, the American Convention on Human Rights, and the International Covenant on Civil and Political Rights, along with the UN Standard Minimum Rules for the Administration of Juvenile Justice:

1. Severe overcrowding exists such that peer interactions become conflict-
ual and physical well-being is threatened. Gymnasiums, classrooms, and
halls are being used for housing, and many facilities have limited, if any,
access to outdoor areas. In adult facilities, double and triple bunking may
result in serious physical and sexual abuse of juveniles.
2. Denials of proper food, clothing, health care, and so forth, act as control
measures. Violence, sexual abuse, and fighting among peers are allowed
in institutions, often between racial and ethnic groups.
3. Staff abuse, both physical and sexual, often does not result in termination, suspension, or other penalties.
4. Inmates are ordered to extended periods of segregation and isolation, often in places of serious sensory deprivation.
5. Denial of appropriate education and education required by law is common, especially special education and vocational training. Lack of the
latter means that many youth will be ill-prepared for employment when
they are released.
6. Health care that has been prescribed is often denied, particularly for mentally ill youth. Lack of proper health care in institutions is a common situation, even for such things as eye and dental examinations. Juveniles are
not provided with regular physical examinations, which are necessary because this is a population at risk due to poverty and lack of previous
health care.[82]
7. Punishments, injurious restraints, and denial of privileges are cruel and
inhumane.
8. Lack of separation of children from adults in adult facilities result in frequent reports of severe abuse by adult inmates.
9. There is a lack of proper nutrition for growing youth, as well as physical
fitness activities.
10. Children convicted of minor or status crimes are held for extended periods and are comingled with youth charged with serious crimes.
11. Exposure to degrading personal searches is common in many facilities.

## Children in Adult Facilities

With respect to youth in adult facilities, the types of punishment and abuse
are not unlike those in juvenile facilities, but they are often more extensive
and continue over long periods. Isolation in segregation units may be one
of the most serious types of punishment, judging from the frequency of sui-
cide attempts and deaths. In addition, where youth are comingled with
adults, sexual abuse is often predatory and violent with the resulting risk of

youths' contracting sexually transmitted diseases in addition to being trau-matized.[83] The use of torture in the form of "stunt belts" and other para-phernalia remains widely practiced. Also, because juveniles resist the rigid scheduling in adult prisons, they are in frequent conflict with staff and end up receiving many "misconducts" that lead to longer stays and placement in high-security facilities, regardless of the crime for which they were com-mitted. Classification systems are such that juveniles may be assigned to facilities on the basis of control requirements rather than needs of the youth.[84]

The lack of any appropriate educational programming for youth who are supposed to be enrolled in school full-time is likely to be found in most adult facilities, especially local jails. Parent and Leiter note that living space, secu-rity control of suicidal behavior, and health care are also lacking.[85] The sui-cide rate for juveniles held in jails is five times that of the general population and eight times that for juveniles in detention facilities.[86] Sexual assault, staff beatings, and weapons attacks were also more common in adult facilities than in juvenile facilities. In adult facilities overall, punishment, torture, and abuse of juveniles are more common, despite their frequency in juvenile institu-tions. Last, juveniles are often sentenced to longer periods for the same crimes than are adults and are often subject to high security because of their adolescent behavior.[87]

The conditions of confinement for juveniles in both juvenile and adult fa-cilities violate many provisions of all of the five conventions noted earlier. What is probably equally disturbing is that little interest is shown through-out the system with adhering to those standards or to even knowing what they are. Compliance with international covenants is complex in the United States because the federal government does not have authority to intervene in the states unless there are challenges due to potential violations of the U.S. Constitution, as in Eighth Amendment violations of cruel and inhumane pun-ishment. There is no central authority charged with systematically monitor-ing the facilities so that the conditions of confinement do not further harm children. During the past quarter-century the majority of state legislatures and executive branches have emphasized punishment and law enforcement rather than rehabilitation or social justice. The federal government could shift toward greater emphasis on rehabilitation, especially for juveniles, by providing incentives to the states to comply with provisions of the CRC and the other conventions. However, the reluctance to sign the international con-ventions or to comply with provisions appears in many instances to be the result of federal political decisions that had little to do with juvenile incar-ceration policy.

## INTERFACE OF CHILD WELFARE WITH
## THE JUVENILE JUSTICE SYSTEM

The juvenile court was established to serve abused, neglected, and dependent children, as well as delinquents. The dual responsibility was based partly on the assumption that the court was to serve and habilitate all children at risk, following the concept of *parens patriae*. Woodhouse's concepts of positive and negative rights seem particularly applicable in these cases because the state is obliged to care for these children, since parental rights have often been terminated, but it is also obliged not to harm them in any way.[88] However, it was recognized that the children needing protective services were victims and therefore deserved care, not punishment. Unfortunately, one unanticipated consequence of this dual responsibility was the drift of protective services clientele to the juvenile justice system, especially those in adolescence. According to the U.S. Children's Bureau, 1.2 percent of the total national population of foster care cases are "AWOL" from placement on any given day.[89] When located, these children often end up in detention, charged with having "violated an order of the court." Thus, a juvenile justice career might begin inadvertently unless the human rights issue of their victimization is noted and addressed. Their victimization has been observed to have long-term as well as short-term consequences.[90]

In 2002 amendments to the federal Juvenile Justice and Delinquency Prevention Act (PL 107-273) recognized the existence of the problem of child welfare clients in the juvenile justice system. The amendments further acknowledged the need to establish policies to provide treatment to children since their treatment falls under federal child welfare legislation as well as juvenile justice statutes. Moreover, the amendments obligate treatment services for all juvenile justice clientele who have experienced child abuse or maltreatment. This provision is particularly important because research findings indicate that most juvenile justice clients, especially females, have experienced neglect or abuse at some point in their lives. States accepting funding are authorized to fund prevention and treatment programs for all of their clientele. They are also to collaborate with child welfare agencies in innovative programming.

The several conventions could be effectively utilized to serve both positive and negative rights for dependent, abused, and neglected children. Children in need of protection do not belong in the juvenile justice system, and barriers should be established to prevent their intake. In addition, alternative mechanisms need to be created to provide care and treatment for them if they do enter so that negative outcomes do not result. Kilkelly argues that European legal structures have been created to address these children under the provisions of the CRC and the European Convention for the Protection of Human Rights.[91] The American Convention on Human Rights also provides for care of these children in need of protection for this hemisphere. The reliance on state authority for most of juvenile justice and child welfare policy and programming deserves further challenge under the U.S. Constitution as well as the international conventions.

## CHILDREN AND THE DEATH PENALTY AND LIFE-WITHOUT-PAROLE SENTENCES

International law clearly prohibits the use of the death penalty for anyone under the age of eighteen. The International Covenant on Civil and Political Rights, ratified by the United States in 1992, states that "the sentence of death shall not be imposed for crimes committed by persons below eighteen years of age." Similar provisions are contained in the CRC and the other conventions and standards that we have considered. The United States signed the International Covenant on Civil and Political Rights but in ratification reserved the right to execute individuals who commit a capital offense under the age of eighteen. Similarly, article 37.a of the CRC states that "neither capital punishment nor life imprisonment without possibility of release shall be imposed for offenses committed by persons below eighteen years of age." Signed but not ratified by the United States, this action has been widely criticized by children's rights advocates and has isolated the United States globally. In 2000 only three countries were known to have executed juveniles: the United States, Congo, and Iran.[92]

Since 1992, eighteen individuals in five states were executed for crimes committed before the age of eighteen.[93] In 2005, nineteen states permitted the use of the death penalty against individuals under the age of eighteen. The federal government and a number of other states set the minimum age at eighteen, but in 1989 the U.S. Supreme Court allowed the death penalty to be applied to sixteen- and seventeen-year-olds in *Stanford v. Kentucky*.[94] According to Amnesty International, several states and the federal government discussed bills that would lower the minimum age for the death penalty.[95]

On March 1, 2005, the U.S. Supreme Court reversed its previous refusals and decided to end the execution of juvenile capital offenders who were under the age of eighteen at the time of commitment of the offense. It decided juvenile executions are a violation of the U.S. Constitution's ban on cruel and inhuman punishment. As of 2005, there were seventy-two inmates on death row nationwide for crimes committed when they were under eighteen years old.

Life-without-parole sentences for juveniles are increasingly said to be Eighth Amendment violations because such sentences inevitably mean many years of incarceration for most juveniles. Youth as young as thirteen have received such sentences in recent years, and changes in transfer provisions have increased the likelihood that more and younger children will be at risk for long sentences.[96] In a recent Illinois case of Leon Miller, the appellants successfully used both the international conventions and customary international law to challenge the sentence of a fifteen-year-old accomplice to a crime.[97] Applications of human rights provisions need to be given further consideration in the cases challenging life-without-parole sentences along with consideration of Eighth Amendment violations for cruel and inhuman punishment.

The growing interest in the use of human rights conventions to challenge life-without-parole sentences needs to be expedited and broadened. The United States became increasingly isolated in the global community because it maintained its authority to execute juveniles despite the fact that all five conventions and the standards condemn both death penalty and life-without-parole sentences for juveniles. It is notable that the U.S. Supreme Court in its 2005 decision referred to international custom as well as the U.S. Constitution.

## CONCLUSION

This discussion highlights the lack of adherence to human rights conventions and standards in the juvenile justice and child welfare systems in the United States. International law provides a framework to measure compliance of policy and practice regarding the treatment of children in the justice systems throughout the world. However, the United States does not adhere to the conventions analyzed in this chapter—access, representation, transfer, minority overrepresentation, conditions of confinement, child welfare overlap, life-without-parole sentences—despite its criticism of other countries for human rights violations. Specifically, the following conclusions may be made with regard to U.S. adherence to human rights standards:

1. Despite the rising costs associated with juvenile crime, children are not afforded access to counsel at all stages of court processing, and sufficient attention is not given to ensure that when provided, counsel is properly equipped to provide effective representation to children.

2. Differences in the administration of juvenile justice and in appellate court decisions negatively affect the ability of attorneys to effectively represent children.
3. Boundaries between the juvenile court and the adult criminal court have become porous, as children are being transferred at younger ages for a variety of person, property, drug, and public-order offenses by a variety of decision makers and often according to offense-related criteria or no criteria. Additionally, evidence indicates that when children are convicted in the adult criminal court, they often receive stricter punishments than do their adult counterparts for the same crimes.
4. Little is known about the treatment of children in the adult criminal court, including the number transferred, the mechanisms of transfer, how they are processed by the system, the effectiveness of defense counsel for children in the adult criminal court, and the outcomes for children processed in the adult criminal court. The lack of attention to human rights violations in this area is notorious. Moreover, state legislatures and prosecutors proceed against juveniles for minor offenses that are wholly inappropriate for the adult court.
5. Conditions of confinement in both juvenile and adult facilities violate many provisions of the conventions that we have examined with respect to punishment, abuse, torture, lack of required programming, overcrowding, segregation, and lack of appropriate supervision. Systems of independent monitoring and evaluation are required to obtain compliance with the provisions of the conventions, and the federal government could demand such compliance as a condition of its appropriations to the states under the Juvenile Justice and Delinquency Prevention Act and several of the block grants that are provided to the states for correctional programming.
6. Overrepresentation of youth of color is one of the most serious problems in the U.S. justice system and reflects longstanding institutionalized racism. This problem requires immediate federal action, as well as state action, if changes are to be effected. The federal authorities could initiate systematic monitoring that would provide the needed information about where and how changes could be effected in accord with the provisions of the U.S. Constitution, the international conventions, and the Juvenile Justice and Delinquency Prevention Act.
7. Despite the clarity of international prohibitions on life-without-parole sentences for juveniles and the fact that the United States has signed the Convention on the Rights of the Child, which prohibits such sentences, the United States continues these sentences for crimes committed while under the age of eighteen years.

8. Crime rates by juveniles have declined significantly since the late 1990s, but the processing and incarceration of juveniles have increased in the juvenile justice and adult justice systems. In addition, reduced funding for programs has resulted in deterioration of conditions of confinement.

9. The best recommendation for immediate action is for concerted action to dramatically reduce the numbers of juveniles who are incarcerated in both juvenile and adult facilities because the majority of the youth being held could be placed in community-based programs, residential and non-residential. Implementation of several of our recommendations regarding court processing could effect some reduction, but more important will be advocacy for legislative change, for restorative justice programs, and for organizational mechanisms to reduce the flow of juveniles into the system. The long-term benefit to the society from such a policy change is both necessary and immeasurable.

10. International human rights conventions and standards provide excellent frameworks to address the multiple injustices and inequalities that exist within the juvenile and adult justice systems in the United States. Hodgkin and Newell have prepared a handbook for promoting the implementation of the CRC.[98] When viewing the system through this lens, it becomes clear that significant reform is needed in all the areas that we outline. Human rights frameworks provide a powerful tool for effecting these changes to ensure both positive and negative rights for juveniles. Concerted action by public interest groups and professional practitioners, as well as concerned policymakers, is needed to effect change because of the powerful opposition that has maintained the United States' lack of attention to its human rights violations toward its own children.

## NOTES

The volume editors added information on the U.S. Supreme Court decision on March 1, 2005.

1. J. Paul Martin, ed., *Twenty-Five+ Human Rights Documents* (New York: Center for the Study of Human Rights, Columbia University, 2001).

2. M. Rosenheim, "The Modern American Juvenile Court," in *A Century of Juvenile Justice*, ed. Margaret Rosenheim et al. (Chicago: University of Chicago Press, 2002), 341–60.

3. Jill Mehlbye and Lode Walgrave, eds., *Confronting Youth in Europe: Juvenile Crime and Juvenile Justice* (Copenhagen, Denmark: AFK, 1998); M. Rosenheim, "Juvenile Justice in Japan: A Historical and Cross-Cultural Perspective," in Rosenheim

et al., *A Century of Juvenile Justice*, 360–81; John Eekelaar, "Child Endangerment and Child Protection in England and Wales," in Rosenheim et al., *A Century of Juvenile Justice*, 381–412; Anthony Bottoms, "The Divergent Development of Juvenile Justice Policy and Practice in England and Scotland," in Rosenheim et al., *A Century of Juvenile Justice*, 413–504.

4. D. S. Tanenhaus, "The Evolution of Transfer out of the Juvenile Court," in *The Changing Borders of Juvenile Justice: Transfer of Adolescents to the Criminal Court*, ed. J. Fagan and F. E. Zimring (Chicago: University of Chicago Press, 2000), 13–43.

5. A. Platt, *The Child Savers: The Invention of Delinquency*, 2nd ed. (Chicago: University of Chicago Press, 1977); E. Scott, "The Legal Construction of Childhood," in Rosenheim et al., *A Century of Juvenile Justice*.

6. D. J. Rothman, *Conscience and Convenience: The Asylum and Its Alternative in Progressive America* (Boston: Little, Brown, 1980); F. A. Allen, *The Decline of the Rehabilitative Ideal: Penal Policy and Social Purpose* (New Haven, Conn.: Yale University Press, 1981).

7. The most important Supreme Court decisions of this period include *Kent v. U.S.* 383 U.S. 541 (1966); *In re Gault* 387 U.S. 1 (1967); *In re Winship* 397 U.S. 352 (1970). The first major juvenile justice legislation, the Juvenile Justice and Delinquency Act, passed in 1974.

8. G. W. Downs, *Bureaucracy, Innovation, and Public Policy* (Lexington, Mass.: Lexington Books, 1976).

9. R. D. Vinter, G. Downs, and J. Hall, *Juvenile Corrections in the States: Residential Programs and Deinstitutionalization* (Ann Arbor: National Assessment of Juvenile Corrections, University of Michigan, 1976); R. Sarri and Y. Hasenfeld, *Brought to Justice? Juveniles, the Courts, and the Law* (Ann Arbor: University of Michigan, 1976).

10. P. Lerman, "Twentieth-Century Developments in America's Institutional Systems for Youth in Trouble," in Rosenheim et al., *A Century of Juvenile Justice*.

11. Franklin E. Zimring, *American Youth Violence* (New York: Oxford University Press, 1998).

12. B. C. Feld, "The Juvenile Court Meets the Principle of Offense: Legislative Changes in Juvenile Waiver Status," in *Bad Kids: Race and the Transformation of the Juvenile Court*, ed. B. C. Feld (New York: Oxford University Press, 1999).

13. H. N. Snyder, "Juvenile Arrests 1980–2000," *Juvenile Justice Bulletin* (Washington, D.C.: U.S. Department of Justice, Office of Juvenile Justice and Delinquency Prevention, Bureau of Justice Statistics, 2002).

14. As of 2001, arrests of juveniles had declined to levels observed in 1983, even for violent crime. H. N. Snyder, "Juvenile Arrests, 2001," *Juvenile Justice Bulletin* (Washington, D.C.: U.S. Department of Justice, Office of Juvenile Justice and Delinquency Prevention, 2003).

15. F. A. Allen, *The Decline of the Rehabilitative Ideal: Penal Policy and Social Purpose* (New Haven, Conn.: Yale University Press, 1981); R. J. R. Levesque, *Adolescents, Sex, and the Law: Preparing Adolescents for Responsible Citizenship* (Washington, D.C.: American Psychological Association, 2000); B. B. Woodhouse, "Children's Rights," in *Handbook of Youth and Justice*, ed. Susan O. White (New York: Kluwer Academic/Plenum Publishers, 2001), 377–410; K. Covell and R. B. Howe, *The*

*Challenge of Children's Rights for Canada* (Waterloo, Ont.: Wilfred Laurier University Press, 2001); U. Kilkelly and L. Moore, *In Our Care: Promoting the Rights of Children in Custody* (Belfast: Northern Ireland Human Rights Commission, 2002).

16. Amnesty International, *Betraying the Young: Human Rights Violations against Children in the US Justice System* (New York: Amnesty International, 1998).

17. California has implemented a statement of foster care rights, California Welfare and Institutions code 16001.9; and the National Resource Center of the Casey Family Programs has published statements of rights for Florida, New Jersey, and Maine.

18. L. Steinberg, T. Grisso, and E. Scott, "Less Guilty by Reason of Adolescence," *American Psychologist* 58, no. 12 (2003): 1009–18.

19. Nancy E. Walker, Catherine M. Brooks, Lawrence S. Wrightsman, *Children's Rights in the United States: In Search of a National Policy* (Thousand Oaks, Calif.: Sage, 1999).

20. Between 1975 and 2003 the American Bar Association adopted a series of policies for the juvenile justice system that refer to rights, programming, statutory changes in the states, conditions of confinement, legal representation, court rules, and support for reauthorization of the Juvenile Justice and Delinquency Prevention Act.

21. 387 U.S. 1.

22. 387 U.S. 1 at 28.

23. 387 U.S. 1 at 31–57. Other rights afforded to children by the Court include notice to charges, opportunity to cross-examine witnesses, and protection against self-incrimination.

24. *Kent v. United States*, 383 U.S. 541 (1966).

25. *In re Winship*, 397 U.S. 358 (1970).

26. *McKeiver v. Pennsylvania*, 403 U.S. 528 (1971).

27. Snyder, "Juvenile Arrests."

28. Standards for the Administration of Juvenile Justice (National Advisory Committee for Juvenile Justice and Delinquency Prevention); Institute for Judicial Administration/American Bar Association (Joint Commission on Juvenile Justice Standards).

29. P. Torbet et al., "State Responses to Serious and Violent Juvenile Crime: Research Report," *Juvenile Justice Bulletin* (Washington, D.C.: Office of Juvenile Justice and Delinquency Prevention, 1996); P. Torbet and L. Szymanski, "State Legislative Responses to Violent Juvenile Crime: 1996–97 Update," *Juvenile Justice Bulletin* (Washington, D.C.: Office of Juvenile Justice and Delinquency Prevention, 1998); F. E. Zimring, *American Youth Violence* (New York: Oxford University Press, 1998); Feld, "Juvenile Court Meets the Principle of Offense"; J. J. Shook, "Changes in Legal Codes and Structured Decision Making: An Analysis of Four States" (unpublished paper, Institute for Social Research, University of Michigan, 2001).

30. Torbet et al., "State Responses"; Torbet and Szymanski, "State Legislative Responses."

31. Shook, "Changes in Legal Codes."

32. M. Sickmund, "Offenders in Juvenile Court, 1997," *Juvenile Justice Bulletin* (Washington, D.C.: U.S. Department of Justice, Office of Juvenile Justice and Delinquency Prevention, Bureau of Justice Statistics, 2002); H. N. Snyder and M. Sickmund,

*Juvenile Offenders and Victims: A National Report* (Washington, D.C.: U.S. Department of Justice, Office of Juvenile Justice and Delinquency Prevention, 1999).

33. R. Sarri et al., *Decision Making in the Juvenile Justice System: A Comparative Study of Four States* (Ann Arbor: Institute for Social Research, University of Michigan, 2001).

34. B. C. Feld, *Justice for Children: The Right to Counsel and the Juvenile Courts* (Boston: Northeastern University Press, 1993).

35. Sarri and Hasenfeld, *Brought to Justice?*

36. B. C. Feld, "*In re Gault* Revisited: A Cross-State Comparison of the Right to Counsel in Juvenile Court," *Crime and Delinquency* 34 (1988): 394–424; Feld, *Justice for Children*; American Bar Association, *A Call for Justice: An Assessment of Access to Counsel and Quality of Representation in Delinquency Proceedings* (Washington, D.C.: American Bar Association Juvenile Justice Center, 1995).

37. American Bar Association, *A Call for Justice*.

38. W. V. Stapleton and L. E. Teitelbaum, *In Defense of Youth: A Study of the Role of Counsel in American Juvenile Courts* (New York: Russell Sage, 1972); M. A. Bortner, *Inside a Juvenile Court* (New York: New York University Press, 1982).

39. Feld, *Justice for Children*; American Bar Association, *A Call for Justice*.

40. R. Hodgkin and P. Newell, *Implementation Handbook for the Convention on the Rights of the Child* (New York: UNICEF, 1998); Amnesty International, *Betraying the Young*.

41. J. Fagan and F. E. Zimring, *The Changing Borders of Juvenile Justice: Transfer of Adolescents to the Criminal Court* (Chicago: University of Chicago Press, 2000).

42. 397 U.S. 358 (1970).

43. P. Griffin, P. Torbet, and L. Szymanski, *Trying Juveniles as Adults in Criminal Court: An Analysis of State Transfer Provisions* (Washington, D.C.: Office of Juvenile Justice and Delinquency Prevention, 1998).

44. *The State of Michigan v. Abraham*, 662 N.W. 2d 836 (2003).

45. Amnesty International, *Betraying the Young*.

46. *People of the State of Michigan v. Martez DeMario Stewart*, 2001 Mich. App. Lexis 1109.

47. Griffin, Torbet, and Szymanski, *Trying Juveniles as Adults*.

48. Shook, "Changes in Legal Codes."

49. Torbet et al., "State Responses"; Torbet and Szymanski, "State Legislative Responses."

50. D. M. Bishop, "Juvenile Offenders in the Adult Criminal Justice System," in *Crime and Justice: A Review of Research*, ed. Michael Tonry (Chicago: University of Chicago Press, 2000), 81–167.

51. Bishop, "Juvenile Offenders in the Adult Criminal Justice System."

52. The exact correlation between crime rate and transfers is not measured here. Legislation has made it easier for judges to transfer juveniles to the adult court, so more children may be transferred in 1997 than in 1988, even with similar crime rates. C. M. Puzzanchera, "Delinquency Cases Waived to Criminal Court, 1990–1999," *OJJDP Fact Sheet* (2003): 4.

53. J. M. Brown and P. A. Langan, *State Court Sentencing of Convicted Felons, 1994* (Washington D.C.: U.S. Department of Justice, Office of Justice Programs, Bureau of Justice Statistics, 1998).

54. U.S. Bureau of the Census, *Current Population Reports* (Washington, D.C.: U.S. Dept. of Commerce, 2001); Lerman, "Twentieth-Century Developments."

55. Snyder and Sickmund, "Juvenile Offenders and Victims."

56. T. P. Bonczar and A. J. Beck, *Lifetime Likelihood of Going to State or Federal Prison*, report no. NCJ-160092 (Washington, D.C.: U.S. Department of Justice, Bureau of Justice Statistics, 1997).

57. J. Miller, *Search and Destroy: African American Males in the Criminal Justice System* (New York: Cambridge University Press, 1996).

58. M. Mauer and T. Huling, *Young, Black, American, and the Criminal Justice System: Five Years Later* (Washington, D.C.: Sentencing Project, 1995); M. Mauer, *Intended and Unintended Consequences: State Racial Disparities in Imprisonment* (Washington, D.C.: Sentencing Project, 1997).

59. A. Blumstein, D. Farrington, and S. Morris, "Delinquency Careers: Innocents, Amateurs, and Persisters," in *Crime and Justice: An Annual Review of Research*, ed. N. Morris and M. H. Tonry (Chicago: University of Chicago Press, 1985), 6; P. Langan, *Race of Persons Admitted to State and Federal Institutions, 1926–1986* (Washington, D.C.: U.S. Department of Justice, Bureau of Justice Statistics, 1990); R. M. Terry, "Discrimination in the Handling of Juvenile Offenders by Social Control Agencies," *Journal of Research in Crime and Delinquency*, no. 5 (1967): 218–30; M. Morash and A. Robinson, *Correctional Administrators Perceptions on Family Programming for Female Offenders* (East Lansing: Michigan State University, 1998).

60. J. Rollin, *The Social Ecology of Criminal Behavior* (unpublished doctoral dissertation, University of Michigan, Ann Arbor, 1997); B. Lander, *Towards an Understanding of Juvenile Delinquency: A Study of 8464 Cases in Baltimore* (New York: Columbia University Press, 1954).

61. T. Bynum, M. Wordes, and C. Corley, *Disproportionate Representation in Juvenile Justice in Michigan: Examining the Influence of Race and Gender* (East Lansing: Michigan State University School of Criminal Justice, 1993).

62. G. S. Bridges and S. Steen, "Racial Disparities in Official Assessments of Juvenile Offenders: Attributional Stereotypes as Mediating Mechanisms," *American Sociological Review* 63, no. 4 (1998): 554–70.

63. D. M. Bishop and C. E. Frazier, "Race Effects in Juvenile Justice Decision-Making: Findings of a Statewide Analysis," *Journal of Criminal Law and Criminology* 86, no. 2 (1990): 392–414; D. Bishop, J. Henretta, and C. Frazier, "The Social Context of Race Differentials in Juvenile Justice Dispositions," *Sociological Quarterly* 33 (1992): 447–58; J. Fagan, E. Slaughter, and E. Hartstone, "Blind Justice? The Impact of Race on Juvenile Justice Process," *Crime and Delinquency* 33, no. 2 (1987): 224–58; T. P. Thornberry, "Race, Socioeconomic Status and Sentencing in the Juvenile Justice System," *Journal of Criminal Law and Criminology* 64, no. 1 (1973): 90.

64. G. S. Bridges and S. Steen, "Racial Disparities in Official Assessments of Juvenile Offenders: Attributional Stereotypes as Mediating Mechanisms," *American Sociological Review* 63, no. 4 (1998): 554–70.

65. Bridges and Steen, "Racial Disparities." In 1998 they observed that probation officers tended to attribute crimes committed by whites to negative environmental factors, but they attributed crimes by African American youth to negative personality traits and "bad" attitudes. They concluded that the different perceptions indirectly influenced juvenile court outcomes by shaping predictions of dangerousness and assessment of the need for court intervention.

66. K. B. Nunn, "The Child as Other: Race and Differential Treatment in the Juvenile Justice System," *DePaul Law Review*, no. 51 (Spring 2002): 679–714.

67. Sarri et al., *Decision Making*.

68. K. Kempf-Leonard and H. Sontheimer, "The Role of Race in Juvenile Justice in Pennsylvania," in *Minorities in Juvenile Justice*, ed. C. E. Pope and W. H. Feyerherm (Thousand Oaks, Calif.: Sage, 1995): 98–128; T. Bynum, M. Wordes, and C. Corley, *Disproportionate Representation in Juvenile Justice in Michigan: Examining the Influence of Race and Gender* (East Lansing: Michigan State University School of Criminal Justice, 1993).

69. Bishop and Frazier, "Race Effects"; Bishop, Henretta, and Frazier, "Social Context."

70. Lerman, "Twentieth-Century Developments."

71. J. Austin, K. D. Johnson, and M. Gregoriou, *Juveniles in Adult Prisons and Jails: A National Assessment* (Washington, D.C.: Bureau of Justice Assistance Institute on Crime, Justice, and Corrections at the George Washington University and National Council on Crime and Delinquency, 2000).

72. Sarri and Hasenfeld, *Brought to Justice?*

73. Amnesty International, *Betraying the Young*.

74. Human Rights Watch, *No Minor Matter: Children in Maryland's Jails* (New York: Human Rights Watch, 1999).

75. Youth Law Center, *Building Blocks for Youth* (Washington, D.C.: Youth Law Center, 2002).

76. R. Vinter, T. Newcomb, and R. Kish, *Time Out: Juvenile Correctional Programs* (Ann Arbor: University of Michigan National Assessment of Juvenile Corrections, 1976).

77. One of the key issues in *Morales v. Terman*, 383 F. Supp. 53 E.D., Texas (1974), was the distance a parent had to travel to visit her son in a state training school.

78. F. Butterfield, "Privately Run Juvenile Prison in Louisiana Is Attacked for Abuse of 6 Inmates," *New York Times*, March 16, 2000, A14.

79. D. Halbfinger, "Care of Juvenile Offenders in Mississippi," *New York Times*, 1 September 2003, 11; R. Satchel, *Lost Opportunities: Our Children Are Not Rehabilitated When They Are Treated and Incarcerated as Adults* (Atlanta, Ga.: Southern Center for Human Rights, 2002).

80. K. Kolker, "State Has Takeover Plan in Case of Emergency at Youth Prison," *News with the Grand Rapids Press*, 30 May 2000.

81. Amnesty International, *Betraying the Young*.

82. R. Satchel, *Lost Opportunities: Our Children Are Not Rehabilitated When They Are Treated and Incarcerated as Adults* (Atlanta: Southern Center for Human Rights, 2002).

83. A. Kotlowitz, "In the Face of Death," *New York Times Magazine*, 6 July 2003, 32–50.

84. S. Rimer, "States Adjust Adult Prisons to Needs of Youth Inmates," *New York Times*, 25 July 2001.

85. D. Parent and V. Leiter, *Conditions of Confinement: Juvenile Detention and Corrections Facilities* (Washington, D.C.: U.S. Department of Justice, Office of Juvenile Justice and Delinquency Prevention, 1994).

86. Community Research Center, *Juvenile Suicides in Adult Jails* (Washington, D.C.: U.S. Department of Justice, Office of Juvenile Justice and Delinquency Prevention, 1980); T. Susman, "Growing Up in Jail," *Newsday*, 20 August 2002, 1–8, www.newsday.com/templates/misc/p...&section=%news.Fnationworld.

87. Office of Juvenile Justice and Delinquency Prevention, *Children in Custody* (Washington, D.C.: U.S. Department of Justice, 1995).

88. B. B. Woodhouse, "Children's Rights," in *Handbook of Youth and Justice*, ed. S. White (New York: Kluwer Academic/Plenum Publishers, 2001), 377–410.

89. U.S. Children's Bureau, *Children in Foster Care: A Growing Number* (Washington, D.C.: U.S. Department of Health and Human Services, 2002).

90. S. Menard, "Short and Long-Term Consequences of Adolescent Victimization," *Juvenile Justice Bulletin* (Washington, D.C.: U.S. Department of Justice, Office of Juvenile Justice and Delinquency Prevention, 2002).

91. U. Kilkelly, "The Best of Both Worlds for Children's Rights? Interpreting the European Convention on Human Rights in the Light of the UN Convention on the Rights of the Child," *Human Rights Quarterly* 23 (2001): 308–26.

92. Amnesty International, "Children and the Death Penalty: Executions Worldwide since 1990," AI Index 50/10/001111 (New York, November 2000).

93. V. L. Streib, "Death Sentences and Executions for Juvenile Crimes, January 1, 1973–December 31, 2003" (unpublished report, Ohio Northern University, Pettit College of Law, 2004); V. L. Streib, "Executing Juvenile Offenders: The Ultimate Denial of Juvenile Justice. Symposium: Children, Crime and Consequences: Juvenile Justice in America," *Stanford Law and Policy Review*, no. 14 (2003): 121.

94. *Stanford v. Kentucky*, 492 U.S. 361.

95. Amnesty International, "Children and the Death Penalty."

96. See *People of the State of Michigan v. Martex DeMario Stewart*, 2001 Mich. App. LEXIS 1109.

97. *People of the State of Illinois v. Leon Miller*, 202 Il. 2d 328; 781 N.E. 2d 300; 2002 Il Lexis 950; 269 Il. Dec. 503.

98. R. Hodgkin and P. Newell, *Implementation Handbook for the Convention on the Rights of the Child* (New York: UNICEF, 1998).

*Chapter Ten*

# The Challenges of Human Rights Education and the Impact on Children's Rights

## Joyce Apsel

Education of the child shall be directed to . . . the development of respect
for human rights and fundamental freedoms, and the principles enshrined
in the Charter of the United Nations.

—Article 29, UN Convention on the Rights of the Child

## A SAMPLER FROM THE CLASSROOM

- During a workshop at a middle school in the Bronx, I asked students what
  they thought their rights should be. One young boy/man around ten years
  old responded, "I think that I should have the right to sleep in the same bed
  every night."
- At a series of March 2002 high school workshops in Connecticut on ID
  cards and civil liberties, many students believed that the government had
  access to all their personal background information anyway and that ID
  cards were "no big deal" and might help protect against terrorists.
- At a New School University course, Human Rights and Cultures of Caring,
  I asked undergraduates to define the term *altruism*. All fifteen undergraduates said they had no idea what the term *altruism* meant.

To what degree are human rights language and education about human rights
developments accessible to students in the United States today? How has the
post–September 11 environment—with terror alerts, war, and legislation
such as the Patriot Act—affected human rights education, including discussion of civil liberties and children's rights? To what extent do the politics of
education preselect what is being taught under the rubric of human rights

and tolerance education? Why is there resistance to teaching economic and social rights as well as political rights? How does this resistance in U.S. educational institutions reflect larger political directives that refuse to ratify the UN Convention on the Rights of the Child (CRC) and other multilateral agreements? Implementation of a human rights–based curriculum would promote new, meaningful debate over issues of education, civil liberties, and law and keep alive some debate on U.S. ratification of the CRC. Human rights education challenges children and their parents to learn about and more vigorously exercise and defend their rights. Projects and resources are available that introduce children to the CRC and other human rights norms and include imagining peace.

## CIVIL SOCIETY AND EDUCATION:
## THE GAP BETWEEN RHETORIC AND REALITY

Articles 28 and 29 of the CRC address the child's right to education and delineate a series of goals for children's education. In the United States, past and present commitment to children and to their education is considered a cornerstone of a well-functioning democracy. The goal of a civil society rests on aware and educated citizens whose childhood learning has prepared them to take their civic responsibilities seriously, from voting to engagement in public policy debates. Articles 28 and 29 reflect the same support for values of civic responsibility and respect that are advocated in the United States. Yet, the gaps between rhetoric, belief, and what is actually going on in educational settings from preschool through the university in the United States and globally remain wide.

Articles 28 and 29 promote the right of the child to education.

Article 28
1. States Parties recognize the right of the child to education, and with a view to achieving this right progressively and on the basis of equal opportunity, they shall, in particular:
   a. Make primary education compulsory and available free to all;
   b. Encourage the development of different forms of secondary education, including general and vocational education, make them available and accessible to every child, and take appropriate measures such as the introduction of free education and offering financial assistance in case of need;
   c. Make higher education accessible to all on the basis of capacity by every appropriate means;

d. Make educational and vocational information and guidance available and accessible to all children;

e. Take measures to encourage regular attendance at schools and the reduction of drop-out rates.

2. States Parties shall take all appropriate measures to ensure that school discipline is administered in a manner consistent with the child's human dignity and in conformity with the present Convention.

3. States Parties shall promote and encourage international co-operation in matters relating to education, in particular with a view to contributing to the elimination of ignorance and illiteracy throughout the world and facilitating access to scientific and technical knowledge and modern teaching methods. In this regard, particular account shall be taken of the needs of developing countries.[1]

While the United States and other countries that have mandatory elementary and secondary education should be applauded, there continue to be significant numbers of the U.S. populace who drop out of school and who are poorly educated, illiterate, and lack skills for employment. The quality of education in the United States differs markedly not only from state to state but within the local community and neighborhood. Issues of state funding, linking community tax base to spending on education, and resource differences (from the training and pay differentials of educators to tutoring and enrichment availability) continue to perpetuate huge differences between schools. The disparities between children who live in poverty and those who do not, as well as racism, are among the factors that directly affect children's opportunity to access and benefit from whatever education is available to them. Hence, the right to education is directly connected to social, economic, cultural, and political rights of children. The CRC's "equal opportunity" for education remains a goal, not a reality, for U.S. students.

Article 29

1. States Parties agree that the education of the child shall be directed to:
   a. the development of the child's personality, talents and
   b. the development of respect for human rights and fundamental freedoms, and for the principles enshrined in the Charter of the United Nations;
   c. the development of respect for the child's parents, his or her own cultural identity, language and values, for the national values of the country in which the child is living, the country from which he or she may originate, and for civilizations different from his or her own;
   d. the preparation of the child for responsible life in a free society, in the spirit of understanding peace, tolerance, equality of sexes, and friendship

among all peoples, ethnic, national and religious groups and persons of
indigenous origin;

e. the development of respect for the natural environment.[2]

This article reflects belief in the progressive development of each child
through access to education that respects the individual and his or her specific
background and abilities and that simultaneously leads toward a more tolerant and peace-filled world. The language conveys affirmation of the human
potential in each child and the broad educational goals for children that represent a vision of a better individual in a better world, with respect for different peoples and for the natural environment.

## WHAT IS BEING TAUGHT UNDER THE
## RUBRIC OF HUMAN RIGHTS CURRICULUM?

Article 29.1.b of the CRC emphasizes that a child's education should be directed to learning about human rights and fundamental freedoms in order to
develop "respect for human rights and fundamental freedoms, and for the
principles enshrined in the Charter of the United Nations." My experiences
conducting workshops with children and adolescents of different ages and
backgrounds across the United States since 1996 is that very few students,
teachers, or parents know the content of the UN Charter and the Universal
Declaration of Human Rights (a 1997 survey by Human Rights USA found
that 93 percent of people in the United States had never heard of the declaration),[3] that even fewer know of the Convention on the Rights of the Child, and
that the United States and Somalia are the only two states not to have ratified
it. Since World War II, international covenants have been drafted on economic, social, and cultural rights, as well as civil and political ones. Further,
a range of international and regional protocols and conventions address elimination of genocide, torture, and all forms of racial and gender discrimination.
Additional conventions have acknowledged the special need to guarantee the
rights of vulnerable groups, such as children, women, refugees, and indigenous people. These important developments in human rights norms are
largely ignored in classrooms across the country. In workshops, I have found
that when students are asked what type of rights they think they have, initially
there is often silence or puzzlement; then some students will talk about freedom of the press and freedom of expression and refer to U.S. history. One notable exception of when students shouted out an answer in one voice—"the
right to stay out as late as we want"—occurred in the Midwest where a teen
curfew had been passed a short time earlier.

Eventually, I began to rephrase the question: What rights do you think you should have? Or, what rights do you think children or young people should have? These questions generated a lot of responses and debates. Sometimes, teachers were uncomfortable with answers ranging from "not to do my homework" or "to have computers" or "to have band uniforms" to "doing anything I want." Explaining the concepts of "wants" and "rights" was often a challenge since students across socioeconomic backgrounds had limited knowledge of terms such as *rights* or *justice* and even less background in universal human rights including the Universal Declaration of Human Rights (UDHR) and the CRC. The idea of children's rights was generally unheard of. In U.S. history courses, pedagogy has historically emphasized political and civil rights, with little attention to social, economic, and cultural rights.

When issues of human rights are taught in U.S. classrooms, the predominant pedagogy teaches about the Holocaust, diversity or tolerance (multiculturalism), and conflict resolution. These subjects are important to introduce into curriculum and can be an effective way to discuss human wrongs and rights in history. However, the hegemonic model of the Holocaust often reduces the likelihood of teaching about international human rights and law or focusing on current human rights and wrongs in the United States or elsewhere. The politics of education from Holocaust mandates passed by state legislatures to institutional structures such as the U.S. Holocaust Memorial Museum and Holocaust centers that do teacher training reinforce the Holocaust as the hegemonic model.[4] The number of curriculum resources, movies, exhibits, and speakers is vast, and the quality of materials varies widely. Hence, given the limited time teachers have to teach about human rights issues, the Holocaust as the hegemonic model reduces the likelihood that students will study comparative genocide and look at the United States' involvement, from the treatment of Native Americans and African Americans (slavery) to foreign policy in Cambodia, Guatemala, and the former Yugoslavia. Less time and resources are often given to current events such as the war in Iraq than to the Holocaust and its significance. A small number of teaching units include discussion of the Nuremberg trials and the Tokyo trials and link with the UDHR as a reaction to the atrocities during World War II. Connections with the international criminal tribunals for the former Yugoslavia and Rwanda and the International Criminal Court could provide another perspective to link with ongoing issues of gross human rights violations and what type of due process and trials terrorists should face. However, most curriculums, even as early as those in elementary school, focus on the Nazis, Hitler, and the Holocaust with recent attention to discussions of rescuers. There is a need to improve the quality of Holocaust education and link with other genocides and related issues of human rights and wrongs, past and present, in the United States and abroad.[5]

Despite the number of post-1945 genocides and the twentieth-century characterization as "the century of genocides," the pedagogical rationale of "never again," rather than the reality of "ever again," continues to predominate in Holocaust curriculum and institutions. A combination of factors, including the number of donors and founding members who are committed to the exclusivity or primacy of Holocaust education, contributes to this trend. However, it should be noted that there are a small but increasing number of Holocaust centers and Holocaust and genocide centers that are including more programs on historic atrocities and genocides as well human rights issues today, most notably, the Holocaust and genocide center at the University of Minnesota, which actually began with a mandate to include broad issues of human rights.[6] Facing History and Ourselves, one of the leading educational organizations over the last three decades on Holocaust education, has expanded its programs and created new texts to address issues from civic education to conflict resolution to *Identity, Religion, and Violence: A Critical Look at September 11*, a resource for teachers and students.[7] The Canadian Zoryan Institute,[8] whose focus is on the Armenian genocide, has developed a summer seminar (there are sites in both a U.S. and a Canadian university) entitled "Genocide and Human Rights" in which a group of international scholars teach a two-week course on genocide and human rights to students and teachers from around the world. Part of the challenge is to have peace studies and human rights educators work with Holocaust educators and institutions to provide a broader perspective and update curriculum to emphasize more post–World War II events and present-day humanitarian dilemmas.

New organizations such as the International Association of Genocide Scholars, founded in 1994, promote study and teaching about a range of genocides, including the Holocaust and other historic atrocities, past and present.[9] A small but growing number of courses on the college level include comparative analysis and link with new case law, international tribunals, truth commissions, as well as developments in the intergovernmental and nongovernmental organizations (NGOs) seeking to address human suffering. Post–September 11 student interest in politics, international relations, and foreign policy has contributed to an increase in course offerings that often include sections on human rights issues.[10] Since the 1994 Rwandan genocide and the ethnic cleansing in the former Yugoslavia, important books have been written critically examining U.S. foreign policy, such as Peter Ronayne's *Never Again?* (2001) and Samantha Power's *"A Problem from Hell": America and the Age of Genocide* (2002) (which is a trade book and winner of the Lemkin award for the outstanding work on genocide and the Pulitzer prize for nonfiction), and reevaluating the role of NGOs, such as Peter Uvin's *Aiding*

*Violence: The Development Enterprise in Rwanda* (1998) and Fiona Terry's *Condemned to Repeat? The Paradox of Humanitarian Action* (2002).

Multicultural[11] or tolerance[12] education introduces different cultures into the classroom with the goals of mutual understanding, respect, and tolerance. Sometimes, the emphasis on difference reinforces stereotypes, but other times diversity education meaningfully promotes prejudice reduction and interest in different cultures and customs. Curriculum on slavery, issues of race, and civil rights may include discussion of legal landmarks. For example, the recent fifty-year anniversary of *Brown v. Board of Education* prompted a series of programs and resources on the subject. Content and accuracy vary widely, and there is often emphasis on heroes and heroines such as Martin Luther King Jr. and Rosa Parks, emphasizing past civil rights achievements without critically examining the brutality of slavery and the complexity of racism and present-day issues. Women's history may include references to legislation giving women the vote or antidiscrimination decrees. Teaching Tolerance is among the most effective organizations in providing education materials for students and adults to "fight hate and promote tolerance."[13] From *101 Tools for Tolerance* to *Responding to Hate at School* to its cybertour *Visit the Civil Rights Monuments*, Teaching Tolerance provides young people with resources to learn about their and other people's rights and how to become active in ongoing struggles against hate and intolerance. Given the increasing violence and number of gangs in schools throughout the United States, conflict resolution has been introduced more and more into the curriculum in recent decades. Private organizations as well as educational nonprofits such as Educators for Social Responsibility[14] and Street Law[15] (for example, see its text *We Can Work It Out*) have designed curricula and presented workshops to try to educate for cooperation and to resolve conflicts peacefully rather than through violence.

The term *peace education* is also used to describe programs that emphasize the need to uphold children's and adults' basic rights and promote cultures of caring and understanding. Its goals coincide with the human rights education model to a great extent and emphasize issues such as disarmament, land mines, child labor, and reduction of conflict and promoting peace within a thriving environment. There is an overlap between peace education and the previous categories discussed, such as teaching about the Holocaust, diversity, and conflict resolution. Two major contributors to peace education are Betty Reardon in, for example, *Educating for Global Responsibility: Teacher-Designed Curricula for Peace Education, K-12*,[16] and John Galtung's works on peace education, which analyze "structural violence" in societies and emphasize the need to reform structures and cultures opposed to peace.[17] *Human Rights Education for the Twenty-first Century* contains important essays by theorists and practitioners of human rights education on theories, teacher training, community-based and academic human rights education, and issues of funding. Peace educator and sociologist Elise Boulding in *Cultures of Peace: The Hidden Side of History*[18] places international human rights norms and institutions such as the United Nations within a historic context and posits new partnerships, including those between children and adults, as ways to encourage peace building in the twenty-first century.

Street Law is a nonprofit group "dedicated to empowering people through law-related education." Through teacher training and resources such as *Street Law: A Course in Practical Law*, Street Law introduces substantive information about law, democracy, and human rights through strategies that promote problem solving, critical thinking, cooperative learning, improved communication and conflict resolution skills, and the ability to participate effectively in society.[19] Street Law connects background about international human rights with its focus on law and the legal system in the United States. Issues of child rights reappear throughout the text under topics such as custody, access prevention, abuse, discipline, adoption, and a variety of other subjects.

It is noteworthy that Street Law points out that many countries have more serious human rights violations than the United States does. Nevertheless, in each chapter of the Street Law book, there is a feature called "Human Rights USA," concerning how effectively human rights are or are not being enforced in specific cases, such as those involving civil rights, in the United States. This integrative model provides a practical law foundation, including hypothetical examples based on case law, "You Be the Judge," and everyday encounters with law. Information on citizen advocacy, methods for solving disputes, parent–child relationships, and civil rights and responsibilities provides background and suggestions for how to learn about and work toward protecting rights. The Street Law curriculum offers a model of empowerment for young people.

## PROGRAMS THAT INTRODUCE THE UDHR, CRC, AND OTHER HUMAN RIGHTS NORMS

While education about the UDHR or CRC remains a minute part of U.S. curriculum, some organizations, such as the family law section of the American Bar Association, promote children's rights by producing materials and lobbying for support of the CRC. Some state law sections have produced educational materials directed at young people, primarily about U.S. law and moot courts. Most human rights initiatives have been initiated by NGOs—notably, Amnesty International–USA's Human Rights Educators' Network. The People's Decade for Human Rights Education (1995–2004) created educator networks and important new resources.

One early program that introduced the issues of children's rights was initiated by Defense of Children International–USA (DCI), which created a curriculum in 1988 and piloted the program to inner-city children on the Lower East Side of Manhattan.[20] DCI produced two texts, *In the Child's Best Interest: A Primer on the UN Convention on the Rights of the Child* and *In the Spirit of Peace*, the latter of which included twenty-three key children's rights through the experiences of children from different cultures. Designed for middle school– and high school–age adolescents, *In the Child's Best Interest* divides the Convention on the Rights of the Child into three main headings: *the right to survival* (adequate food, shelter, clean water, and primary health care); *the right to protection* (from abuse, neglect, and exploitation, including the right to special protection in times of war); and *the right to develop* (in a safe environment, through the provision of formal education, constructive play, advanced health care, and the opportunity to participate in the social, religious, and political life of the culture—free from discrimination).[21]

An examination of the content of this curriculum exercise reveals that teaching about rights often includes challenging students to think critically about their own lives, including their schools and ways of life. Discussion questions begin with "As a student, how can you make sure you get a good education?" to "Why would free universal public education be essential in a democratic society?" Teaching young people about the CRC and their rights means empowering them to become aware of what they are supposed to have and teaching them to compare that with what they in fact do have. Figures of high rates of illiteracy, inequity in school funding, low graduation rates in segregated inner-city schools, and lack of permanent teachers in low-income schools raise student awareness of the right to education and the reality of disparity in opportunities and access. Hence, in many respects, this curriculum challenges students to question the status quo and to engage in actions that better their lives through trying to obtain access to better education.

*Human Rights for Children: A Curriculum for Teaching Human Rights to Children Ages 3–12* uses the ten principles of the 1959 UN Declaration of the Rights of the Child to offer multidisciplinary activities to develop "both self-worth and empathy for others." "These feelings are the foundation children need if they are to understand their rights as children and the basic rights of all children."[22]

The People's Decade for Human Rights Education (1991–2000), an enabling agent for the UN Decade for Human Rights Education (1995–2004), composed of educators and human rights advocates worldwide, has produced some excellent resources that provide an immediate window of opportunity to increase human rights education in the United States. Two excellent works include peace educator Betty A. Reardon's *Education for Human Dignity*[23] and the collection edited by human rights educator Nancy Flowers, *Human Rights Here and Now: Celebrating the Universal Declaration of Human Rights.*[24] The section "Taking Action for Human Rights" gives examples of human rights service-learning projects that students created from a youth speakers' bureau—for example, International Children's Day, a human rights quilt containing symbolic representations of the articles on the CRC, and a catalogue to explain each article.[25] *Raising Children with Roots, Rights, and Responsibilities: Celebrating the UN Convention on the Rights of the Child* is a curriculum designed for young children and their parents.[26] *Economic and Social Justice: A Human Rights Perspective*, by David A. Shiman, is a companion to *Human Rights Here and Now.*[27]

The Hague Appeal for Peace and Justice for the Twenty-first Century includes peace education as central to its efforts and has developed curriculum and workshops to "educate for peace, human rights and democracy."[28] Betty A. Reardon and Alicia Cabezudo developed a peace education resource packet entitled *Learning to Abolish War: Teaching toward a Culture of Peace,*[29] which is based on the Hague Agenda for Peace and Justice for the Twenty-first Century. The booklets include sample learning units for primary, middle, and secondary schools (most of the material is from earlier writings of Reardon and other human rights educators) as well as teacher-training resources. A section on international humanitarian and human rights law and institutions includes a unit on the CRC as being "essential to the lives of children." The resource packet provides a valuable starting kit for introducing human rights education, from conflict resolution to disarmament to the UN Declaration of Human Rights and the CRC, including issues of child labor and child soldiers. Study units range from the conflict in Chechnya, Russia, to peacebuilders locally and globally to environmental issues. Sections of "imagining peace" are particularly important, such as "Cora's Vision" and "Vision for Women in the 21st Century," which promote "moral imaginings" and dreams of social justice and peace.[30]

Two recent publications by UNICEF in cooperation with Peace Child International Network, *Stand Up; Speak Out* and *Stand Up for Your Rights*, are outstanding collections on human rights. *Stand Up; Speak Out* focuses on the CRC and is a collaboration of "facts, interviews, opinions, stories, poems, and photographs from young people all around the world" on the content and meaning of the convention.[31] This book provides an excellent way to introduce students to how the CRC connects to children's own lives, with chapters ranging from children's rights as people, education, special needs, and refugees to children in danger, child labor, street children, drugs, child soldiers, and war).

The book includes children's views and references to NGOs such as Save the Children, Amnesty International, and others promoting children's rights. Finally, there is a section on children and the law and a reference section that includes addresses and action ideas.

## PARADIGM SHIFT: CURRICULUM FOR HUMAN RIGHTS, CHILD RIGHTS, AND A CULTURE OF PEACE

Democracies do not just happen, as illustrated around the world, from the struggle for democratization in Russia and other states in the region to implementation of constitutions in Afghanistan and Iraq. The 2000 U.S. presidential election underlines how even those rights that many people assume are theirs, such as the right to vote, cannot be taken for granted. The September 11 terrorist attacks and their repercussions have made the balancing of individual freedom, civil liberties, and national security especially challenging. Creating a viable democracy reflects an education for participation and commitment. Continuing a viable democracy also reflects commitment to educating children about rights and responsibilities locally and globally. Until municipal, state, and federal governments, as well as important lobbying groups, support human rights curriculum that includes learning about the development of international human rights norms and agencies, the language and content of human rights will remain foreign to most U.S. children. The current war on terrorism and domestic security concerns have reinforced the long-standing educational trend to downplay educating about human rights in the United States.

More than ever before, imagining peace and creating alternative visions of reducing conflict and promoting disarmament are needed. One of the most effective pedagogical tools of peace education is futures "imaging," or imagining transformations of the world that embody the conditions of peace and justice, to cultivate the "moral imagination" of learners in order to enable them to see peace as an actual condition of a preferred and possible future.[32] From elementary through adult education, more imagining peace exercises and discussions are urgently needed.

A series of factors may help explain why human rights education is not more widely integrated into the U.S. curriculum, such as inadequate methods of distributing materials, resistance or reluctance by educators and administrators to teach the subject, a political climate unfavorable to raising issues of human rights implementation in the United States, and a lack of effective training in integrating different aspects of human rights into classroom curriculum. There continues to be a disconnect between the availability of high-quality and user-friendly teaching resources and actually getting these materials into the hands of teachers in classrooms across this country. Free publications can be obtained through United Nations agencies, such as the UN Department of Public Information Office and UNICEF (United Nations Children's Fund), including works on the CRC, and online at the UN Cyberschool Bus.[33] More teacher-training workshops and human rights education centers are necessary for educators, parents, and children. One-day projects such as Human Rights Day, UN Day, or Anti-Violence Day are important beginnings, but integrating human rights throughout the curriculum from language to drama to social studies is the goal. As Amnesty International's *Human Rights Education: The Fourth R* states, "Teaching of human rights is as basic as teaching the traditional three Rs. The *Fourth R* should occupy as central a place in the curriculum as reading, writing and arithmetic."[34] From its *Fourth R* magazine to its activist networks and meetings, Amnesty International–USA, which is largely made up of volunteers, has been among the most effective advocates of human rights education in the United States and around the world. William F. Schulz, executive director of Amnesty International–USA, reflects this philosophy in the title of his book *In Our Own Best Interest: How Defending Human Rights Benefits Us All.*[35]

Teaching curriculum on human rights is challenging and often promotes questioning of the status quo and making students aware of the range of national and international rights they possess as human beings. Rather than avoid these subjects, teachers should be encouraged to use human rights for "critical thinking" assignments as well as in basic skills, civics, and other subjects. As the choruses for educating for "moral character" and "civil society" increase, a human rights education connected to present-day realities raises student awareness and engagement. However, the fact is that human rights and peace education are often labeled "too Left" or "too critical" of conditions or foreign policy in the United States, and teachers are reluctant to teach subjects that may offend parents or administrators and undermine their jobs. This self-censorship and hostile environment are major obstacles to human rights curriculum.

Mainstreaming human rights into departments of education is an important way to legitimize the field. Teachers' and administrators' knowledge can be fostered through training sessions and courses in graduate and undergraduate departments of education (courses on teaching social justice, peace education) as well as through continuing education credit courses or workshops. Presentations on human rights in professional organizations such as the National Council of Social Studies annual conference or regional and local professional groupings may provide another way to legitimize human rights curriculum.[36] Educators and administrators need to be creative and flexible and allow children to study and talk about rights that are meaningful to their lives. Supporting and continuing the work of the UN Decade for Human Rights Education is important to open access and provide opportunities to discuss concepts of human rights and learn about the rights and responsibilities of the CRC and their relevance to children's lives here and around the world.

Encouraging the support of nonprofit organizations is another avenue to promote human rights education. For example, the Stanley Foundation helped underwrite producing and making available free copies of *Human Rights Here and Now*. Perhaps, most important, the politics of education in the United States needs to shift to an emphasis on learning not only about prejudice, violence, and destruction in human history but also of law and rights— economic, social, as well as civil and political—now and in the past, both in the United States and worldwide. Since September 11, a new series of issues face human rights educators, from detention of immigrants (including children) to curbing civil liberties and the Patriot Act. Traditional nonprofits are trying to address these challenges. For example, the American Civil Liberties Union (ACLU) has increased its membership and introduced new educational programs and legal challenges. Amnesty International–USA is among the best sources for human rights education; its fall 2003 *Fourth R* magazine highlights "Embracing Controversy: Teaching Human Rights in Today's Conservative Environment." Through enrichment programs, grassroots initiatives in literacy and human rights, international movements such as the Hague Appeal for Peace, and child–adult partnering, human rights education may be grounded not in rhetoric but in learning about domestic and international law, concepts of rights and justice, and educating for moral awareness of children as human beings with rights.

The UN Convention on the Rights of the Child is an important milestone in attempting to articulate the rights of young people throughout the world, yet U.S. policy at present opposes and undermines multilateral institutions, such as the International Criminal Court and international treaties, such as the CRC. Skepticism about the United Nations and ignorance about what UNICEF and other UN agencies are accomplishing around the world further taint curriculum on human rights and peace education. In fact, children's rights remain a largely unpopular or unknown subject in the United States on the whole.

It is imperative to push forward in the twenty-first century in human rights education including children's rights, to educate a new generation of young people about the content, complexity, and power of human rights. A new vocabulary of essential terms—including *justice, children's rights, law, civil liberties*, and *altruism*—must be introduced, debated, and incorporated into everyday speech and life. Educators, parent groups, concerned citizens, and children and young adults all can develop awareness and work together to create networks that first empower the participants and then connect them with the larger society through the media, teacher unions, various professional organizations, and political institutions. The important work of UNICEF in its peace education initiatives and other international agencies, as well as NGOs such as Amnesty International, and local education projects provide models and support.

There are a range of grassroots groups that exist nationwide who introduce human rights initiatives into their communities. Local projects are initiated by volunteers and promote children's rights, from Save the Planet Day to Global Citizen Day. Some of these local groups develop links with larger networks. For example, *A Curriculum of Hope for a Peaceful World Newsletter* began in 1985 when a group of Connecticut teachers introduced teaching about peace in their classrooms and worked with other teachers in the K-4 elementary school to develop peace projects and assemblies with the cooperation of other local educators. Through their professional organization, Delta Kappa Gamma, an international organization of women educators, they networked with other educators interested in working on peace and writing a newsletter. The *Curriculum of Hope for a Peaceful World Newsletter* is published three times a year and mailed to over 750 people (primarily teachers and parents) in the United States and abroad. Its mission is "to study and promote critical thinking, conflict resolution and cooperative learning skills toward a more peaceful world."[37] Such local human rights groups are among the most hopeful signs of educating about human rights in the United States today.

This chapter has emphasized the need to work toward reconciling the politics of education with human rights education. Through educating a new generation of students about children's rights and making children, parents, teachers, and all citizens aware of the content of the CRC and other human rights conventions, U.S. democracy is strengthened and the potential for positive social, political, and economic changes increased. In the post–September 11 environment, a range of compelling civil liberty and security issues gives human rights education particular urgency. It is up to each of us to pursue a breakthrough in integrating human rights into each child's life and classroom. All of our futures depend on it.

## NOTES

1. J. P. Martin and R. Rangaswamy, eds., "UN Convention on the Rights of the Child," in *Twenty-five Human Rights Documents* (New York: Center for the Study of Human Rights, Columbia University, 1994), 86.

2. "Convention on Rights of Child," 87.

3. Human Rights USA poll, cited in Nancy Flowers and Kristi Rudelius-Palmer, "Fifty Years Old and Still Not in School: Human Rights Education in the United States," *Human Rights Education: The Fourth R* 9, no. 2 (Winter 1999): 3.

4. See Peter Novick, *The Holocaust in American Life* (Boston: Houghton Mifflin, 1999). A good example of the rationale of Holocaust-centered curriculum is "Florida's Holocaust Mandate," passed in 1994 by the Florida legislature. The Florida commissioner of education's Task Force on Holocaust Education includes integrating the Holocaust into K-12 classrooms and states that "the Holocaust is to be taught as a uniquely important event in modern history, with emphasis placed upon the systemic and state-sponsored violence which distinguish it from other genocides. Florida teachers are enjoined to teach about the gradual unfolding and escalation of the Holocaust ('the ramifications of prejudice, racism and stereotyping'), with special attention paid to both the apathy and the altruism of the world community ('what it means to be a responsible and respectful persons'). Finally, the Holocaust is to be taught in ways that encourage a pluralistic perspective and democratic practices" (reprinted in the *Pinellas Holocaust Studies Curriculum*, Pinellas County, Florida, 3.)

5. See Joyce Apsel, "Learning about and Protecting Human Rights: Teaching Anne Frank: Some Suggestions" in *Human Rights Resource Guide for Communities and Educators*, ed. Judithanne Hill (Boise: Idaho AFH Rights Center, 1998).

6. See, for example, Stephen C. Feinstein, ed., *Absence, Presence: The Artistic Memory of the Holocaust and Genocide* (Minneapolis: Center for Holocaust and Genocide Studies, University of Minnesota, 1999). For events and genocide alerts, see www.ushmm.org/conscience.

7. See www.facing.org for information on publications and workshops nationwide. For a brief discussion of curriculum issues in teaching about genocide and Facing History and Ourselves, see Joyce Apsel, "Looking Backward and Forward: Genocide Studies and Teaching about the Armenian Genocide," in *Looking Backward, Moving Forward, Confronting the Armenian Genocide*, ed. Richard G. Hovannisian (New Brunswick, N.J.: Transaction Books, 2003).

8. See www.zoryan.org for information on the Genocide and Human Rights summer course. While the course emphasizes "the Armenian Genocide as the archetypical genocide of the 20th century," it uses a comparative model to study the Holocaust and the genocides in Cambodia, Rwanda, Bosnia, Kosovo, and most recently in the Sudan.

9. See Roger W. Smith, introduction to *Genocide: Essays toward Understanding, Early-Warning, and Prevention*, ed. R. N. Smith (Williamsburg, Va.: AGS and College of William and Mary, 1999). For more information on the International Association of Genocide Scholars and its affiliate, the Institute for Study of Genocide, see www.isg-iags.org.

10. For a collection of syllabi and other teaching resources, see Joyce Apsel and Helen Fein, eds., *Teaching about Genocide*, 3rd ed. (Washington, D.C.: American Sociological Association, 2002). See also, Joyce Apsel, "Education, Genocide, and Human Rights," in *Encyclopedia of Genocide and Crimes against Humanity*, ed. Dinah Shelton (New York: Macmillan Reference, 1994).

11. For example, see James A. Bank and Cherry A. McGee Banks, eds., *Multicultural Education: Issues and Perspectives*, 3rd ed. (Boston: Allyn and Bacon, 1997); Maurianne Adams, Lee Anne Bell, and Pat Griffin, eds., *Teaching for Diversity and Social Justice: A Sourcebook* (New York: Routledge, 1997). Neither of these valuable texts includes human rights in the index or discusses international human rights norms and how they intersect with teaching issues of multiculturalism and social justice.

12. The term *tolerance* has fallen into some disfavor because of its connotation of putting up with someone else rather than extending him or her mutual acceptance and respect. Nonetheless, the nonprofit Teaching Tolerance (a project of the Southern Poverty Law Center in Montgomery, Alabama) includes an excellent magazine (*Teaching Tolerance*) and educational materials free to educators, providing some of the best-quality resources on tolerance available. See also, Sara Bullard, *Teaching Tolerance: Raising Open-Minded, Empathetic Children* (New York: Bantam, 1996), a classic work in educating parents, teachers, and others about prejudice and giving concrete suggestions of how to promote open-minded and tolerant children.

13. See www.tolerance.org for extensive information and suggestions to foster tolerance and fight hate.

14. For example, see *Teaching Young Children in Violent Times: Building a Peaceable Classroom: A Pre-school–Grade 3 Violence Prevention and Conflict Resolution Guide* (Cambridge, Mass.: Educators for Social Responsibility, 1994); William J. Kriedler, *Educators for Social Responsibility: Conflict Resolution in Middle School: A Curriculum and Teacher's Guide* (Cambridge, Mass.: Educators for Social Responsibility, 1997). An initial emphasis of Educators for Social Responsibility was antinuclear education.

15. Lee P. Arbetman and Edward L. O'Brien, *Street Law: A Course in Practical Law*, 6th ed. (Cincinnati, Ohio: West Publishing, 1999). See www.streetlaw.com for further information and resources.

16. Betty Reardon, ed., *Educating for Global Responsibility: Teacher-Designed Curricula for Peace Education, K-12* (New York: Teachers College Press, Columbia University, 1988). See Reardon, "Human Rights as Education for Peace," in *Human Rights Education for the Twenty-first Century*, ed. George J. Andreopoulos and Richard Pierre Claude (Philadelphia: University of Pennsylvania Press, 1997), 21–34.

17. See Johan Galtung, *Human Rights in Another Key* (Cambridge, Mass.: Polity Press, 1994); Johan Galtung and D. Ikeda, *Choose Peace* (London: Pluto Press, 1995).

18. Elise Boulding, *Cultures of Peace: The Hidden Side of History* (Syracuse, N.Y.: Syracuse University Press, 2000).

19. Arbetman and O'Brien, *Street Law*, vi.

20. Dennis Nurkse and Kay Castelle, *In the Spirit of Peace: A Global Introduction to Children's Rights* (New York: Defense for Children International–USA, 1990), iii. This program took place for several years; the U.S. chapter of the DCI is presently inactive.

21. Kay Castelle, *In the Child's Best Interest: A Primer on the UN Convention on the Rights of the Child* (New York: Foster Parents International and Defense for Children International, 1988). The articles of the convention are explained in basic terms;

some violations are discussed; and drawings done by children worldwide interpret the convention articles (Nurkse and Castelle, *In the Spirit of Peace*, iv).

22. Virginia Hatch, *Human Rights for Children: A Curriculum for Teaching Human Rights to Children Ages 3–12* (Alameda, Calif.: Hunter House, Amnesty International Human Rights for Children Committee, 1992).

23. Betty A. Reardon, *Educating for Human Dignity: Learning about Rights and Responsibilities: A K-12 Teaching Resource* (Philadelphia: University of Pennsylvania Press, 1995).

24. Nancy Flowers, ed., *Human Rights Here and Now: Celebrating the Universal Declaration of Human Rights* (Minneapolis: Human Rights Center, University of Minnesota, 1999). Flowers, coedited with Julie Mertus and Mallika Dutt, *Local Action/Global Change: Learning about the Human Rights of Women and Girls* (New York: United Nations Development Fund for Women, 1998). *Human Rights Here and Now* was a cooperative effort of human rights organizations and educators, including Amnesty International, the Human Rights USA initiative, and the private Stanley Foundation. It is highly recommended as a starting text for human rights education. For more information on this and other books in the Human Rights Education Series, see www.hrusa.org.

25. Flowers, *Human Rights Here and Now*, 91.

26. Lori Dupont, Joanne Foley, and Annette Galiardi, *Raising Children with Roots, Rights, and Responsibilities: Celebrating the UN Convention on the Rights of the Child* (Minneapolis: Human Rights Resource Center, University of Minnesota, 1999).

27. David A. Shiman, *Economic and Social Justice: A Human Rights Perspective* (Minneapolis: Human Rights Resource Center, University of Minnesota, 1999).

28. "The Hague Agenda for Peace and Justice for the 21st Century," UN Ref A/54/98, 13. For example, the Hague Appeal for Peace has produced a collection by Jo Tyler and Adam Berry with the support of the European Youth Foundation, *Time to Abolish War! A Youth Agenda for Peace and Justice* (New York: Hague Appeal for Peace, 2000), which includes resource material and suggestions on topics ranging from youth and conflict, education for peace, disarmament, and child soldiers to international law and human rights, economic justice, and contact lists. See also, Verdiana Grossi, ed., *Report of the International Peace Education Conference of Geneva*, November 26–29, 1998 (Geneva, Switz.: International Peace Bureau and Hague Appeal for Peace), a collection of essays from peace educators around the world. For publications and activities, see www.haguepeace.org for information on publications and workshops.

29. Betty A. Reardon and Alicia Cabezudo, *Learning to Abolish War: Teaching toward a Culture of Peace* (New York: Hague Appeal for Peace, 2002).

30. Betty A. Reardon and Alicia Cabezudo, *Sample Learning Units: Learning to Abolish War: Teaching toward a Culture of Peace*, book 2 (New York: Hague Appeal for Peace, 2002), 33ff.

31. Peace Child International, *Stand Up; Speak Out: A Peace Child International Project Celebrating Children's Rights Around the World* (New York: UNICEF and Peace Child International, 2002), 2.

32. *Stand Up; Speak Out*, 34.

33. United Nations, *Convention on the Rights of the Child* (New York: United Nations, Department of Public Information, 1991) includes a brief introduction and highlights and reproduces all the articles of the convention. For additional resources e-mail inquiries@un.org. UNICEF has a website (www.unicef.org), which provides information on and publishes resources about children. See especially, Susan Fountain, *It's Only Right! A Practical Guide to Learning about the Convention on the Rights of the Child* (New York: UNICEF, 2000). A wonderful new book for children from kindergarten and up is *For Every Child: The UN Convention on the Rights of the Child in Words and Pictures*, text adapted by Caroline Castle (New York: Fogelman Books, published in association with UNICEF, 2000). A few recent UNICEF publications include *The State of the World's Children 2003* (New York: UNICEF Publications, 2003), an annual report of children around the world; *The Convention on the Rights of the Child* (New York: UNICEF, 1999), a leaflet on the convention; and Susan Fountain, *Peace Education in UNICEF* (New York: UNICEF Staff Working Paper, 1999). For the UN CyberSchool Bus Global Teaching and Learning Project, see www.un.org/CyberSchoolBus. The Hague Appeal for Peace materials include *The Hague Agenda for Peace and Justice for the 21st Century* (1999) and, most recently, the peace education resource packet compiled by Reardon and Cabezudo (at www.haguepeace.org).

34. Flowers and Rudelius-Palmer, "Fifty Years Old," 2.

35. William F. Schulz, *In Our Own Best Interest* (Boston: Beacon Press, 2001).

36. The National Council of Social Studies has devoted one issue of its publication *Social Education* to human rights (1987) and one to the CRC (1993).

37. The Committee for a Curriculum of Hope for a Peaceful World is a standing committee of the Delta Kappa Gamma Society International, an honorary organization of key women educators in fourteen countries. See www.deltakappagamma.org/CT/chope.html.

# Conclusion: Some Progress, Many Challenges

## Mark Ensalaco and Linda C. Majka

As today's children are the citizens of tomorrow's world, their survival, protection, and development are the prerequisite for the future development of humanity. Empowerment of the younger generation with knowledge and resources to meet their basic needs and to grow to their full potential should be the primary goal of national development. As each child's individual development and social contribution shapes the future of the world, investment in children's health and education is the foundation of national development.[1] What was offered as a simple truth fifteen years ago at the World Summit for Children—"The survival, protection and development of children is the prerequisite of the future development of humanity"—now seems more like an indictment of the international community's failure to take effective action to confront the multiplying challenges confronting children. The summit's declaration did not call for miracles; the 1990 Plan of Action set reasonable, measurable, and *attainable* goals. Kofi Annan notes the progress made toward fulfillment of the international community's promise to children in his decade-end review *We the Children*. But there was a tone of disappointment in his report—not that the international community set goals that were "too ambitious or technically beyond reach" but because of the international community's "insufficient investment" in children.[2]

There would have been the need for new goals and renewed investment in children even if the progress had been greater and even if the international community had attained or surpassed all the goals set down in 1990, because the challenges confronting children are so many and so formidable. This book has offered an assessment of both the progress made since the World Summit for Children in 1990 and the challenges to be confronted as the international community strives to achieve the goals that the 2003 special session of the

247

General Assembly set down in *A World Fit for Children*. By way of a conclusion, three observations need elaboration.

The first observation concerns the importance of adopting human rights
standards in public policy debates about the needs and best interests of children. Investment in children is sound public policy because, as the leaders
who assembled for the World Summit for Children observed, "today's children are the citizens of tomorrow's world." But investment in the survival,
protection, and development of children is more than sound public policy: it
is a state obligation arising from ratification of the Convention on the Rights
of the Child. A human rights standard uncompromisingly demands that the
best interests of children be given priority in domestic public policy debates
about issues specific to children as well as in the broader political debates
about economic and fiscal policy and national development strategy. Indeed,
because some of the most urgent issues are global in scope—for example,
children in armed conflict, children living in abject poverty, trafficking of
children, and HIV/AIDS—it is imperative that the world's economically developed nations give due consideration to the rights of the child in their foreign policy and foreign assistance debates. Thus, as the Committee on the
Rights of the Child, the convention's treaty body, asserts, "Implementation of
the human rights of children must not be seen as a charitable process"; rather,
"states must see their role as fulfilling clear legal obligations."

As noted in chapter 1, it took more than three-quarters of a century—from
1924, when the League of Nations adopted its Declaration on the Rights of
the Child, until 1990, when the CRC entered into force—for the international
community to conceive of the survival, protection, and development of children as legal obligations rather than charitable processes. The adoption of the
Convention on the Rights of the Child represents real progress because it
serves to transform the public policy debate about children, while the near-
universal ratification of the CRC, a legally binding treaty, strengthens the
ability of human rights and children's rights advocates to influence the debate. In a world composed of stubbornly sovereign states, the fact that virtually every state has ratified the CRC has transformed what was once just a
moral appeal to make a better life for all children into a legitimate demand for
compliance with a treaty obligation.

However, the CRC does not provide for enforcement mechanisms, a fact
that makes the convention's language of legal entitlement and legal obligation
seem empty. Instead, the CRC obligates states to adopt all necessary legislative and other measures to give the convention the force of domestic law. Ensuring that states comply with this obligation is a necessary first step in the
implementation of a treaty that has gained near-universal acceptance. There
are opportunities to litigate the rights of the child where domestic legislation

is in place. As noted in chapter 3, it is critical that human rights and children's advocates maximize "the potential of existing mechanisms for the enforcement of children's rights," including national and international courts as forums to demand implementation of the principles embodied in the CRC. Both the European Court of Human Rights and the Inter-American Court of Human Rights have explicitly cited the CRC in recent rulings involving juvenile justice, physical punishment and abuse, and family law and identity. Litigation in international human rights constitutes an important element in a comprehensive strategy to implement the CRC because no state can ignore a legal ruling of a domestic court or a regional human rights court (i.e., the European or Inter-American human rights court) without incurring a potentially high political cost. For this reason, again as noted in chapter 3, "the importance of using the CRC as an interpretive tool in international and domestic courts cannot be underestimated, particularly given the number of states that have ratified the Convention."

The second observation concerns the need for effective collaboration among nongovernmental organizations (NGOs) and between nongovernmental and intergovernmental organizations (IGOs) for the purpose of pressuring governments to implement the CRC. Progress toward improvement of the well-being of all children is dependent on the ability of NGOs and IGOs, acting in unison, to pressure states to fulfill their treaty obligations under the CRC and to make good on the commitments contained in a *World Fit for Children*. NGOs are the driving force of the human rights movement. Without their tenacious advocacy, it is doubtful that states would ever have drafted meaningful human rights treaties or would ever comply with their treaty obligations.

As noted in chapter 2, an alliance of NGOs headed by the International Save the Children Alliance and Defense for Children International was instrumental in drafting many of the provisions of the CRC, negotiating compromises among states during the drafting process, and educating the public and policymakers about the merits of ratifying the convention. The NGOs' lobbying efforts undoubtedly contributed to the rapid and virtually universal ratification of the CRC. Since the convention entered into force, this alliance of NGOs has succeeded in expanding the normative standards relating to children through the adoption of the optional protocols to the CRC on the involvement of children in armed conflict and on the sale of children, child prostitution, and child pornography, as well as International Labour Organization Convention 182, on the worst forms of child labor. Beyond these efforts at standard setting, human rights, and child advocacy, organizations have succeeded in developing statistical measures of the well-being of children and in incorporating references to children into the declarations and plans of action of no less than six world conferences between 1992 and 2000. In the process, NGOs have developed a collaborative relationship with the United Nations—UN-specialized agencies such as UNICEF, as well as the ILO, the WHO, and the World Bank. Without that collaboration, the goals set forth in *A World Fit for Children* will be beyond reach. NGOs have a further role to play in promoting human rights education, as noted in chapter 10. A global agenda for public and private actions to implement children's rights in effect requires young people to mobilize to hold their governments accountable to ameliorate the factors that cause instability in children's lives. Without the persistent efforts of young people who are prepared to participate in the decisions of public and private institutions, national leaders will find themselves unwilling to address the full consequences of a huge growth of youth unemployment that is predicted to occur in developing countries.

The "soft power" of human rights NGOs has been apparent in the global campaigns against human trafficking, including the trafficking of children for economic and sexual exploitation, and against the use of child soldiers. As noted in chapter 4, since the early 1990s, an alliance of NGOs in Poland, the Czech Republic, Ukraine, and Bulgaria, working closely with the Netherlands-based Foundation Against Trafficking in Women, has been engaged in a campaign to stop trafficking that has effectively utilized all the strategies of human rights advocacy. These NGOs have provided direct assistance to victims through counseling services; they have gathered data about the extent of the human-trafficking problem; they have raised awareness of the human tragedy of trafficking through the publication of reports, the organizing of conferences, and the adept use of the media; and they have lobbied governments and the European Union to take legal action. As a result of these efforts, the European Union established the Stop Trafficking of Persons (STOP) program in 1996, and by the end of the twentieth century at least ten European states had enacted legislation criminalizing trafficking. The adoption of the optional protocol to the CRC on the sale of children, child prostitution, and child pornography in 2000 considerably strengthens the campaign against trafficking of children for sexual exploitation in Europe and elsewhere.

There has been similar progress with respect to the movement to save children from the scourge of armed conflict. In 1998 a number of NGOs, most prominently Amnesty International and Human Rights Watch, formed the Coalition to Stop the Use of Child Soldiers. As noted in chapter 5, the NGOs forming the coalition, like the alliance of NGOs against trafficking in Europe, are engaged in an array of activities. They provide direct assistance to child soldiers in the form of medical assistance and psychological counseling; they pressure government and rebel forces to cease using children as combatants; and they undertake to demobilize child soldiers and to reintegrate them into society. The Coalition to Stop the Use of Child Soldiers continues to document and denounce the pervasive practice of forcing children into combat, sustaining the momentum generated by the 1996 Machel report commissioned by the UN secretary-general. Thus, the collaboration between the coalition and the United Nations attests to the "importance of transnational advocacy networks and the symbiotic relationship between NGOs and IGOs." The adoption of the optional protocol to the CRC on the involvement of children in armed conflict—which, like the protocol on the sale of children, child prostitution, and child pornography, was also adopted in 2000 – attests to the effectiveness of the Coalition to Stop the Use of Child Soldiers and strengthens the coalition's ability to advocate on behalf of children caught up in war.

The collaboration among NGOs and between NGOs and IGOs has contributed to measurable progress in the cause of children's rights in terms of both setting universal standards and achieving some measure of global implementation. But the challenges for small NGOs engaged in community-based initiatives to improve the well-being of children in the communities where they live are truly formidable. Often possessing minimal resources and organizational capacity, community-based NGOs must struggle against structural poverty, governmental indifference, and the forces of globalization.

As noted in chapter 6, any improvement in the welfare of marginalized youths in Managua, Nicaragua, has depended largely on community-based actions of NGOs and civic groups. Yet, the experience with civic organizations working to address youth alienation and violence in the poorest districts of the Nicaraguan capital yields some disturbing lessons about the limitations of NGOs faced with sharp reductions of public services in an era of globalization and neoliberal economic reform. In Managua, civic organizations have had to assume the responsibility of addressing problems that are properly the responsibility of local and national governments precisely because those governments have abdicated their responsibility to address them. Yet the NGOs possess neither the organizational capacity nor the financial resources to ameliorate problems that are structurally grounded in poverty and aggravated by the disintegrative effects of globalization. In such a situation, access to foreign aid directed at NGOs becomes critical, a reality that makes competition among NGOs, rather than collaboration between them, more likely. Moreover, the sustainability of community-based initiatives becomes dependent on the sustained flows of external resources, leaving important community-based projects vulnerable to the shifting priorities of foundations with global reach or the geopolitics of the foreign aid policies of wealthy states. Finally, in a situation in which local NGOs are transformed into "subcontractors for international donors," those NGOs are likely to be deterred from "challenging the very structures of power that underlie the situations of mass poverty and social injustice."

The experiences of civic organizations in communities as different as Nogales, Mexico, and Dayton, Ohio, provide similar lessons about the formidable challenges facing civic organizations seeking to improve the well-being of children. In both communities, complex transformations in the global economy have placed tremendous economic and social pressures on families and have negatively affected the life chances of children. Those same pressures have severely constrained the communities' abilities to respond to families and children in crisis, a problem exacerbated by a tendency to view children as a "social problem rather than a community responsibility." But the experience of both cities demonstrates that to protect children's rights, it is imperative that various stakeholders in the community collaborate effectively to strengthen families' abilities to nurture and provide for children. Consequently, the most effective way to protect children's rights is to promote institutional change and to build a community where social justice is valued and practiced. In the final analysis, the basic lesson to be drawn from the experiences of Nogales and Dayton is that pursuit of social justice in the community is "at the heart of the human rights project" of protecting children.

The final observation concerns the formidable challenges addressed in *We the Children*, which are reflected in the select issues discussed in this book. Four chapters examine some of the practices that pose the most serious threat to children—trafficking for the purposes of sexual exploitation, the use of child soldiers, the exploitation of child labor, and deficiencies in administration of juvenile justice. This research demonstrates that these problems exist in the wealthiest states as well as in the poorest.

As noted in chapter 4, sex trafficking of young women and girls for the purpose of prostitution and pornography "is flourishing in this era of globalization." Trafficking is the fastest-growing segment of illegal profits for organized crime. The human consequences of trafficking are catastrophic. The girls and young women who are trafficked are thrust into harsh conditions in brothels, bars, apartments, and other places of confinement. They are victims of rapes, beatings, and murder. The damage to their physical health and psychological well-being is tremendous and long-lasting. Experts concur that trafficking for sexual exploitation is an "insidious form of violence."

There is a complex set of supply-side and demand-side factors that contribute to the flourishing of trafficking. The supply-side factors include social and economic dislocation associated with economic transformations of post-Communist Eastern Europe. Women and children are especially hard hit by the social and economic hardships associated with these transformations. The desire to escape from poverty in their native lands to the prosperity of Western Europe or to flee conflict and political turmoil makes young women and girls vulnerable to traffickers. The opening of frontiers after the fall of the Berlin Wall has ironically facilitated such trafficking and enslavement in Europe.

The estimated three hundred thousand child soldiers fighting in the world's brutal internal conflicts tragically embody the literal meaning of the Latin word for foot soldiers, *infantry*. The children who fill the ranks of rebel or government forces in conflicts in Latin America, Asia, and especially Africa as "volunteers" or conscripts are forced to serve in multiple capacities, including as combatants who kill or are killed. For those that are not killed, the physical injuries and psychological effects of soldiering are grave. Beyond the wounds of war, child soldiers suffer high incidences of drug addiction, sexually transmitted diseases, and HIV/AIDS, as well as deep psychological harm. Child soldiers tend to be "permanently traumatized." Notably, the physical and psychological harm done to child soldiers who are forcibly conscripted is not unlike that done to child prostitutes who are forcibly trafficked.

As with human trafficking, the reasons for the widespread use of child soldiers are complex. The intrastate wars of the post–Cold War era, many of them fueled by underlying ethnic conflicts, invariably involve the civilian population. In this circumstance, the consequences of armed conflict for children are dire even when they are not combatants. Extreme poverty fuels these ethnic conflicts, which tend to be zero-sum struggles among impoverished peoples for scarce resources. Moreover, in conditions of extreme poverty, prostitution and soldiering can be the only livelihoods available to children.

The exploitation of child labor is a global problem that, like trafficking and child soldiers, is connected to poverty. Adults exploit children for their labor everywhere, even in the United States, despite its fabulous wealth. As noted in chapter 8, "conditions for the most vulnerable members of the American labor force, minor teen and child workers, reached an unacceptable level of risk and harm during a period of record-setting business prosperity." The impact on the physical, moral, and spiritual development of children is profound. A child who is compelled by the poverty of his or her parents to work as hired labor in crop agriculture is a child who is unlikely to receive an education, who is at increased risk of injury by exposure to toxic pesticides, and who is even at risk of death by accidents on dangerous farm machinery. The exploitation of child labor in violation of the CRC or ILO convention 182 on the worst forms of child labor calls attention to the need to change institutional policies and practices. In an increasingly economically integrated world, child labor (perhaps more than any other practice that harms children) calls attention to the need to scrutinize not only the policies of states but also the activities of corporate and transnational organizations.

The administration of juvenile justice in the United States is the focus of chapter 9. Serious social problems are associated with the high rate of incarceration of juveniles, the application of sentences to minors of life without parole, the processing of children as adults, the state of legal representation of children, and the overrepresentation of youth of color. Immediate action by public interest groups, professional practitioners, and concerned policymakers is needed to address the consequences of a lack of attention in the United States to institutionalized human rights violations toward its own children.

*A World Fit for Children* addresses the challenges treated in this volume in addition to others not explored here. *A World Fit for Children* renewed the United Nations commitment to protect children from harm and exploitation and from war. Eliminating the worst forms of exploitative labor is imperative because the exploitation of children for economic gain is so pervasive. Thus, *A World Fit for Children* calls for effective measures intended to prohibit and eliminate the worst forms of child labor as a "matter of urgency," and it calls attention to the need to rehabilitate, reintegrate, and educate exploited children, including children of migrant workers, such as those hired in crop agriculture in the United States. But the document is quite clear that success will require "enhanced international cooperation" in the form of support for socioeconomic development and poverty eradication in developing countries.[3]

*A World Fit for Children* also calls attention to the need for "concerted national and international actions" to criminalize and halt the trafficking and sexual exploitation of children. Just as the document calls for the strengthening of the collection and analysis of data about child labor, it calls on the international community to monitor and share information about the trafficking of children. Cooperation among governments, IGOs, and NGOs is crucial in this respect, but so too is the cooperation of the private sector, specifically the tourism industry. As with so many emerging human rights challenges associated with globalization, the involvement of the private sector—both as a source of human rights violations and a potential partner of the human rights movement—is increasingly important. A major challenge involves preventing the criminal use of the unregulated Internet for the sale of children, child sex tourism, and child pornography.[4]

Protecting children from armed conflict is another priority. The problem is broader than halting the recruitment and use of child soldiers, the practice that receives the most media attention. The protection of children from war requires that the international community undertake a comprehensive set of measures: weigh the negative impact of economic sanctions imposed by the UN; stem the flow of small arms and light weapons; remove landmines and unexploded ordnance; care for refugees and internally displaced persons; facilitate family reunification; and ensure that children living under military occupation receive the treatment demanded by international humanitarian law. *A World Fit for Children* makes special note of terrorism, demanding protection of children from all forms of terrorism, including hostage taking.[5] Although the document does not acknowledge it, protecting children from the scourge of war ultimately demands international cooperation to more effectively achieve the principal purposes of the United Nations—to maintain international peace and security and to prevent and remove any threats to the peace.

*A World Fit for Children* addresses the issue of juvenile justice through recommendations for general measures of protection against abuse, exploitation, and violence.[6] The context is noteworthy. The document does not specifically address the increasingly widespread practice of prosecuting children as adults and, incarcerating them with adults. But the document stresses the need to create "justice systems specifically applicable to children" that are guided by the principle of "restorative justice." Its language with respect to the imposition of capital punishment is more forceful. Appearing in the same context as the call to protect children from torture, *A World Fit for Children* calls on governments that have not abolished the death penalty to comply with the "obligations they have assumed" under the CRC as well as the International Covenant on Civil and Political Rights (ICCPR) to refrain from sentencing to death persons who were minors at the time of their offenses. The United States is not a party to the CRC. It is a party to the ICCPR, although to the dismay of human rights advocates it continues to sentence minors to life without parole.

*A World Fit for Children* also addresses issues related to education, health, and HIV/AIDS that were not the subject of chapters in this volume. The General Assembly correctly concludes that education for all children, girls as well as boys, is "a key factor in reducing poverty and child labor, as well as a fundamental human right."[7] But with an estimated one hundred million children not even enrolled in primary school and with one-third of enrolled children dropping out of school before attaining basic literacy, the international community is challenged to accelerate efforts to promote quality education. The problems related to quality education are many: undertrained and underpaid teachers; crowded, unhealthy, and poorly equipped classrooms or no classrooms at all. Because of the importance of a quality education, the General Assembly sets a lofty goal: ensuring as a matter of "high priority" that by 2015 all children complete a free, compulsory, and quality primary education. *A World Fit for Children* gives special attention to girls' free and equal access to education. Girls represent the majority of the estimated one hundred million children not enrolled in school. The gender disparities both in access to education and educational achievement thwart economic growth and are rooted in cultural practices that are exceedingly difficult to abolish or modify. Accordingly, *A World Fit for Children* calls for changes in "social and cultural attitudes" as well as the "legal and economic circumstances" that contribute to gender disparities in education.

*A World Fit for Children* presents a vision of a world in which all children have a safe and healthy start in life.[8] Accordingly, the document's goals with respect to health and nutrition are dramatic: 90 percent immunization of children under one year of age; a two-thirds reduction of mortality rates for mothers, infants, and children under five; a one-third reduction in the number of households without access to sanitation or safe drinking water; the global eradication of polio (poliomyelitis) and Guinea worm disease. Some goals, such as the eradication of polio, are to be achieved by 2005, others by 2015. Similarly, *A World Fit for Children* calls for a global effort to contain the spread of the AIDS epidemic. These goals are also dramatic: 25 percent global reduction of HIV infection among young women and men by 2010; 50 percent reduction of infants infected by HIV in the same period.

Except for the issue of children in armed conflict, all of the challenges to the survival, protection, and development of children exist in the wealthiest states as well as the poorest. But whether in wealthy states or poor ones, these challenges are associated with poverty and exacerbated by the accelerating pace and unequal benefits of globalization and economic integration. *A World Fit for Children* correctly identifies chronic poverty as "the single biggest obstacle to meeting the needs, protecting and promoting the rights of children" and reaffirms the utopian-sounding "vow to break the cycle of poverty within a single generation." It affirms that globalization offers opportunities, but the document also observes that globalization creates challenges and that "developing countries and countries with economies in transition face special difficulties in responding to those challenges."[9]

For these obvious reasons, *A World Fit for Children* appeals for the mobilization of additional resources "to complete the unfinished agenda" of the 1990 World Summit for Children, mindful that "the resources that were promised at the Summit at both the national and international levels have yet to materialize." *A World Fit for Children* makes it clear that there can be no excuses for the lack of investment: "Promoting healthy lives, including good nutrition and control of infectious diseases, providing quality education, protecting children from abuse, exploitation, violence and armed conflict and combating HIV/AIDS are achievable goals and are *clearly affordable for the global community*."[10]

States have the legal obligation to make good-faith efforts to achieve progress in each of these areas. But in a world being transformed by the forces of globalization and by the sharp division between rich and poor, the goals enunciated in *A World Fit for Children* mirror the commitment articulated in the United Nation's Millennium Declaration "to free our fellow men, women and children from the abject and dehumanizing conditions of extreme poverty."[11] In September 2000 the United Nations held the highest-level assembly ever convened to deliberate on peace and development. The Millennium Summit produced a consensus declaration, later adopted by the General Assembly, specifying a series of Millennium Development Goals (MDGs). The MDGs form perhaps the most important development agenda ever composed, whose implementation would effectively reduce global poverty. The declaration states, "As leaders we have a duty therefore to all the world's people, especially the most vulnerable and, in particular, the children of the world, to whom the future belongs."[12] Experts from the UN Secretariat, World Bank, International Monetary Fund, and the Organization of Economic Cooperation and Development drafted a consensus framework of eight goals, eighteen targets, and forty-eight indicators of progress.[13] The MDGs thus signal a global agreement for direct support from the developed world in the areas of aid, trade, debt relief, and investment in exchange for sustained political and economic reform in the developing world. World leaders agreed to a set of time-bound measurable goals and targets to be achieved by 2015 directed at reducing poverty, hunger, disease, illiteracy, environmental degradation, and gender discrimination. The declaration also outlines a consensus about the need to promote human rights, including the right to development, democracy, and accountable governance.

The vision expressed in *A World Fit for Children* reflects the Millennium Declaration. The MDGs have particular impact on children: to halve extreme poverty and hunger; to achieve universal primary education; to reduce maternal mortality and mortality in children under five; to empower women and promote gender equality, especially in education; to reverse the spread of killer diseases, especially malaria and HIV/AIDS, with special assistance to children orphaned by disease. A key goal is to ensure environmental sustainability, promote accessible and affordable clean water, and free children "from the threat of living on a planet irredeemably spoilt by human activities, and whose resources would no longer be sufficient for their needs."[14]

A critical MDG concerns the commitment to provide substantial development assistance in the form of external resources, expertise, and advocacy for the large majority of nations who will reach the MDGs only with outside aid, debt relief, and improved terms of trade. Without such a commitment, progress is certain to be uneven and too slow. In many developing countries, public funding spent on social services is less than that spent on debt relief alone. Thus, the declaration states, "We believe that the central challenge we face today is to ensure that globalization becomes a positive force for all the world's people. For while globalization offers great opportunities, at present its benefits are very unevenly shared, while its costs are unevenly distributed."[15] A new global partnership is needed to reorient development policies and priorities and to connect with partners in civil society and the private sector. Beyond a conventional view of partners, enlightened grassroots social movements in every nation will be needed to mobilize national efforts and hold their leaders accountable for progress.

The Millennium Declaration states, "Global challenges must be managed in a way that distributes the costs and burdens fairly in accordance with basic principles of equity and social justice. Those who suffer or who benefit least deserve help from those who benefit most."[16] It is therefore essential that UN action be based on national campaigns and strategies that take into account uneven national resources. In the South, emphasis is on the fights of poor people to realize the MDGs. The role of the United States and other advanced industrial democracies is to supply additional aid, design more effective assistance programs, provide debt relief, and increase trade and technology transfers for poor nations.

Moreover, the United States should ratify the major human rights treaties, including especially the CRC, and promote full national observance. Then the United States could legitimately assume leadership status in the international community in promoting the standards of children's human rights. It is difficult to imagine the policy changes happening without sustained pressure on Washington by an aware and engaged citizenry, who are informed about local and global challenges to the human rights of children. What is certain is that a meaningful public debate about the human rights of children in the United States will resonate throughout the rest of the world and contribute to progress toward the realization of a world fit for children.

## NOTES

1. Plan of Action for implementing the World Declaration on the Survival, Protection, and Development of the Child in the 1990s, para. 3.
2. *A World Fit for Children*, part I, para. 33.
3. *A World Fit for Children*, part III, paras. 33–39.
4. *A World Fit for Children*, part III, paras. 40–47.
5. *A World Fit for Children*, part III, paras. 20–32.
6. *A World Fit for Children*, part III, paras. 7–8.
7. *A World Fit for Children*, part III, paras. 38–39.
8. *A World Fit for Children*, part III, paras. 35–37 and 45–47.
9. *A World Fit for Children*, part II, paras. 7, 18–19.

10. *A World Fit for Children*, part III, para. 48 (italics added).

11. United Nations Millennium Declaration (8 September 2002), A/RES/55/2, part III, para. 11.

12. UN Millennium Declaration, part I, para. 2.

13. See Road Map Towards the Implementation of the United Nations Millennium Declaration, A/56/326.

14. UN Millennium Declaration, part IV, para. 21.

15. UN Millennium Declaration, part I, para. 5.

16. UN Millennium Declaration, part I, para. 6.

# Index

*Note:* Page references in *italics* indicate a table on the designated page.

abduction, as method in sexual
  trafficking, 88–89
Abraham, Nathaniel, 208
acquired immunodeficiency syndrome
  (AIDS), global epidemic in child
  populations of, 1, 20. *See also*
  HIV/AIDS
Ad Hoc NGO Group, 34
adverse effect wage rate (AEWR), 188,
  190
African Charter on the Rights and
  Welfare of the Child, 44, 116
Agricultural Job Opportunity, Benefits,
  and Security Act (AgJOBS), 188–89
*Aiding Violence: The Development
  Enterprise in Rwanda* (Uvin),
  234–35
Albania, sexual trafficking in, 96
Alemán, Arnoldo, 129, 134
American Bar Association (ABA), 203,
  206, 223n20, 236
American Civil Liberties Union
  (ACLU), 241
American Convention on Human Rights
  (ACHR): as framework for juvenile
  justice in U.S., 197, 202, 214, 218;
  reference to CRC standards in, 69, 71

America's Defense Monitor, 113
Americorps Program, 158–59
Amnesty International, 112, 121, 214,
  218, 236, 239, 240–42, 250
Anderson, Elijah, 160
Angola, use of child combatants in, 43
Annan, Kofi: on child and sexual
  trafficking, 85, 89, 97, 104; on
  children affected by war and conflict,
  111; decade-end review in *We the
  Children,* 19, 20, 43, 247
Anzaldua, Gloria, 151, 165n1

Barnen, Rädda, 112
Beck, A. J., 211
Belli, Humberto, 134
Bill and Melinda Gates Foundation, 32,
  45–46
Bonczar, T. P., 211
Borderlinks, 159
border security, after 9/11, 104
Border Volunteer Corps, 158
Bosnia, 94, 98
Boulding, Elise, 236
Boutros-Ghali, Boutros, 33, 41
Bracero Program, 181
Bridges, G. S., 212

261

Brussels Declaration, 102
Bush, George W., policy on use of child soldiers, 121–22
Bynum, T., 212

Cabezudo, Alicia, 238
California: Agricultural Labor Relations Act of, 183; farm labor contractor (FLC) system in, 180, 181–84, 189; on foster care rights, 223n17; H-2A workers in, 188–89; minimum wage policies of, 189
Canada, CRC standards in juvenile court decisions, 54, 73–74
capital punishment, 218–19
Center for Defense Information, 112, 116, 120, 121
Central America, civil conflicts in, 18
Central and East European (CEE) states: alcohol and drug abuse in, 92; crime rates in, 93; economic displacement and hardships in, 88–89, 90–94; erosion of social and family stability in, 92–94; human and sexual trafficking in, 85–104, 252–53; regional and national corruption in, 96; rising unemployment in, 91–92
Chamorro, Violeta, 134
Charter of Fundamental Rights of the European Union, 57
Chaskin, Robert, 151–52
child combatants: defined, 82; demobilization and reintegration of, 115; human rights of, 41–44, 111–26, 251, 253; increased usage of, 3, 4, 42, 112–15, 124n8, 124n10; physical and psychological effects of, 114–15, 253; press-ganging of, 113–14; prevalence of, 41–42, 82, 112, 115–17, 119–20, 251, 253; U.S. policy on, 119–22
child development, human right of, 22–26
child labor: consequences of, 177–78; history in U.S. of, 186–91; ILO

convention on, 11–12, 27n9, 40, 44, 174, 249, 253, 254; obstacles to enforcement of CRC standards on, 179, 253; rights of migrant farm workers in U.S., 169–70, 173–91, 253
child pornography: in Central and East European (CEE) states, 81, 87, 90, 97–98; governmental and societal responses to, 3, 4, 98–103, 104, 250; optional protocols on, 40–41; promoted on the Internet, 82, 90, 97–98, 104
child prostitution: in Central and East European (CEE) states, 81, 85–104; governmental and societal responses to, 98–103, 104, 250; international and national activism against, 3, 4, 103–4, 250; optional protocols on, 40–41, 250; in sexual tourism, 90, 250
children's parliaments, 37, 49n21
children's rights: enforcement of, 53–80, 248–49; evolving standards of, 10–13, *13,* 14–17; gaps in national resources for, 81; global conferences on, 38–39, *39;* human rights approach to, 2; interdisciplinary research for, 3; intergenerational dialogue on, 171–72; protection at local and community levels of, 149–65; rhetoric and reality of, 229–42; on the right to be heard, 75; studies of realities at local levels for, 81–84
Children's Rights and the Tenuousness of Local Coalitions 95, 133
Children's Rights Information Network (CRIN), 37
Child's Rights Indicators Project, 44
Childwatch International, 38, 44
Clinton, William J.: antipoverty policies of, 189; legislation against human trafficking, 100–101; policy on use of child soldiers, 119, 121, 125n35

Coalition to Stop the Use of Child Soldiers, 43, 116, 250, 251

Code of Childhood and Adolescence, 141

Cold War, end of, 18, 31, 253

Colombia, use of child combatants in, 118

Committee on the Rights of the Child: monitoring implementation of CRC standards, 8, 16, 25, 27n14, 53, 54, 74–75, 248; on recruitment of child combatants, 41

Communal Movement, 129

communities: norms of family and neighborhood involvement in, 161–63, 251–52; principles of children's rights in, 4, 149–67; realities of children's rights at local level in, 81–84, 149–65, 251–52. *See also* Dayton, Ohio; Nogales, Sonora, Mexico

*Condemned to Repeat? The Paradox of Humanitarian Action* (Terry), 235

Convention against Discrimination in Education, 57

Convention against Torture and Other Cruel, Inhuman, or Degrading Treatment or Punishment, 198, 202–3

Convention Concerning the Prohibition and Immediate Action for Elimination of the Worst Forms of Child Labour, 40

Convention on Adoption, 57

Convention on the Elimination of Discrimination against Women (CEDAW), 33

Convention on the Legal Status of Children Born Outside Wedlock, 57

Convention on the Rights of the Child (CRC): development and drafting process of, 31–51; education and increased awareness of, 37–38, 236–38; on exploitation and dangers of child labor, 173–74, 253, 254;

framework for enforcing children's rights of, 53–75; goals of, 143, 230–33, 238, 241; human rights approach in, 22–26; implementation of, 8, 16–17, 25, 27n15, 31–48, 248–51; international adoption of, 4–5, 7, 12, 26, 74–75; as interpretive tool in international and domestic courts, 53–75, 197–98, 217–18; near-universal ratification of, 12, 31, 54, 119, 174, 200, 202, 232, 258; optional protocols of, 2, 28n16, 116, 117, 120; principal articles and provisions of, 34–35, 54; provisions for children's health and education, 44–47, 51n48, 256; on sale of children, child prostitution, and child pornography, 40–41, 250; states obligations to, 7, 14–17, 27nn11–12, 247–48; on use of child combatants, 41–42, 112, 115–17, 119–20, 251, 253

Convention on Torture, 44

Coomaraswamy, Radhika, 33

Corley, C., 212

Council of Europe, 57, 60, 61, 82, 103

coyotes/smugglers, 182

*Cultures of Peace: The Hidden Side of History* (Boulding), 236

*A Curriculum of Hope for a Peaceful World Newsletter,* 242

DAPHNE initiative, 100

Davidson, Miriam, 151, 160

Dayton, Ohio: Child Protection Task Force of Montgomery County in, 150, 152–57, 163; partnership of university and community for child protection system in, 84, 149–57, 163, 252

death penalty, 218–19

deception, recruitment method in sexual trafficking, 88–89

Declaration on the Elimination of Violence Against Women, 33

Declaration on the Rights of the Child, 3, 10, 22, 26, 57, 248
Declaration on the Right to Development, 22–26, 29n29
Defense of Children International (DCI), 32, 38, 237
Delta Kappa Gamma, 242
Democratic Republic of the Congo, use of child combatants in, 43, 118
Doherty, Mark, 214
Donnelly, Jack, 25
Duncan, G. J., 152

earned income tax credit (EITC), 189, 190
Eastern Europe, sexual trafficking of children in, 103–4, 252–53
East Timor, use of child combatants in, 118
*Economic and Social Justice: A Human Rights Perspective* (Shiman), 238
economic inequality, effects on world's children, 2
*Educating for Global Responsibility: Teacher-Designed Curricula for Peace Education, K-12* (Reardon, ed.), 235
education: children's rights to, 11–12, 255; CRC standards for, 44, 46–47; decreased enrollments in CEE states, 93; developing a curriculum for human rights, child rights and culture of peace, 5, 164–65, 171–72, 229–41, 246n33; dropout rate of youth farm workers, 177; equal access by girls to, 38, *39,* 46, 255; of marginalized youth in Nicaragua, 133–34; multicultural and tolerance in curriculum of, 235–36, 244nn11–12; on norms of children's rights, 236–39; teaching issues of human rights in curriculum of, 229–42
*Education for Human Dignity* (Reardon), 238

Educators for Social Responsibility, 235
End Child Prostitution in Asian Tourism, 41
enticement, recruitment method in sexual trafficking, 88–89
Esperanza Foundation, 159
Espinoza, Doña Esmeralda, 135–36, 142
ethnic cleansing, 18, 94
European Conference on Preventing and Combating Trafficking in Human Beings, 102–3
European Convention against Trafficking in Human Beings, 104
European Convention on Human Rights (ECHR), CRC standards and case law of children's rights in, 55–69, 218
European Court of Human Rights, CRC standards in decisions on juvenile justice, 8, 54–55, 56, 57, 75, 249
European Court of Justice, 57
European Experts Group on Trafficking in Human Beings, 102
European Forum on the Fight against Trafficking, 102
European Union (EU): Charter of Fundamental Rights of the European Union in, 57; Council Framework Decision on Combating Trafficking in Human Beings, 102; DAPHNE initiative of, 100; on human trafficking by organized crime, 87; STOP (Stop Trafficking of Persons) program, 100, 250

Fair Labor Standards Act, 170, 178, 179
family law, ECHR case law citing CRC standards on, 66–69
farm labor: Bracero Program of, 181; citizenship of workers in, 180; living and working conditions of, 184; minimum wage violations in, 179, 180; policies of immigrant-sending countries of, 179; rights of child workers in, 173–91; risks of injury

and health problems in, 177–78;
United Farm Workers (UFW) in, 183
farm labor contractors (FLCs), 170, 180,
181–84, 189
Farm Labor Organizing Committee
(FLOC), 188–89
Feld, B. C., 200, 206
Fitz, Raymond, 152–53
Florida: Migrant Farmworker Justice
Project in, 186; modern-day slavery
of farm workers in, 184–86
Flowers, Nancy, 238
Ford Foundation, 47
Fortas, Abe, 203–4
Foucault, Michel, 143
Foundation Against Trafficking in
Women (STV), 100, 250
Fourth Conference on Women (Beijing),
38, *39*
Fox, Vicente, 187
France, case law on child's right to
identity in, 68–69

Galtung, John, 235
Geneva Declaration of the Rights of the
Child, 10, *13,* 18
genocide, as subject in education
curriculum, 233–35, 243n4
Gill, Elizabeth, 179
Global Alliance for Vaccines and
Immunization (GAVI), 45
Global Citizen Day, 242
globalization, impact on children's
rights, 2, 21, 31, 169, 253
Gradin, Anita, 100
Grant, James P., 34
Grisso, T., 201
GTZ, study of reproductive and sexual
health in Managua by, 138–41,
146n36
Guatemala: on rights of street children
in, 70–71; use of child combatants
in, 113, 114, 253
Gulf War, 18
Guzman, Cecilia, 158

The Hague Appeal for Peace and Justice
for the Twenty-first Century, 238,
245n28
Hasenfeld, Y., 206
health: adequate nutrition for, 45, 256;
CRC standards for, 44–47, 256;
effects of HIV/AIDS on child
populations, 20, 31, 42, 46, 97, 253,
255, 256; immunization programs
for, 45–46, 256; improved sanitation
and safe water for, 45, 256;
measuring achievement in advances
of, 44–46, 256; risks and injury in
teen/minor farm workers, 177–78
Hickey, Maeve, 157
HIV/AIDS, global epidemic of, 31, 42,
46, 253, 256, 257
Hodgkin, R., 221
Holocaust, 233–34, 243n4
Htoo, Johnny, 111
Htoo, Luther, 111
human development, children's rights
to, 22–26, 28n25
human rights: approach to children's
rights, 2; conventions of, 32–33, 44,
202–3; human development approach
to, 22–24, 28n25; impact on
children's rights, 229–46; rhetoric
and reality of, 229–42
*Human Rights Education: The Fourth R*
(Amnesty International), 240, 241
*Human Rights Education for the
Twenty-first Century* (Andreopoulos,
ed.), 235
*Human Rights for Children: A
Curriculum for Teaching Human
Rights to Children Ages 3-12*
(Hatch), 237
*Human Rights Here and Now:
Celebrating the Universal
Declaration of Human Rights*
(Flowers, ed.), 238, 241, 245n24
Human Rights Watch, 112, 121, 214, 250
human trafficking: governmental and
societal responses to, 98–103, 104,

250; mail-order brides and dating services through, 97–98; media and public attention to, 99–102, 250; for prostitution in Europe, 87–104, 250; transnational market of, 86–87, 250, 252–53

Hungary, pornography industry in, 98

*Identity, Religion, and Violence: A Critical Look at September 11* (Hovannisian, ed.), 234

Ignatieff, Michael, 119

immigration, U.S. policies after 9/11, 104, 170

Immigration and Naturalization Service (INS), 72, 180

Immigration Reform and Control Act (IRCA), 182, 187

*In Our Own Best Interest: How Defending Human Rights Benefits Us All* (Schulz), 240

Integrated Management of Childhood Illness, 45

Inter-American Commission of Human Rights, 69

Inter-American Court of Human Rights, citing CRC standards in decisions by, 54, 69, 70–71, 249

intergovernmental organizations (IGOs), collaborations with NGOs, 41–44, 112, 115, 119, 122–23, 251, 254

International Association of Genocide Scholars, 234

International Conference on Population and Development, *39*

International Convention on the Elimination of All Forms of Racial Discrimination, 197, 203, 210, 213

international courts: on children's rights to be heard, 75; CRC guidelines used in, 304

International Covenant on Civil and Political Rights (ICCPR), 5, 15, 27n12, 36, 60, 72, 73, 197, 202, 214, 218

International Covenant on Economic, Social, and Cultural Rights, 15, 27n12

International Criminal Court (ICC), 33, 43, 118, 198, 233, 241

International Labour Organization (ILO): Convention Concerning the Prohibition and Immediate Action for Elimination of the Worst Forms of Child Labour by, 11–12, 27n9, 40, 44, 174, 249; Convention 182 on child farm workers, 5; on implementation of CRC, 47, 190, 250; Statistical Information and Monitoring Programme on Child Labour by, 40

international law, norms of children's rights in, 3–4, 8

International Monetary Fund (IMF), 257

International Organization of Migration, 85

International Peace Academy, 43

International Programme on the Elimination of Child Labour, 40

International Save the Children Alliance, 32, 34, 45, 249

International War Crimes Tribunal, 43

Internet: child and sexual trafficking through, 82, 97–98, 104; mail-order brides and dating services through, 97–98

Intersectoral Commission for Integrated Care of Adolescents (CIS), 132–33, 138–40, 141, 142, 143

*In the Child's Best Interest: A Primer on the UN Convention on the Rights of the Child* (Castelle), 237, 244n21

*In the Spirit of Peace: A Global Introduction to Children's Rights* (Nurkse and Castelle), 237

Ireland, legal cases on juvenile justice in, 60

Jebb, Eglantyne, 10

*judicial waiver,* 207

justice system, international standards on treatment of juveniles in, 5, 170–71, 197–227, 254, 255

juvenile justice: access to education in facilities of, 216; child welfare interface with, 217–18; conditions of confinement in, 213–16; death penalty and life-without-parole sentencing of, 218–19; European legal cases on, 57–63; history of American system of, 198–99; human rights in, 219–21; international conventions on, 197–98; juvenile access to counsel in, 203–7, 223n28, 254; prevalence of youth of color in, 210–13, 226n65; processing children in adult criminal courts in, 204, 207–10, 215–16; UN on matters of, 27n8, 197–98; U.S. adherence to international conventions on, 197–227, 254, 255

Juvenile Justice and Delinquency Prevention Act, 203, 210, 211, 217, 220

Keck, Margaret E., 122
Kilkelly, U., 217
King, Martin Luther, Jr., 235
Kosovo, 98

labor: adverse effect wage rate (AEWR) in, 188, 190; exploitation of child labor in, 11–12, 27n9, 169–70, 173–91, 253, 254; H-2A workers in the U.S., 188–89; international standards on, 189–90; revolving door of farm workers in, 187–91; unionization in, 189–90

Lantos, Tom, 120
La Strada, 100
Latin America: resources for implementation of CRC in, 127–28; traditional views of children and adolescents in, 134

Lauren, Paul, 31

League of Nations, 3, 7, 10, 11–12, 22, 248

*Learning to Abolish War: Teaching toward a Culture of Peace* (Reardon and Cabezudo), 238

Leiter, V., 216
Lerman, P., 213
L'Heureux-Dube, Claire, 74
Liberia, use of child combatants in, 42, 114

Lord's Resistance Army, 43–44

MacArthur Foundation, 47
MacDonald, Laura, 130
Machel, Graça, 41–42, 43, 111–12, 115, 122, 251

*machismo,* 160
malnutrition, 1
Managua, Nicaragua: CIS-supported activities in, 138–41; civic activities in District VI of, 132–44; community and NGO initiatives for marginalized youth in, 127–44, 144n3, 251; GTZ study of reproductive and sexual health in, 138–41; Social Action Committee (SAC) in, 135–36; Villa Libertad school program in, 135–37, 141, 142, 143

*maquiladoras,* 150, 157, 159
Maryknoll Sisters of St. Dominic, 121
Melton, Gary, 151
Mexico: educational opportunities in, 187; farm workers immigrating from, 169–70, 173–91; Nogales community partnerships for child protection in, 150–52, 157–61, 163, 252

Migrant Farmworker Justice Project, 186

migrant farm workers: exploitation of children in, 4, 169–70, 173–91; living and working conditions of, 190; rights of child workers in U.S. agriculture, 174–91; temporary resident status (TRS) of, 188

Millennium Development Goals (MDGs), 257–58
Miller, Leon, 219
Moldova, 91
Montgomery County, Ohio, community-based child protection systems in, 150, 152–57
Moon, Donna, 152–53
Moore, K. Michael, 185–86
Morenilla, J. M., 59
Myanmar, use of child combatants in, 42

National Agricultural Workers' Survey (NAWS), 174–76, 178, 182, 183
National Council of Churches, 121
National Council of Social Studies, 240
*Never Again?* (Ronayne), 234
Newell, P., 221
Nicaragua: Centro de Información y Asesoría en Salud (CISAS) of, 132; Children's Rights and the Tenuousness of Local Coalitions 95 civic group in, 133; Code of Childhood and Adolescence of, 83, 127, 128, 131–32, 141, 143–44, 146n24; Communal Movement in, 129, 133, 136, 137; community and NGO projects advocating children's rights in, 4, 81–84, 127–44, 149–65, 251–52; Intersectoral Commission for Integrated Care of Adolescents (CIS) in, 132–33, 138–40, 141, 142, 143; Sandinista government in, 128, 129; strength of civil society in, 129–32; study of marginalized urban youth in Managua, 132–44; traditional views of children and adolescents in, 134; Villa Libertad school for at-risk youth in, 133, 135–37, 141, 142, 143; youth crimes in cities of, 134, 146n29. *See also* Managua, Nicaragua
Nogales, Sonora, Mexico: Casa Misericorde youth center in, 159, 163; children in tunnel systems of,

158, 159; *colonias* of poverty in, 151, 159, 161; community partnerships for child protection systems in, 150–52, 157–61, 163, 252; corporate participation in child protection in, 159–60; Mi Casa Nueva center in, 158–59, 163; rapid business and population growth in, 150–51, 157–60
nongovernmental organizations (NGOs): antitrafficking activism by, 99–102, 250; coalitions against use of child combatants, 41–44, 112, 115–16, 119, 120–23, 251, 253; in drafting process of CRC, 33–35; educator networks of, 236–37; on exploitation of children, 82–83; information networks of, 37–38; in local community implementation of CRC in Nicaragua, 127–44, 144n3, 251–52; maintaining funding for, 83; role in implementation of CRC, 3, 4, 7–8, 32, 37, 47–48, 249–51
North American Free Trade Agreement (NAFTA), 160
North Carolina Growers Association, 189
Northern Ireland, use of child combatants in, 118
Nunn, K. B., 212

O'Donnell, Guillermo, 147n43
official development assistance (ODA), 21
O'Manique, John, 23
Ombudsman for Children, 53, 75n3
*101 Tools for Tolerance* (Teaching Tolerance), 235
Optional Protocol against Smuggling of Migrants by Land, Sea, and Air, 86
Optional Protocol to CEDAW, 33
Optional Protocol to the Convention on the Rights of the Child on the Involvement of Children in Armed Conflict, 28n16

Optional Protocol to the Convention on
the Rights of the Child on the Sale of
Children, Child Prostitution, and
Child Pornography, 28n16, 90
Organization for Security and
Cooperation in Europe (OSCE), 103
Organization of Economic Cooperation
and Development, 257
organized crime, role in human and
sexual trafficking, 85–104, 250
Otunnu, Olara, 43, 111, 116–17, 118,
125n27

Parent, D., 216
Parks, Rosa, 235
Patriot Act, 241
Peace Child International Network, 238
People's Decade for Human Rights
Education, 237
Peru, use of child combatants in, 114
physical punishment and abuse, CRC
standards on, 63–66
Plan of Action for Implementing the
World Declaration, 18
Poland, human trafficking in, 101, 250
poverty: effects on world's children, 2,
256; feminization of, 82, 92–94;
increase of child soldiers related to,
113, 124n8; as "silent" emergency,
47; social isolation of, 151, 161, 256
Power, Samantha, 234
press-ganging, 113–14
Prison Litigation Reform Act (1995),
214
*"A Problem from Hell": America and
the Age of Genocide* (Power), 234
Protocol to Prevent, Suppress, and
Punish Trafficking in Persons,
Especially Women and Children, 33,
86, 101

Quaker Peace and Service, 41

racial discrimination, in juvenile justice
systems, 210–13

*Raising Children with Roots, Rights,
and Responsibilities: Celebrating the
UN Convention on the Rights of the
Child* (DuPont, Foley, and Galiardi),
238
Raudenbush, S., 152
Reardon, Betty, 235, 238
*Responding to Hate at School* (Teaching
Tolerance), 235
right to development, human right of,
22–26, 28n25
right to identity, ECHR case law citing
CRC standards on, 66–69
Rockefeller Foundation, 45, 47
Romania, 91
Ronayne, Peter, 234
Rotary International, 46
Russia: conflict in Chechnya, 238;
sexual trafficking by organized crime
in, 88, 89, 90, 91, 95–96, 250; street
children and runaways in, 92–93
Rwanda, crimes of genocide in, 18, 233,
234

sale of children, national and
international standards against, 3, 4,
28n16, 40–41, 90, 250
Sarri, R., 206
Save the Children, 10, 38, 239
Save the Plant Day, 242
"Say Yes to Children," 48
Schulz, William F., 240
Scott, E., 201
Sengupta, Arjun, 23–24, 28n26
September 11, 2001, focus on human
rights issues after, 239, 241
sex tourism, 40–41, 90
sexual trafficking: in Central and East
European (CEE) states, 81–82,
85–104, 252–53; economic
dislocation as cause of, 4, 104;
geographic patterns of, 89–90, 250;
governmental and societal responses
to, 98–103, 104, 250; media and
public attention to, 99–103, 250;

physical and psychological effects of, 89–90, 250; in postcommunist Europe, 85–110, 250, 252; recruitment methods for, 88–89; role of organized crime in, 85–104; through the Internet, 82, 97–98, 104

Shiman, David, 238

Shining Path, 114

Shook, J. J., 209

Sierra Leone, use of child combatants in, 42, 43, 114, 118

Sikkink, Kathryn, 122

Sjoberg, Gideon, 179

slavery: modern-day case in Florida of, 184–86; in school curriculum, 235

Smith, Jan Florez, 158

Snyder, H. N., 204

social justice: children's rights in, 4, 149–67; community building and, 163–64; defined, 163; studies of private-public partnerships for children and, 83–84

Somalia: humanitarian crisis in, 18; refusal to ratify the CRC by, 4–5, 12, 31, 119, 232

Special Agricultural Workers program, 182

Special Representative for Children and Armed Conflict, 43

*Stand Up; Speak Out: A Peace Child International Project Celebrating Children's Rights Around the World* (UNICEF and Peace Child International), 238

Stanley Foundation, 241

*The State of the World's Children* (UNICEF), 34, 45, 46

*The State of the World's Mothers Report,* 45

Statistical Information and Monitoring Programme on Child Labour, 40

Steen, S., 212

Steinberg, L., 201

STOP (Stop Trafficking of Persons) program, 100, 250

street children, rights of, 70–71, 92–93

Street Law, 235, 236

*Street Law: A Course in Practical Law* (Street Law), 236

sub-Saharan Africa, child health and education in, 46, 47

Taylor, Lawrence, 157

Taylor, Ronald B., 190

Teaching Tolerance, 235

temporary resident status (TRS), 188

Terry, Fiona, 235

Thompson, Ross, 151

Torres, Hope, 159

Torres, José, 159

Trafficking Victims Protection Act (2000), 100

Trafficking Victims Protection Reauthorization Act (2003), 100

transnational advocacy networks, 111–23, 253

Transparency International, 96

Trechsel, S., 59

2000 Millennium Declaration, 21, 257

Ufford-Chase, Rick, 157

Uganda, use of child combatants in, 43–44, 113, 118

Ukraine: cooperation with Poland against trafficking, 101, 250; postcommunist economic hardships in, 91; sexual trafficking in, 88, 95–96, 250

UN Centre for Human Rights, 36

UN Commission on Human Rights, 33–35, 41

UN Committee on the Rights of the Child, 32

UN Conference on Population, 46

UN Conference on the Environment and Development, 38, *39*

UN Cyberschool Bus, 240

UN Decade for Human Rights Education, 241

UN Declaration of the Rights of the Child (1959), 11–12, *13,* 26n6

UN Department of Public Information Office, 240, 246n33

UN Drug Control Program, 139

UN Economic and Social Council (ECOSCO), 36, 41

UNESCO (United Nations Educational, Scientific, and Cultural Organization), 57

UN General Assembly: adoption of protocol on use of child combatants, 42; Committee on the Rights of the Child in, 36, 49n13; CRC norms and standards adopted by, 12; Declaration of the Rights of the Child (1959) by, 11–12; on Declaration on the Elimination of Violence Against Women, 33; plan of action on children's rights by, 1, 2, 4, 10, 20–22, 25, 48, 248–50, 254–57; sanctions decade of, 18–19; 2000 Millennium Declaration by, 21, 257

UNICEF (United Nations International Children's Emergency Fund), 8; children's books on human rights by, 238–39; creation of, 10–11; in drafting process of CRC, 33–35; education outreach programs in Nicaragua, 139; humanitarian relief provided by, 45; on improving children's health and education, 44–46, 51n48; monitoring compliance of ILO Convention 182, 40; peace education initiatives of, 240, 241–42; on poverty as "silent" emergency, 47; role in implementation of CRC, 32, 37, 47–48, 250; on sale of children, child prostitution, and child pornography, 41, 89; "Say Yes to Children" campaign by, 48; on use of child combatants, 42, 117–18

United Farm Workers (UFW), 183, 188, 189

United Kingdom, legal cases on juvenile justice in, 59, 60, 61–64, 63–66, 71–72

United Nations: Charter of, 231, 232; establishment of, 10–12; on matters of juvenile justice, 27n8, 197–98; optional protocols on human trafficking, 86, 90, 250

United Nations Convention against Transnational Organized Crime, 86, 101

United Nations Development Program, 23, 28n27

United Nations Millennium Assembly: adoption of protocol on sale of children, child prostitution, and child pornography, 41, 90; on children's right to development, 21, 25, 257

United Nations Millennium Declaration (2000), 21, 25, 257

United Nations Rules for Protection of Juveniles Deprived of Their Liberty, 198, 203

United Nations Standard Minimum Rules for Administration of Justice, 171

United Nations Standard Minimum Rules for Administration of Juvenile Justice, 198, 203, 204, 207, 214

United Nations Standard Minimum Rules for Noncustodial Measures, 198, 203

United Nations Standard Minimum Rules for the Treatment of Prisoners, 198, 203

United Nations World Summit for Children: on dangers to world's children, 1, 2, 3, 4; end-decade follow-up review for, 19, 20–22; framework for children's right to development by, 25, 26; goals of, 7, 8, 10, 46, 127; Plan of Action for Implementing the World Declaration by, 18, 127

United States: adoption of protocol against use of child combatants, 42, 122–23; adult court compared with juvenile court in, 199–200; children's access to counsel in justice systems of, 203–7, 223n28, 254; children's rights in, 4, 173–96, 197–227; Commission on Agricultural Workers in, 175; conditions of confinement of juveniles in, 213–16; criteria for transferring youth to adult criminal courts in, 207–9; death penalty and life-without-parole sentencing of juveniles in, 218–19; Department of Labor in, 174–76, 179, 188; Fair Labor Standards Act of, 178, 179; farm labor contractors (FLCs) in, 170, 180, 181–84, 189; Foreign Relations Authorization Act, 119; General Accounting Office (GAO) of, 174, 178, 192n26; Health, Education, and Human Services Division in, 179; human rights and juvenile justice in, 170–71, 197–227, 254, 255; Immigration and Naturalization Act of, 72–73; Immigration Reform and Control Act (IRCA) of, 182, 187; inequalities between juvenile and adult justice systems in, 197–221; juvenile crime in, 200, 209, 222n14, 224n52; Juvenile Justice and Delinquency Prevention Act of, 203, 210, 211, 217, 220; National Advisory Commission on Migrant Health in, 174, 177; National Agricultural Workers' Survey (NAWS) in, 174–76, 178, 182, 183; National Institute for Occupational Health and Safety in, 174; Occupational Health and Safety Administration of, 179; Patriot Act of, 241; policy on use of child soldiers, 119–22, 125n36; Prison Litigation Reform Act of, 214; processing children in adult criminal courts, 204, 207–10; Racketeering, Influenced, and Corrupt Organization statute of, 101; refusal to ratify the CRC by, 4–5, 12,

31, 71, 119, 174, 200, 202, 232, 258; relevance of CRC norms in court decisions of, 71–73; rights of child farm workers in, 173–91; Special Agricultural Workers program in, 182; Supreme Court initiatives on juvenile justice system in, 199, 203–7, 222n7; Trafficking Victims Protection Act (2000) of, 100–101

United States Constitution, 214, 216, 218–19

United States-Mexico border: "borderlands" of, 150, 158; child protection systems in area of, 150; effects of poverty on children's rights in, 83–84, 164–65, 256; grassroots advocacy of protecting children, 84, 164–65; illegal crossings of, 180–81; *maquiladoras* along, 150, 157, 159

Universal Declaration of Human Rights (UDHR): on children's rights, 7, 11–12, *13,* 26n6, 72; educational materials about, 232, 233, 236; human development approach of, 22–24; on inherent dignity of all humans, 10, 26n4

UN Office of the Special Representative, 82

UN Secretariat, 257

UN Security Council: on issue of child combatants, 43, 82, 116, 117, 125n29; role in implementation of CRC, 32; on transnational advocacy networks, 122

UN Special Representative on Children and Armed Conflict, 32

U.S. Centers for Disease Control and Prevention, 46

U.S. Children's Bureau, 217

USA's Human Rights Educators' Network, 236

Uvin, Peter, 234–35

Vienna World Conference on Human Rights, 32, 33

Villa Libertad school program, 133, 135–37, 141, 142, 143

*We Can Work It Out* (Street Law), 235
Weiss, Thomas, 47
Wells, Miriam, 184
Wellstone, Paul, 119–20
Wessells, Mike, 115, 124n8, 124n10
West Africa, use of child combatants in, 18, 42, 253
West Timor, use of child combatants in, 118
*We the Children: End-Decade Review of the Follow-up to the World Summit for the Children,* 19, 20, 22, 25, 247
Williams, Norma, 179
Woodhouse, B. B., 217
Wordes, M., 212
World Bank, 32, 44, 45, 47, 250, 257
World Conference on Education, 46
World Conference on Human Rights, 25, 38, *39,* 41
World Conference on Women (Beijing), 46

World Declaration on the Survival, Protection, and Development of Children, 18
World Education Forum, *39*
*A World Fit for Children* (2002), 2, 20–22, 25, 248–50, 254–57
World Health Organization (WHO): on improving children's health and education, 44, 45–46; role in CRC implementation by, 32, 250
World Summit for Children. *See* United Nations World Summit for Children
World Summit for Social Development, 25
World Summit on Social Development, *39*

Youth Law Center, 214
Yugoslavia, crimes of genocide in, 18, 233

Zimring, Franklin E., 200
Zoryan Institute, 234, 243n8

# About the Contributors

**Joyce Apsel,** Ph.D., J.D., is a Master Teacher of Humanities in the General Studies Division at New York University. She is also director of RightsWork International, a human rights education project, and conducts workshops introducing students, teachers, and community members to resources on human rights and social justice issues. She is past president of the International Association of Genocide Scholars. She is co-editor of *Teaching about Genocide* (3rd ed, 2002) and is editing a volume on Teaching Human Rights to be published by the American Sociological Association. Her article "Moral and Pedagogical Challenges of Teaching about Genocide" will appear in the Spring 2005 issue of *Human Rights Review*.

**Jaro Bilocerkowycz** is associate professor of political science at the University of Dayton. He is the author of *Soviet Ukrainian Dissent: A Study of Political Alienation* (1988). He has delivered numerous papers at scholarly conferences, contributed many articles to encyclopedias, and written book reviews and review essays for academic journals. He has taught abroad in Russia and Germany. He is a founding member of the University of Dayton Human Rights Committee.

**Mark Ensalaco** is associate professor of political science at the University of Dayton. He is director of the University of Dayton's International Studies and Human Rights Programs and is cofounder and director of the International Human Rights Education Consortium. He is the author of *Chile under Pinochet: Recovering the Truth* (1999) and is completing its sequel, *The Mark of Cain: The Prosecution of Pinochet.*

**Raymond L. Fitz, SM**, served as seventeenth president of the University of Dayton, Ohio's largest independent university and one of the nation's largest Catholic universities, from 1979 to 2002. He is active in facilitating participation and collaboration with respect to difficult regional problems of poverty and other social ills. Locally, Brother Ray chaired the Montgomery County Child Protection Task Force, a task force of local leaders that revolutionized how this area deals with child abuse and its causes. He also chairs the Dayton Public Schools Community Advisory Council and is involved in the Miami Valley Research Foundation and the Miami Valley Higher Education Coalition.

**Jill Marie Gerschutz** is a master of arts candidate in international peace and conflict resolution. She graduated in May 2002 with political science and Spanish degrees and an international business certificate. She recently completed a summer of study in Chile, where she focused on the activities of government and nongovernmental organizations in promoting and protecting the rights of at-risk children. She worked as an advocate for street children in Central America with Casa Alianza in Costa Rica.

**Mary B. Geske** was assistant professor in the Government Department at Smith College in Northampton, Massachusetts. Her research interests were in the area of globalization and U.S. foreign economic policy. Other interests included debates surrounding human rights, with a focus on women's human rights and child soldiers. Her publications have appeared in *Alternatives* and *International Politics*. Mary Geske died in October 2001, following a lengthy illness.

**Margaret P. Karns** is professor of political science at the University of Dayton and was the founding director of the university's Center for International Programs. She is the author of numerous articles on international organizations and global governance. With Professor Karen Mingst, she has published *The United Nations in the Post–Cold War Era* (2nd ed., 2000) and *International Organizations: Politics and Processes of Global Governance* (2004).

**Ursula Kilkelly** is a law lecturer at University College Cork, Ireland, where she teaches children's rights and juvenile justice. She is the author of *The Child and the ECHR* (1999) and the editor of *ECHR and Irish Law* (2004), and she has also published on a variety of children's rights subjects in international, United Kingdom, and Irish law journals. She provides training to lawyers and the judiciary in Central Europe and Eastern Europe on children's rights issues. She is currently involved in a number of research projects, including one for the Commissioner for Children and Young People on respect for children's rights in Northern Ireland.

**Laura M. Leming, FMI**, is assistant professor of sociology in the Department of Sociology, Anthropology, and Social Work at the University of Dayton. Her main research area is American Catholicism, with a particular emphasis on lay movements. She is currently working to develop international experiences within the sociology curriculum. Before completing doctoral studies at Boston College, she did extensive work in campus ministry in Catholic higher education and has published on the millennial generation on Catholic campuses.

**Richard Maclure** is associate professor in the Education Department of the University of Ottawa. He is the author of numerous journal articles and chapters on education, social policy, and children's rights in Africa, Latin America, and Canada. He is a member of the Faculty of Graduate and Postdoctoral Studies. His teaching fields are comparative and international education, the education of marginalized youth, and basic education in developing countries.

**Linda C. Majka** is professor of sociology at the University of Dayton. Her research on child labor in U.S. agriculture is an extension of her historical studies on the farm labor market and unions. She coauthored *Farm Workers, Agribusiness, and the State* (1982) and coedited *Families and Economic Distress* (1988). She has contributed articles, chapters, and review essays to a variety of publications on social problems, labor and employment, and families. Her teaching interests concern social inequality, gender, and family policy. She is active in the Ethnic and Cultural Diversity Caucus, a multicultural initiative in the Dayton community.

**Theo J. Majka** is professor of sociology at the University of Dayton. He is the coauthor of *Farmers and Farm Workers' Movements* (1995), and coauthor of *Farm Workers, Agribusiness, and the State* (1982). His publications and research interests involve immigration issues in the farm labor market and the unionization process. He teaches about racial and ethnic minorities, community, and immigration and immigrants for the human rights concentration at the University of Dayton. He is currently active in the local community as cochair of a community summit, inspired by the UN World Conference against Racism, that is concerned with eliminating local practices that disadvantage minorities.

**Rosemary Sarri** is a faculty research associate at the Institute for Social Research of the University of Michigan and a professor emerita of social work.

*About the Contributors*

She has a long history of policy and research work and writing on juvenile justice and adult women offenders. She codirected a national study of juvenile corrections in the United States and has authored several studies of courts and correctional programs in Michigan. She served as a member of a presidential commission on juvenile justice, a member of several state and regional commissions, and a monitor for the federal court on women in prison in Michigan. At present she is completing a four-state study of structured decision making in juvenile justice and is engaged in a study of comparative program impact on adolescent female high-risk and delinquent teens.

**Jeffrey Shook** received his bachelor of arts in economics from Grinnell College in 1992, his juris doctorate from American University in 1996, and his master of social work from the University of Michigan in 1999. He is a doctoral candidate in the joint PhD program in social work and sociology at the University of Michigan. His research interests include juvenile and criminal law, children's rights, the juvenile court, children in the adult criminal court system, and social policies for children and youth. Currently he is working on a four-state study of juvenile court decision making and his dissertation, examining the processing of children in the adult criminal court.

**Melvin Sotelo** is at the Centro de Informacion y Servicios de Asesoria en Salud (CISAS) in Nicaragua. His publications include *Los Jóvenes: Otra Cultura* (1995), *Politica Nacional de Atención Integral de la Niñez y la Adolescencia* (coauthor, 1996), and *Conocimiento, Actitudes y Practicas de la Sexualidad en Adolescentes* (with Richard MaClure, 1997); and he has published articles in *Third World Quarterly* and *Journal of Latin American Studies* and in the national press, *La Prensa* and *El Nuevo Diario*.